Baladi Women of Cairo

D1339188

Baladi Women of Cairo

Playing with an Egg and a Stone

Evelyn A. Early

Lynne Rienner Publishers • Boulder & London

Published in the United States of America by
Lynne Rienner Publishers, Inc.
1800 30th Street, Boulder, Colorado 80301
www.rienner.com

and in the United Kingdom by
Lynne Rienner Publishers, Inc.
3 Henrietta Street, Covent Garden, London WC2E 8LU

ISBN 978-1-55587-268-7 (pbk. : alk. paper)

Printed and bound in the United States of America

The paper used in this publication meets the requirements
of the American National Standard for Permanence of
Paper for Printed Library Materials Z39.48-1992.

To my parents,
Aleene Tate and Firman Anderson Early,
who followed me twice to the Middle East to support my work,
and to the memory of my sister Anne Elizabeth

Contents

Preface

My introduction to Egypt was in 1969 when I spent a summer in Cairo studying Arabic. I was struck by the resilience, humor, and generosity of the Egyptian people. This spirit is exemplified in the *baladi* (traditional) women of Bulaq Abu 'Ala, who are the subject of this work. For three years (1974–1977) I joined them to sit on curbsides to watch saints' festivals, ride buses across town to visit their relatives, travel by train to the countryside for family visits punctuated by marriages and marketing, or simply clean rice and sip tea together. Since I began my research and friendship with them, the standard of living of the women of Bulaq Abu 'Ala has steadily deteriorated, yet their cheerfulness and hospitality has never flagged. Without their goodwill, which moved them to include me in their most intimate life, I could never have written this book. I celebrate their baladi spirit, and their savvy, here. It is the latter, their self-proclaimed ability to play with an egg and a stone at the same time without breaking the egg, which inspired the subtitle of this book.

In the fall of 1970 I made one of many return visits to Cairo, the day before Gamal Abdul Nasser's funeral. The next morning I watched the funeral cortege wind its way across the Nile bridge as the crowds swept away police barriers to tear a piece of the flag from the coffin. In some dozen visits since then, I followed the lives of my women friends—first as a student researcher, then as a professor at the University of Notre Dame and the University of Houston to consult as a medical anthropologist for United States Agency for International Development (USAID) health projects, and several times in the late 1980s on personal trips while director of the American Cultural Center in Khartoum, Sudan. The political and economic events of these years affected the lives of baladi women: sons and husbands died in war or migrated to other Arab states in search of employment. Constant struggle for survival was punctuated by periods of both optimism and despair as the women pieced together a family life. It is these women, whose lives I knew intimately for almost two decades, that I present here via their own narrative accounts.

My parents were my best advocates. Having trekked to Lebanon in the late 1960s while I was studying for my master's degree at the American University of Beirut, my parents remained strong of heart and followed me to Cairo while I was a Ph.D. candidate at the University of Chicago. They arrived laden with gifts for my friends in Bulaq, following the list I had sent them line by line, down to the wall calendars and the arthritis salve. They visited with my Bulaqi friends and thus filled out my social identity for my friends.

Another backer of my research was my Egyptian thesis supervisor, Dr. Wafiq Ashraf Hassouna, who ensconced me at the Institute of National Planning and introduced me into a network of health service researchers. His support enabled me to conduct research in 1974, before Camp David and the warming of U.S.-Egyptian relations, when no other American I knew of was "in the field."

With this support, I was able to meet my Bulaqi women friends, the prime source of inspiration for this book. I am particularly indebted to Fatima, the cheese merchant who took me to her village countless times. During my last visit to Cairo in fall 1991, I learned that she had died. Zahara, an MCH (mother–child health) clinic client, identified me early on as a potentially useful friend, but she also took a chance by integrating me into her extensive network of family and friends. I met most of the rest of my friends through one of these two women, and some (such as Ihlam, originally a nurse in Ras el Barra in the north, and Aniyat, a recent southern migrant) offered me frequent refuge. I could visit them at any time, nap, sip tea, unwind, tell my own tales of life in Cairo, or simply sit and watch the world go by in the street below. In this book I have changed the names of all my women friends, but they would recognize themselves.

Egyptian residents living outside Bulaq were also helpful. Zainab Anous and her son Mustafa el-Shafa'i answered all my questions about Arabic and Egyptian customs and entertained me in their home regularly. My Cairo roommate, Sandra Langtry, agreed to type some of my field notes if I would run the household; mine was the better bargain, since Sandra not only typed but also edited for me. She, sadly, met an untimely death and so never saw this book. Nawwal el-Messiri, Sawsan el-Messiri, Assad el-Nadim, and Sayyid Oweiss shared their own research with me and gave me strong encouragement. Mary Taylor Hassouna provided not only moral support and hospitality but also collaborated with me in research on fertility behavior, lending her rigorous eye as a behavioral scientist to my work. She and my maid, Halima Muhammad, nursed me back to health when I fell sick with hepatitis in 1975. My brother Jim Early and sister-in-law Jayne sent numerous musical tapes and chocolate chip cookies to keep my spirits high. Fawzi Rahman contributed to my understanding of baladi culture while assisting me on another study, of Egyptian kiosk (popular) literature. Other colleagues in Egypt who deserve my heartfelt thanks include: Judith Gran, Peter Gran, Laila Hamamsy, Enid Hill, Mona Kamal and (the late) Fuad, Ahmed Khalifa, Lutfi el-Kholi, Galal el-Nahal, and Cynthia Nelson.

Before I left for the field I worked closely with my committee chair, Lloyd Fallers, a giant in scholarship as well as in humility. His death while I was in the field was a blow for me and for humanity. His wife Margaret picked up his interest, providing her own insights for my work. Janet Abu Lughod was a never-flagging supporter who devoted long hours to helping me interpret my research back in the United States and, on a three-day visit to Cairo in 1976, she carved out an entire day to accompany me to Bulaq. At the University of Chicago, Bernard Cohn cheerfully assumed chairmanship of my committee—meeting me in as an unlikely a place as the London Records Office to discuss my work. Jean Comaroff walked me through thorny issues of medical anthropology and read my manuscripts carefully. Victor and Edith Turner generated animated discussions on popular Islam in seminars in their home. I treasure our walks on the shores of Lake Michigan the fall before Victor's inopportune death. Leonard Binder offered me not only a desk away from the jawbones perched next to my originally assigned desk in the dental anthropology lab of the University of Chicago, but also many deep dialogues on Middle East politics. Joan Guard deserves praise for her management of my research grants.

At the University of New Mexico, where I was visiting assistant professor of anthropology in 1979–1980, Mari Lyn Salvador and I discussed narrative theory and compared popular Islam in Egypt with popular Catholicism in the Azores. She read numerous drafts of my manuscripts and, with Vernon Salvador, provided valuable intellectual and moral support. Other faculty at the University of New Mexico, especially Alfonso Ortíz, Marta Weigle, and Louise Lamphere, also helped me refine my ideas. In the early 1980s, Donna Lee Bowen of Brigham Young University and I received a National Endowment for the Humanities grant to edit a humanistic source reader on everyday Middle East Muslim life. Our collaboration has been a personal and intellectual source of inspiration. Jane Gaffney and I exchanged notes on the popular culture of Kuwait, Syria, and Egypt in several Middle Eastern capitals, including Beirut and Kuwait City, where she invited me to lecture. Jane also contributed many hours to reviewing the cultural details of the manuscript. Elizabeth W. Fernea has been a constant source of encouragement and provided invaluable counsel.

In the early 1980s, while teaching at the University of Notre Dame, I helped to found the Midwest Middle East Consortium based at the University of Chicago, which allowed frequent dialogue on Middle East culture and society with such colleagues as Cathy Ewing, Erika Friedl, Jan Johnson, Lynn Killean, Farouq Mustafa, Donald Whitcomb, and Marvin Zonis. When I was an assistant professor at the University of Houston in the mid-1980s, Sybil and Ted Estess and Artis and John Bernard asked questions that kept me analyzing my work. My brother John and his wife, Jean, welcomed me on many trips to Washington, D.C., where I consulted with Middle East colleagues. I can only cite a partial list of associates and friends who have listened to me hone topics, read drafts, made me cups of coffee, and told me what to change and what to leave; they include Anne H. Betteridge, William O. Beeman, Frederick M. Denny, Dale F. Eickelman, Michael M. J. Fischer, Felicia Holgate, Joyce Holfeld, Sharon O'Brien, Karen Ericksen Paige, Marcie Patton, and Ann Radwan. Lastly, I thank my daughter Amelia Aleene Elisabeth for resisting the temptation to sweep sticky fingers across the computer keyboard where, for several months after Amelia Aleene's arrival in Morocco, her mother hovered, sorely neglecting her daughter's preference for walks in forests.

I wish to thank the University of Chicago Middle East Center, the Fulbright Commission, the Social Science Research Council, the National Institute of Mental Health, and the University of Houston Faculty Research Grants for support of my research. In Egypt I was affiliated with the Institute of National Planning, whose support I appreciate. The National Center for Sociological and Criminological Research and the Ministry of Health also facilitated my work.

Finally, Yahya Armajani and David McCurdy at Macalester College in St. Paul, Minnesota, launched this study by introducing me to Middle Eastern society. My study was conducted under research grants as a Ph.D. candidate, as a professor, and during leave time from my current job as press attaché for the U.S. Information Service. (I wrote this book as a cultural anthropologist, so none of the material herein should be taken to represent official views of the U.S. government.)

My research was conducted in colloquial Egyptian. I have tried to restrict transliterations to words with a cultural significance. Most of the common nouns will appear transliterated as they sounded to my nonlinguistic ear. However, proper names of people and places are transliterated according to foreign or local usage as appropriate. For simplicity I do not indicate velarized letters or long vowels; I have collapsed both the letter "hamza" and the letter "'ayn" into apostrophes. There is a glossary of Arabic terms at the back of the book.

Evelyn A. Early

The Bulaq Abu 'Ala Quarter of Cairo

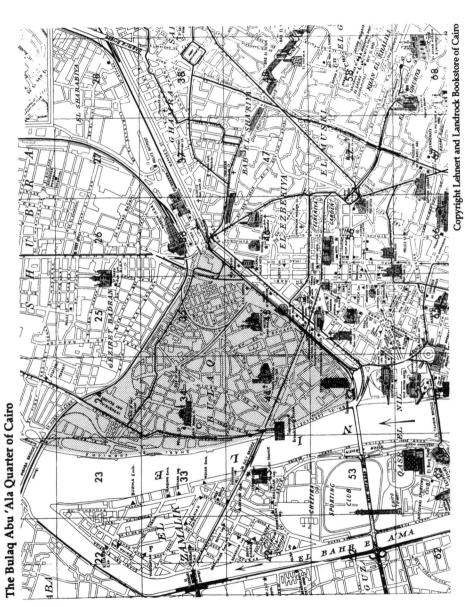

1

Spontaneous Performance and Everyday Life

I t was the day to pick my research site, the launching that all
anthropologists anticipate. I sat in the director's office in the
Ministry of Health in Cairo, Egypt, inhaling turpentine odors of
newly polished floors mixed with acrid odors of the antifly aerosol
"Piff Paff." The official pronounced the magic words: "We will go
ahead and send you to an MCH [mother child health] clinic to start
your research."

I had spent three months circulating from office to institute
trying to find a sponsor for my research. It was the pre–Camp David
era of April 1974, when the United States and Egypt had no
diplomatic relations and the U.S. interests section operated in the
annex of the "American-turned-Spanish" embassy garden. In those
days, only some thirty or forty Americans huddled in that embassy
garden each Fourth of July to eat hot dogs especially flown in for the
occasion, whereas a decade later the U.S. community would number
in the thousands. No one at the American University of Cairo
offered me affiliation; it would only hinder me, they said. I met no
Americans doing social research outside of the archives, although
Egyptological expeditions continued apace.

I asked no more questions at the Ministry of Health, so I only
learned later that the benevolent director had persuaded his
ministry's security office to approve my research provisionally
pending a formal nod from the all-powerful Office of Mobilization
and Statistics. In Egypt, only this office could authorize field
research, which they generally defined as studies involving
questionnaires and statistics. Ethnographers who eschew
questionnaires for more informal observation puzzled this office. As
part of my application I had constructed a questionnaire about
medical practices (which I never implemented), more to justify my
use of the clinic as an initial research site than to design medical

1

research. Initially, my actual plan was to conduct a neighborhood study of how recent rural migrants to Cairo used social networks to adapt to the city. I chose to work in a *baladi* (traditional) quarter because I understood it would have more rural migrants than an *afrangi* (modern) quarter.

I had already settled on an appropriate baladi quarter, Bulaq Abu 'Ala, for research, both because many Egyptians I queried recommended it and because it made sense. Conveniently located a ten-minute walk from my apartment behind the Egyptian museum, Bulaq's population was the mix of long-term residents and recent migrants I had targeted for the comparative study of migrant adjustment to the city that I initially conceived. As my research progressed, my interest shifted from the adjustment of migrants to this study of baladi culture and everyday life.

My perspective on health moved through three distinct phases during my three years in Cairo: first, health research was a strategy to provide a locus (the clinic) for a neighborhood study; second, health research provided data for analysis of baladi medical culture; third, medical culture became a critical template for my initial perception of the baladi:afrangi cultural dichotomy, which redounded through not only the medical but every other social action system. For me, health behavior was transformed from mere mechanism to method. To study health, to study business, to study rites of passage, or whatever, was to study baladi culture and everyday life. While I have described baladi medical culture elsewhere in some detail (Early 1982; 1985), I discuss health in this book not as a subject in itself but as an exemplar of baladi culture in action.

Luckily, Bulaq Abu 'Ala remained an appropriate site after my research interests shifted; it had originally attracted my attention because it was renowned as a tough quarter whose inhabitants had resisted both Napoleon and the British, but it proved in the long term an accessible and typical baladi neighborhood.

I was sure of Bulaq, but I still had no idea which Bulaq clinic to request! The director, surely reading my mind, continued: "We need a list of clinics" and dispatched a tea server to fetch the supervisor of MCH clinics. She arrived shortly carrying a hand-written list of clinics, not the computer print-outs that would be routinely churned out in the late 1970s when USAID (United States Agency for International Development) began to finance MCH clinic reconstruction and to bring consultants such as myself (by then with three years of MCH observation under my belt) to evaluate health services.

We started at the top of the list. I recognized the first address:

it was on the major thoroughfare Ramses—hardly the intimate "neighborhood clinic" I sought as the base for a neighborhood study. The next clinic was an MCH clinic on Behig—a street none of us knew. A quick poll of office messengers and tea servers indicated that Behig was a back street in the heart of Bulaq's workshop district. Behig looked promising! The next MCH clinic on the list was in a multipurpose clinic on a major street next to the river— again, not cozy enough for me. I settled on Behig.

The next day, ministry letter in hand, I set off for "my" clinic. Years before when I researched rural-urban migration in a southern Lebanese village, I ritualized my weekly trip there from Beirut by drinking one last cup of French coffee Friday afternoon at Uncle Sam's restaurant, with its reassuring formica-topped tables and familiar location near the American University of Beirut. Then I would catch the service-taxi for south Lebanon in the dizzily busy Bourj taxi station. This spring morning in Cairo, I ceremonially munched an American breakfast of eggs and toast before I left for Bulaq.

My taxi dropped me at "a clinic," which turned out to be the Ramses clinic. Who had heard of Behig anyway? I queried the clinic staff. A nurse whose path crossed Behig seized the excuse to leave early, and she departed promptly with me in tow. As we walked, I strained to locate, or to create, landmarks that would allow me to retrace my steps. Beware the deceptively easy markers, such as neon-green plastic sandals on display, which disappear when shops close, I told myself. Look for never-changing structures— street pumps, building arches, painted doors.

The Behig Street MCH clinic proved to be every bit a neighborhood clinic; that day and every other a group of women discussed the latest market and medical news in the doorway. I soon came to recognize these women as the regulars of the clinic's foster-parent program. Astute maximizers in a subsistence economy, the foster mothers benefited from government stipends to raise orphans. Most of these women were also conscientious and loving guardians, and several eventually adopted their orphan charges.

This first morning, my volunteer guide left me at the gate to make my own way to the head doctor's office. I was late and it was noon. She had already cleared her desk, and looked ready to leave. Later I realized that the head doctor rarely had anything on her desk; in and out boxes were unheard of, since all business required personal intervention for a signature. The head nurse, smiling pleasantly, joined us as I presented my ministry letter of introduction. I am sure they wondered why I wanted to study mothers' attitudes toward health, but the ministry had spoken. It had sent a social researcher to this crumbling, three-story clinic. I began my observations among the baladi women frequenting Behig clinic.

Baladi Women of Bulaq Abu 'Ala

The baladi women of Bulaq Abu 'Ala are generally from families that have migrated to Cairo from the Delta (northern) or Upper (southern) Egypt within the past thirty years. The few long term residents live similar lives and often have rural relatives. Women of Bulaq usually manage a household with money from a husband, whose average monthly salary in the mid-1970s as a government employee was thirty pounds, but who as a blue collar worker might have earned from a hundred up to several hundred pounds a month depending on his level of skill. In the mid-1970s, meat sold for about sixty piasters a kilo and bread for one piaster a loaf (a pound is one hundred piasters).

The quarter of Bulaq lies a ten-minute walk north of the Nile Hilton, but many of its one-room apartments located in three-story, mud-brick buildings and rented for a couple of pounds a month, have neither running water nor electricity. Multiple-room apartments with electricity cost five to ten pounds a month, one-sixth to one-third of a typical government worker's salary and usually beyond their means. Selected as an industrial site by Muhammad Ali, the ruler of Egypt in the early nineteenth century, Bulaq rapidly lost the attractive vestiges of a medieval elite Mameluke suburb and became a grimy popular quarter with an iron foundry and textile, spinning, and dye factories.

Twentieth-century Bulaq still provides critical carpentry and ironworks service; the sleek cars of contractors edge along streets, past donkeys and ducks, to commission work in the informal economic sector. Shoppers crowd the famed Wikalat al Balah "seconds" market in Bulaq to buy car parts or used clothing. The film based on the Nobel-prize-winning Egyptian novelist Naguib Mahfouz's *Wikalat al-Balah* has immortalized the life of a young proprietress of a scrap metal yard and her undercover narcotics agent admirer/protector who poses as a crippled beggar.

Baladi women have historically held important economic roles, but their place of employment has changed since the nineteenth century, when the family was the basic unit of production. The cottage industries have been replaced as the primary source of income with the advent of wage labor (Gran 1977; Fernea 1985; Friedl 1989; Maher 1974; Tucker 1985). Bulaqi women now work as merchants and creditors; sometimes, if her husband or father dies, a woman takes over the family workshop. With the growing oil industry of recent years, women with a little capital may travel to Libya or the Levant to buy household goods and clothes to sell door-to-door in Bulaq; those without any means may work as a domestic in Cairo or abroad. Some women find employment in textile, pharmaceutical, and other factories, but jobs are limited, and a woman must often wait for a family member to retire to claim a work slot. Young women with diplomas queue two to three years for guaranteed government office jobs.

Baladi women merchants, known as *mu'allimat*, or masters, are tough women with mannish demeanor who run shops or cafes. Respected and feared by all, they remain untouched by innuendos of loose morals reserved for some women in public places. A *mu'allima* (also the word for teacher, but never confused with that role) talks sternly, even roughly, with customers and curses as if she were a man. A popular story recounts how, shortly after the 1967 defeat by the Israelis, an Egyptian coffee-house proprietress barred an army general's entrance with a stream of expletives promising that this "pimp of the Israelis" would never darken *her* door. Tough in the street and shop, a mu'allima discards her "street" facade at home. When I told a woman that I thought we had met before, she replied: "Oh, you don't recognize me now because when we met you were buying bread from me, and I was dressed in black and acting like a tough mu'allima; now you see me as a normal housewife!"

Bulaqi women energetically create marketing and social opportunities. Inflation accompanying the *infitah* (policy of economic liberalization initiated by the late President Anwar Sadat) hit Bulaqis hard. When I returned to visit Bulaq in 1979, some of my older women friends had begun small-scale peddling or sewing to supplement the household income. Many men had either left to work in the Gulf or had begun moonlighting. One man worked mornings in a ministry, evenings in a coffee shop, and rented out a food cart he had built himself. Baladi women invest any extra money in gold—carrying a "bank" on their arm as a double hedge against inflation and divorce. They pawn jewelry, much as one would parlay stocks and bonds, to finance such family ventures as paying the onetime lump-sum deposit to rent a new apartment, or buying furniture. Another source of capital is the baladi savings association. Members give, say, ten pounds each month to the association organizer and receive the lump sum of one hundred pounds once in the ten-month cycle. The organizer determines when everyone takes their payment. First is not always best; a woman calculates payment to coincide with a major expense, such as a wedding. Savings associations pay no interest, but they do prevent one from frittering money away on daily trifles.

Most Bulaqi families are of very modest means and live in one or two rooms in an apartment building that has been subdivided to house ten or twelve families. Several families may share a landing onto which family rooms open. But there are also some lower-middle-class families scattered throughout Bulaq. Although their furnishings and life-style resemble those of low-income baladis, they may occupy the entire floor of a building, host more elaborate weddings, and travel abroad. Workshop proprietors in the carpentry, welding, and lathing mazes of Sharia Shannin and other Bulaqi streets netted anywhere from five hundred to several thousand pounds a month in the mid-1970s. Their wives clanked an impressive row of gold bracelets on their arms, and some worked as creditors—financing sales of cloth and household goods to less-fortunate neighborhood women.

Thus, the Bulaqi women I studied were mainly low income but were by no means trapped in a "culture of poverty." They practiced an eclectic mix of popular and orthodox Islam, and folk and cosmopolitan medicine. The businesswomen among them worked at the intersection of the domestic and the public, of the informal baladi economy and the formal afrangi economy. They participated in national and international markets and labor migration—whether as merchants, domestics, or relatives processing remittances of migrant laborers in Libya or the Gulf. Bulaqi women mobilized both material and social capital; their individual lives revealed delicate counterpoints of resources with rural, national, and world markets. Their children were educated and entering the professional job market.

Everyday Life on Behig Street: From Clinic to Community

It was Bulaq's fame for feisty resistance to outside occupiers in the past that first attracted me, but the Bulaq of the 1970s was better known for its drug dealers and street gangs. The quarter's reputation moved a leading Egyptian social scientist to caution sternly: "I understand you're observing in the MCH clinic in Bulaq, but certainly you are not planning to visit in homes." Such friends feared, presumably, that I would be harmed during a street fight or a drug raid. For me, research without home visits was impossible. By the end of my three years in Bulaq, I had walked in the streets at all hours of the day and night, and spent the night in friends' houses before predawn trips to the cemeteries at feast time. The most

The Behig Street MCH clinic in Bulaq

serious harassment I ever encountered was some sassy comments from young boys—who were immediately disciplined by adult onlookers before the boys had uttered much more than a few phrases.

I never rented an apartment in Bulaq. First, there were no suitable empty apartments even if it would have been acceptable for a woman to live alone in Bulaq. Second, had I lived with a family, I would not have had a room to myself or a way to write field notes in privacy. Third, had I lived in Bulaq, I would have become a "neighbor," whose naive questions—tolerated as long as I was an outsider—would have appeared stupid coming from a Bulaq resident.

My initial research goal was to explore how recent migrants mobilized their social networks to cope with urban life. As with ethnographers in search of a tribe, a community, or a family with whom to settle, I sought a "social mooring" in the chaos of Cairo's back streets, but I was dead set against using a servant's family or experimenting with any hangers-on I might attract while walking the streets.

Why a clinic? One day my thesis adviser Janet Abu Lughod and I had sat hunched over coffee in a south-side Chicago greasy spoon reviewing my typed list of "ways to start in Cairo." Rejecting clubs, village associations, and benevolent societies, we alighted on clinics. What better locus of research than a clinic, sure to attract recent migrants? To prepare for clinic research, I spent the summer in Chicago's public clinics collecting information to share with Egyptian health officials. Once in Egypt, I discovered that Egyptian clinic personnel were much more interested in what life was like in the United States and in pictures of my family than they were in Chicago's public health system.

Every day when I arrived at the Behig clinic I signed in upstairs, a handy practice allowing me to greet the director daily without tarrying. The rest of the day I observed, striking up conversations in the waiting areas, examination rooms, and labs. I avoided chatting with the clinic staff; this would have identified me with the administrative "powers" and would have led to client requests for mediation and staff attempts to "rescue me" from the discomfort of crowded waiting areas. I also wanted to avoid delaying the staff's work, although no one else who passed through the clinic to visit seemed to worry about this. I socialized with clinic staff before and after hours lest they think me standoffish.

Clinic staff anticipated that a social researcher would work with the clinic social worker. Fortunately she was on maternity leave, so I was spared assignment to her office, where I would have been isolated from clinic operations and forced to choose between the "official" social worker of the "official" world that had sent me and the foster mothers of the neighborhood that I proposed to study. Instead, I became acquainted with the foster mothers first, and used their social network to enter the life of the quarter.

Initially, I spent all my time in the clinic. As days passed, women invited me to their homes. Usually my first visit started out formally; my hostess sat me in a chair, on which baladi women rarely sat, and offered me tea in an afrangi cup. I protested that I preferred to sit on the floor and drink tea from a baladi glass. As my reputation preceded me, I dispensed with formalities and joined the women, sitting on straw mats. Some already knew that I drank tea without sugar, a habit they considered odd. While I joined women in their work, I left them to twist and turn bread and to stuff vegetables, and chose such simple tasks as cleaning rice.

In my early research I accepted any invitation to visit, but soon I concentrated on women who were potentially good informants and who represented a demographic spectrum on such variables as length of residence in the city, geographic origins, and household types. Through a key foster mother at the clinic, Zahara, and through a particularly empathetic woman, Aniyat, who became one of my best friends in Bulaq, I met long- and short-term migrants from northern and southern Egypt as well as long-term urbanites. My contacts snowballed, and I was able to cultivate informant friends from within the two clusters of women with whom Zahara and Aniyat associated. I also sought out clinic-attenders who struck me as particularly articulate. One such woman was Ihsan, who lived, alienated from all her neighbors, in a hovel off the courtyard of a building with multiple apartments.

My status throughout my fieldwork remained that of foreign student, Ministry of Health "employee," and friend, even after I ended formal observations at the Behig street MCH clinic in January 1975. By then I was established well enough to continue to visit women at home, which I did until I finished my fieldwork in the winter of 1977. In January 1975, just as I ended clinic work, I was grounded by hepatitis for four months. When I returned to Bulaq, I followed the lives of some dozen women closely, and nearly a hundred other women via friends' accounts and chance encounters. I accompanied my friends on excursions to visit relatives and friends, religious shrines, and on other typical urban errands such as hospital visits. I traveled to a friend's village in Menoufiyya many times, and the regional home town of another friend in northern Egypt several times to observe their roots and—in the case of the village where my friend Fatima marketed—the source of their economic livelihood.

I developed my own patterns of reciprocity, which somewhat resembled baladi practices. With closest friends, I felt free to drop by, drink tea, eat meals, and rest; I refused food if I chose, an action unthinkable with formal associates. With mere acquaintances, I visited during "normal" visiting hours. Although I never was drawn into the complex exchange system of *nuqta*, in which women give each other money or food gifts of prescribed magnitude at life-crisis events, I did bring fruits and sweets to families and I did distribute money to children at feast times. My general rule was not to present anything that could not be consumed—thus avoiding comparison of my gifts among women. The one exception I made was when my parents visited and brought gifts on my behalf to my friends.

Let Them Tell Stories: Reflexivity and the Researcher

The Behig Street MCH clinic became a theoretical bonus when my research tactic, using a clinic as an entree to a neighborhood, created one of my research subjects, health behavior. By the end of my first year in Bulaq my interests had shifted from migrant adjustment to the city to this study of baladi culture as demonstrated in medical, religious, social, business, and other activities. The contrast between baladi and afrangi culture also struck me as permeating every decision and explanation in everyday life of Bulaq. Baladi women mocked afrangi languor as they worked hard to sell vegetables, and envied clean afrangi streets while decrying baladi filth. I examine in detail in Chapter 3 baladi ambivalence toward afrangi life and how baladi women blend elements of the two daily.

In Bulaq, I found myself catching slices of cultural explanations in the bedlam of normal visiting, particularly when a distressed woman was moved to bare her soul. Several years later in Chicago, when I had the luxury of time to reread my early, painstakingly typed, field notes, I revisited these cultural episodes in grouped paragraphs quoting a woman on neighbors' gifts, a recent quarrel, a marriage prospect, and so on.

As I began to feel my way through everyday life in Bulaq, I started collecting what I later called "well-being narratives." These commentaries by women in the clinic waiting area proved compelling exemplars of everyday life and culture. One could argue that every issue is ultimately tied to well-being, and it is certainly true that when I spoke with women about past pregnancies, all manner of topics—the search for housing, making religious vows, neighborhood relations, or government bureaucracy—spilled out with talk of babies born and babies died. It was no accident that much of my data was about health or raising a healthy family, as that weighed on baladi women's minds—as it does on minds of mothers around the world—and figured heavily in their everyday discourse.

For example, on 28 September 1975, after I had been in the field almost a year and a half, I wrote in my notes:

Zainab took me to Um Nadia's [Um means "mother of"] on the fourth floor of her building to have Nadia measure me for a dress. I later recorded all the conversations during the visit, including a long one on miscarriage—since a relative visiting had just lost a baby—and another one on birth control. Then the women—Zainab and her sister Sayyida, and several visitors to Um Nadia—began to discuss children.

Sayyida related how her twins stole meat in the apartment building. One woman hit a twin when the twin took meat, and that night Sayyida's cat came and scratched the woman while she slept.

Um Nadia: "I had heard about a story of Christians and a cat in

the Aylouli district and had meant to ask you if you knew about
it."

Sayyida: "Yes, after that happened, my son was passing by the
door of some Christians. It was during their fast from meat.
They called to my son and said, 'We don't have any meat for
you,' and then they called him names. The next day I went and
confronted them about this. Those kids of mine! My twin came
home today, after walking all the way to the Bata store in
Shoubra way past the Shoubra bridge. You [turning to the
woman who had just miscarried] don't want kids."

As we continued to discuss children, Sayyida related two
separate incidents when she tried to embarrass her husband:
"We were sitting with his sister in her house, and she exchanged looks with him, clearly telling him to let me leave
first because she had something to tell him. Being no fool, I left,
but I curved around by another route and came upon my husband
with a woman on each arm—his sister and the new wife his sister was proposing. I was carrying my baby with me. I tapped my
husband on the shoulder and threw my baby down on the ground
and screamed: 'So this is what you do while I am home caring
for the children?' The baby's head was cut open.

"Another time I followed my husband to the Shoubra cinema
where he had gone with another woman. I told the usher that
my husband was inside and that his father had just died so I
must find him. The usher helped me with his flashlight until
we found him. Then I began to scream at him. They turned off
the movie. He had to leave the other woman, just like one
leaves a dog, and come home with me."

All the women listening to Sayyida approved of her tac-
tics—even that of hurting the baby, for after all it was for the
ultimate good of the children that she picked this fight.
Sayyida demonstrated her actions—standing in the middle of
the room gesturing and re-enacting how she had thrown her
baby on the ground—saying "I did it for my children. I do good so
that God will reward me with children." The women nodded
sympathetically and said to Sayyida that now that she had
shown her courage her husband would not play around any more.

Sayyida's account replays earlier dramatic encounters with her
spouse. The rerun is better than the first show because women
listeners can contribute their opinions, and because Sayyida has
time to give them background to set them up for her best lines.
Sayyida worked her story into the naturally situated discourse
surrounding another woman's miscarriage.

Studies of "personal narrative" (Allen 1978; Robinson 1981; Stahl 1977) note how raconteurs link stories to context and jockey for positions in conversation. Tales such as Sayyida's percolate up anytime baladi women have a few minutes to swap experiences. Their tales are not epic works, and their audiences do not mull over and critique the stories in the way, say, that formal storytelling audiences do in Afghanistan (Mills 1991:24). Baladi audiences expect informal recounting with more embellishments: they are more attentive to affect than to text as they encourage a woman such as Sayyida to try to maintain her family. These cultural performances can have a therapeutic as well as creative effect. "The impact of narratives on their raconteurs and audiences is enhanced by the power of such cultural themes as envy, *mushahara* (infertility), or modest behavior when they are coupled with biographic immediacy" (Early 1985:179).

Like many social researchers, I generated my own notes and my own texts and thus perhaps dismissed my informants to the periphery as I constructed my view of the life of a Bulaqi woman. I may have typified those for whom writing and the "making of texts . . . has emerged as central to what anthropologists do both in the field and thereafter" (Clifford 1986:2). I like to think, however, that note-taking restrictions kept me closer to baladi texts, since as numerous studies of reflexivity pound home, the texts of the people studied, and not the field notes of the researcher, are the important source.

While I have no illusions about the purity of my texts, I judge that many were naturally situated because of my conditions of research. Unlike many field workers of the 1960s and 1970s, I did not have the luxury (or perhaps the obstacle) of recording notes in the field. My Bulaqi friends understood that I was a researcher, and I told them that I was writing a book on the lives of women in Bulaq and on child-rearing practices. Some of their daughters had similar work as social workers or students. I found that my hostesses would tell the other visitors to talk to me "because I liked to ask questions and was writing a book about them." Nevertheless, I was continually foiled by runaway chickens or crying children who interrupted my chats with women.

I found it almost impossible to write notes or to use a tape recorder, for two distinct reasons. First, even close friends lost interest when I began to take notes. When I asked my good friend Fatima to write down the names of family members that we would be meeting on our trip to her village, she responded, "Well, you'll meet them won't you? Why do you need to write them now?" Baladi society is fast moving, and I simply decided to catch information on the wing, as best I could. That increased the quality of my cultural information, but it also tried my memory. Second, as a high-profile foreigner in a poor quarter where residents might question my interests in poverty (as had occurred with friends of mine stopped for taking pictures of a baladi area by self-appointed guardians of public interest), I felt it best to avoid advertising my research with a tape recorder.

To collect notes as accurately as possible, I jotted down key themes for each day as soon as I left the field. Sometimes I paused at the orange juice stand just outside the quarter of Bulaq to write notes. As soon as I returned to my apartment, I typed up my notes with triple carbons. What this meant in terms of fieldwork methodology was that all of my texts were reconstructed from outline notes or my own tape recording of events and women's talk that I recorded as soon as I left Bulaq. I developed gimmick "signposts" (such as "the three reasons Zainab is angry with her husband and the two explanations of her baby's illness" or "the fat lady and baby nutrition") to jog my memory. Texts were not always complete, and that was frustrating. It was not frustrating that I never could conduct directed, recorded interviews. I suspect that had I stuck a recorder under my friends' noses they would have frozen. I was not looking for life histories, but for spontaneous evaluations of life situations. These could not be preprogrammed, and their grounding in everyday discourse more than compensated for the awkwardness of their collection.

The medical narratives I collected in early research were dramatic accounts of interpreting symptoms, justifying recourse, and explaining eventual recovery or death. But they were just one instance of spontaneous accounts; when I turned to my religious, economic, and social field data, I found poignant biographic events of piety, of conflict, and of death linked with cultural ideals such as religious practice, morality, and fate.

As I conducted research in the mid-1970s, anthropology was shaking itself loose from rusty moorings of "emic" versus "etic" perspectives and sailing toward the texts of research subjects. We had become painfully aware of how our presence in the field had influenced our data. Folklore was moving in a similar direction, focusing on how personal narratives described action and gave the narrator's interpretation of the incident recounted (Allen 1978; Labov and Waletsky 1967; Robinson 1981; Stahl 1977).

Different genres of narratives (medical, religious, business, and so on), along with descriptive, affective, informative, and information-seeking statements, compose the "stuff" of daily discourse in Bulaq. Baladi women of Bulaq have their stories to tell, but the women are neither epic poets nor local notables. In between the pulses of daily life, they recount tales that may not be elaborate, but can be dramatic. This study of everyday Bulaqi life relies heavily on cultural information conveyed in informal performance. The baladi, traditional, way is a rich cultural approach to life that is both authentic, and creatively cosmopolitan and eclectic. The kernel of my contention is this: baladi is at its best when it tries to bridge the gap between the reality of the moment and that hoped for, between the real and the ideal. Baladi people select from a menu of pragmatic, stop gap alternatives that includes both the simple and traditional as well as the complex, Western-oriented, modern afrangi. Most situations fall far short of the ideal, and baladi people draw from both sides of the baladi:afrangi cultural dichotomy.

Baladi Egyptians, like people everywhere, daily face disparity between their situation and the ideal. Performances, interpretation of events, and the retelling of myths allows "extensive opportunity for imaginative manipulation of content . . . a special freedom of situation usage in contrast with other forms of discourse" (Basso 1985:1, 5). Ethnographies are no longer *the* story but rather *a* story. Multiple voices resound in baladi and other texts (Marcus and Fischer 1986:162). Not only is there the research and the research subject; not only are there the biographic details negotiated against shared cultural understandings. There is also the fact that everyone has their own story to tell, no matter what form it takes. "Storytelling comes in many genres. Renewed attention to the relation between these forms or genres and the information conveyed has reinvigorated recent thinking about ethnography. . . . Experience . . . tends to be shared knowledge encapsulated in stories that everyone can recognize" (Fischer and Abedi 1990:xix, 6). The narrator of a story embedded in everyday discourse fashions an individual interpretation that weaves the text, the story, to the context. These threads are more predictable in such epiclike stories as the *ceili* hearthside tales of Ballymenone, although the event itself is quite casual:

> Ceilis are not planned. They happen. At night you sit to rest and perhaps a neighbor or two will lift the latch and join you at the hearth. Or perhaps you will rise to your feet after supper and go out along the black lanes to one of the local homes known as a "ceili house." . . . For years our perceptions were so conditioned by literary convention that we had nothing better to call tales than prose. Recently noting similarities between spoken narra- tive and modern verse (much as critics have noted similarities

between folk art and modern painting), we have begun to think of them as poetry. . . . Stories begin and end in conversations. During their course they refer to their social situations by returning to the thick, uncadenced sound of chat (Glassie 1982: 71, 39).

A similar performance is the *veglia* of Tuscany, which are characterized by fireside evenings and their homespun performances (Felassi 1980).

Text and Context: Narrative and Performance

Folklorists have addressed the issue of emergent intertextuality (Bauman 1986; Bruner 1984; Briggs 1988; Chock and Wyman 1986) in performance and how "a story can be dialogic with itself, simultaneously conveying mixed or opposed messages, and thus be open-ended, ambiguous, and paradoxical" (Mills 1991:22). Performance-generated meaning is clear in such baladi rituals as negotiation of social relations, disputes over familial duties, or coffee-ground reading. My study does not attempt to present a particular genre of ordinary baladi discourse, such as the baladi dispute that has its ritual complement in the *radih* or rhymed insults that baladi women trade in the lanes. Rather, my study uses field notes, some of which are certainly also baladi text: first, to examine the cultural opposition baladi:afrangi in situated discourse as a window to understanding everyday baladi life; second, to consider the expression of sentiment and creation of meaning in the baladi performances that wed biographic immediacy with cultural understandings. I do not pretend to present a baladi text totally free of my views, and I am certain that I meddled in the baladi texts I present; I note those that were elicited rather than spontaneous. "One cannot stand clear out of the way while the other speaks, because one is the way, the conduit through which more or less alien ideas and forms, crafted sometimes in a thoroughly alien language, are transmitted to an interested audience of strangers" (Mills 1991:16). Nevertheless I allow spontaneous discourse and narrative recountings to reveal a culture in action that my baladi women friends would recognize.

An important example of this spontaneous discourse was the unsolicited talk on the periphery of formal ritual. I began to notice how helpful this talk was after a year or so in the field. An instance of this counterpoint of the ritual and the mundane in my fieldwork occurred the day my friend Karima called me away from the *zar* (spirit exorcism ritual) for which I had waited half the day. I wrote in my field journal in January 1976:

> I had been waiting six hours for the zar to begin. Just a few minutes after the drumming started and before anyone had even gone into a proper trance, I felt a tap on my shoulder. It was the daughter of my friend Karima summoning me to her house to meet visitors. "Couldn't she wait?" I countered. Surely Karima, my friend, could appreciate how important a zar was to my work. I turned back to watch.

In the end, I gave up and left the ritual to meet Karima's friends. Karima's claim on me was reasonable. She had introduced me to her friends so I could conduct research, and now she wanted to show me to a cousin to impress her.

As the cousin and I sat talking, I witnessed a spontaneous dispute. While I had seen many run-of-the-mill street fights, this was more complex. Each sister employed cultural themes of sibling responsibility and of honor to score points. Witnessing the dispute influenced my research far more than observing one more zar, because it was part of the unconscious process that alerted me to the importance of quotidian conversation. I found myself hurrying home to record what people said when they quarreled, when they explained their work, when they advised on finding apartments, or when they defended their curative strategy. While women baked sweets for weddings or naming ceremonies, they recounted dramatic versions of past matches and past births. While they awaited the groom's procession of gifts to the bride in a rural wedding, they speculated excitedly over the number of dresses likely to be sent and the quality of food to be served at the ceremony—combing all clues such as visits by the groom's family to market or arrival of urban relatives bearing parcels. While they boiled rice for a birth celebration pudding, they talked of neighbors' responsibility to help at birth or of fathers working abroad. My mind was so full of these collections of everyday texts that on the days I found visitors at my apartment on my return from the field, I excused myself until I had finished my initial recording of notes.

It was the medical, or well-being narratives, that alerted me to the cultural importance of other business, social, and religious accounts. I found them framed with such characteristic expressions as "although it was unbelievable" or "I'll tell you how it was" (Early 1982:1492). Such characteristic expressions or linguistic devices such as pitch change are metacommunicative devices. Opening and closing formulae in verbal art like the "Once upon a time" and "And they lived happily ever after" signal the start and end of a fairy tale (Briggs 1988:9). Stylistic patterns such as gesture and prosody (pitch, loudness, stress, vowel length, phrasing, and so on) set off stories or narratives (Briggs 1988; Bauman 1977; Goffman 1974; Robinson 1981).

As there is often a confluence of the context and text, my most important clues about baladi culture emerged willy-nilly in the midst of cooking, racing for a bus, or visiting a shrine. It is their context that vitalizes baladi women's stories. Similarly, a study of woodcutters in the U.S. Southwest revealed the "difficulty of producing a proverb text apart from a social context that provided a raison d'etre. . . . The nature of performance lies not in repeating texts but in developing the competence to embed textual elements in an ongoing interaction" (Briggs 1988:4).

This situation of symbolic expression in action, this coupling of conceptual structures with biologically mediated experiences, is widely discussed in the literature (Basso 1985; Bourdieu 1977; Baumann 1977; Geertz 1983; Fischer and Abedi 1990). Culture constitutes and contains within itself "explanations of human life and thought and of social, psychological, environmental, and cosmological events and process" (Basso 1985:1–2). As an individual's situation is often not what one hopes, so there may be a disjunction between a text and life. Baladi women of Bulaq often harkened back to the "good old days" of life under the British and the glories of the afrangi lifestyle to work out the incongruence between days of glory and the reality of their baladi Cairo.

It may be flippant to say that the privileged have their psychoanalysts and the poor have their folk medicine and religion. (I found to my great surprise that middle-class Egyptians who snickered about therapy in the 1970s were attending group therapy in the 1980s). Baladi Egyptians use home and herbal pharmacist remedies for simple complaints, much as Westerners self-prescribe megadoses of vitamin C for the common cold. They resort to modern clinics, however, if symptoms warrant. Both spontaneous and religious rituals have a salutary effect on baladis (Early 1985).

These ritual pronouncements are woven into the context of conviviality and informality, and often draw their strength as ritual text from that very context. For example, one evening while we sat drinking coffee and talking about proposed urban renewal, Um Amal volunteered to tell the future of a visiting in-law by reading the grounds in the visitor's coffee cup. Her reading was a spontaneous performance the cultural exegesis of which depended on the social context. Um Amal was both hostess and counselor that particular evening. She contrasted cultural ideals of bad and good behavior, and suggested "therapy" for her visitor, the father of her son-in-law, who was both worried because his son Muhammad had not returned from a visit to the village and also angry because Muhammad's injured mother needed him to drive her in his taxi to the doctor. Um Amal told her visitor:

> How can Muhammad know his mother's leg is broken, and that she must change her bandages every few days at the doctor? If he knew, he would not stay so long in the village. But, his mother is usually a ball of fire and finishes all her housekeeping early in the day. Now, she cannot move and must stay home, worried to death because her son is gone. If you were the son and away in the village, wouldn't you write a letter or at least call your mother? My nephew Mimi phoned his own sister in the village to find out how her daughter's exams went.

Um Amal's counselor persona had blossomed that evening in the midst of a conversation about her broken television, which Muhammad had taken for repair six months earlier, and which he promised to pick up every day. Muhammad's father then told of his experience with a television repairman who charged only five pounds, which pleased him so much that he gave the man two extra pounds. "People pleased with reasonable prices tip well."

Our conversation moved on to urban renewal. Adjacent streets had been leveled and residents were expecting their area to be next. Six months earlier they had been ordered to evacuate. Um Amal packed only her clothes. She regaled us with a personal narrative about moving, set off from the normal chatting by heightened voice pitch and dramatic gestures:

> Why would I want to take this pile of junk with me? The furniture is worth almost nothing and the refrigerator is about ready to break down. . . . We returned to the building on our own when we saw they were not going to tear it down. One woman stayed at her daughter's, another at her cousin's, etc., but most of us were uncomfortable. In simple Arabic, I don't like to visit anyone. Amal was a splendid hostess, but do you believe that when I stayed with her, I made my own tea? I can only be comfortable in my own home.

Eventually our conversation returned to the errant son, and as he spoke of his worries, the father (Abu Muhammad) accepted Um Amal's earlier offer to read his cup, and handed it to her.

Um Amal: I see in your cup a victory and that it is you who will be victorious. I can see you will have the answer to an important question in five days.

Abu Muhammad (counting to himself): Yes, that is definitely true.

Um Amal: Do you have any vows you have made to the saints?

Abu Muhammad: No, nothing.

Um Amal: You have no intention to make a promise to any saint?

Abu Muhammad: No.

Um Amal: Well, the thing you should do does not actually have to be a vow. It can be rather simple. Find a poor person sitting in the street; give him five loaves of fresh bread and a ten-piaster coin; and have him recite the Quranic chapter "The Family." I see your son Muhammad in your cup. I see that you are very worried.

Abu Muhammad: Of course I am worried and upset, for I have a sick wife and a son I can't find. I have a problem in every place! Why shouldn't I be worried!

Um Amal: But I see that good will happen; but remember to give the loaves of bread and the ten piasters to the poor person (Early 1985b:177).

This fortune-telling performance, which I witnessed quite by accident and could never have "scheduled" to view, is typical of many other spontaneous performances—whether invitations, arguments, or accounts of daily trials—I observed and recorded in my field notes. It was nothing I elicited; indeed my only comments that evening were about the problems of urban renewal. The "ritual efficacy" and "cultural information" of these performances (already known to the participants, but revealing clues to an outside researcher) are similar to those of such formal rituals as exorcism, but their genesis is always a social encounter, a personal problem, or some other social serendipity. The cultural information of these spontaneous ritual performances was always rich.

Um Amal's performance did more than tell the future; it calmed a man frantic both because his wife was sick and because he feared for his son's safety. Such a mundane performance can quietly evaluate, endorse, and counsel. The cup reading, much as formal ritual, was set off from ordinary discourse by the ringing declaration "I see in your cup" plus the accompanying gestures of holding and peering at the cup. Um Amal's performance was clearly directed "at" her visitor to calm him and to encourage him to judge his son and her daughter less harshly. In much the same way, Western Apache historical tales are both about a past event and "about" the person at whom it is directed to teach them a lesson (Basso 1984:39). While baladi women would normally make a vow at a shrine in such cases, Um Amal provided a male-tailored alternative (a good deed) much as she might have prescribed a household remedy.

Um Amal's role as "fortune teller" is a logical extension of the adviser role typical of older baladi women who, often specialized as midwives or as excisors (performers of female circumcision), also provide social and medical counsel. Um Amal is not a midwife but she frequently suggests both home remedies and cosmopolitan medicine to neighbors. In fact, when I returned in the 1980s after completing fieldwork to consult on Egyptian infant oral rehydration programs, Um Amal asked me to explain rehydrants to her so she could advise her relatives and friends.

Um Amal's fortune-telling and the host of other everyday performances framed by declarations such as "I'll show you" that I witnessed during my research helped to crystallize cultural truths for me. While my original focus on health yielded many healing and well-being performances, I inevitably witnessed a host of other performances, each with its unique cultural focus: marriage narratives that expressed anxiety of young brides, or ritual money exchange that announced social alliances. Baladi women signaled the importance of their statements as they paused and set them off with a high-pitched voice and dramatic gestures. Undeniably, I, as researcher, made the final interpretation.

My journey toward everyday performance was not straight and simple. In the field I found myself carefully noting the events I only later identified as "everyday performances." At the time I simply found them rich exemplars of baladi culture, but in retrospect I can see how they socialized me into baladi society. For example, one day a woman accidentally dumped water on me as I walked down the street. Drenched, I leapt to the middle of the street and, without reflecting, raised my fist and my voice simultaneously:

Me: How dare you drench my dress. See, I can never go to work this way! Have you no upbringing?

Woman: I didn't see you. I intended nothing.

Me: You should look before you throw water out the window. Why, you could have been throwing something heavy and hurt my head, knocked me cold. Have you no respect—if not for my sake, than at least for your children's!

Woman: I am sorry. Why don't you come up and I will give you my daughter's clothes to wear?

Me: I can see from here that your daughter is much smaller than I. Do you also want to insult me by dressing me in clothes that they will mock at work?

By then I felt I had put the woman in her place, and passers-by were encouraging me to stop fretting, that all would be well. I moved on down the road to see my friend Fatima. When I did not find her home, I settled down to recount my wash-water tale to a worker who was carding cotton stuffing in the courtyard. With a jolt, I realized how baladi I had become. Certainly fights and telling tales are universal, but I felt myself invoking the very baladi cultural categories of proper action and respect that my friends would. As with them, I felt better after recounting the entire episode.

In my research, I began to anticipate places in conversation where such tales would appear. It was clear that they were most likely to happen while a group of women were sitting together cooking or drinking tea. At some point I unconsciously sought out these richer venues in my work and tried to participate in group outings that took us out of the quarter, and away from the distracting bustle of shopping or neighbors dropping by to borrow things or chat. Baladi women's performance-rich "retreats" were not unlike those I experience with my own women friends when we stay together at a hotel for an academic conference. Our meals out and evenings at the hotel are certain to be crammed more with tales of each woman's past year than with theoretical discussions! What better venue for self-expression and group support than a hotel room away from our families and colleagues?

When I later reviewed my field notes, I found cultural jewels in narratives of individual, biographic incidents that illuminated cultural themes such as envy, fate, motherhood, devotion, and right action. In a 1982 article, before I had read any of the by-now voluminous literature on "narrative" and "performance," I analyzed baladi medical culture and its "illness narratives." I found the same phenomena—narratives, stories, spontaneous performances about religion, business, and society that framed poignant biographic events of piety, of conflict, of death, linking them with cultural ideals—when I turned from my medical to my general ethnographic data. The personal narrative comments on the progression of life events (Labov and Waletzky 1966:13; Robinson 1981; Stahl 1977:10). To understand it and other more formal epic and folkloric texts, one must comprehend the "indissoluble unity of text, narrated event, and narrative event" (Bauman 1986:7). As theorists paid more attention to context, they moved from the study of formal ritual to the edges of formal ritual, where it more spontaneously interacts with the prodigious problems of getting on in life (V. Turner 1982, 1985; E. Turner 1987). An Ndembu ghost doctor tailors his healing rituals to a woman's experience with miscarriage: "African ritual reaches down easily in the particularities of each case, by divination—with no holds barred as to the sensitive nature of a dangerous one-night stand, for instance, with suicide threats or the inner dread of a pregnant woman continually feeling in herself an impending miscarriage" (E. Turner 1987:33).

As social scientists have sought to let their informants speak for themselves, we have heightened our age-old concern with the impact of the researcher's presence on the quality if not kind of data. At the same time, researchers of performance-oriented narratives are aware that context shifts from moment to moment, and that "participants in a communicative event provide each other with cues that signal how words and actions are to be interpreted" (Briggs 1988:14). Stylistic features provide a metacommunicative framework to link style of performance to social and cultural patterns. All this may not be apparent to the researcher, for audiences mull over and review storytelling performances to which they bring prior and posterior understandings (Mills 1991:26).

My concern with analysis of text emerged gradually in the course of my research. While I always aimed to let baladi women speak for themselves and see how listeners responded, affirmed, and critiqued any discourse—both mundane and that set off in narrative or spontaneous performance—I did not initially differentiate between general ethnographic data collection and special stories. Further, I sometimes played a role similar to that of a baladi woman when I was the sole interlocutor. At other times, I interjected comments and questions that undoubtedly were more motivated by my research interests than my interest in simulating a baladi woman's performance. In the texts in this book, I have indicated where I was the interlocutor by means of italics. Since I often heard similar cultural explanations in other settings, I do not feel that my occasional participation impacted greatly on the quality of the data.

Middle Eastern Discourse

Linguistic eloquence and literary expression are central to Middle Eastern culture. Arabic holds a special status for Muslims because the Quran was revealed to the Prophet Muhammad in Arabic, and Quranic references and Quranic Arabic often appear in everyday parlance. Muslims who have memorized the Quran are highly respected. "The Islamic emphasis on the oral or dialogic over the textual might be compared with that of eighteenth-century Japanese 'nativism.' In neither case does the oral exclude the literate; rather, the literate is problematized and kept from being a tyrannical authority" (Fischer and Abedi 1990:xxiii). The cultural value placed on reciting the Quran and poetry extends to the electronic media. Radio programs in the Middle East carry long segments of Quranic recitations or poetry; a similar incidence of Biblical recitations or nineteenth-century poetry recitations on popular radio stations in the West is unthinkable. Studies of Islamic rituals such as those of sufi orders and Quranic reading (Crapanzano 1973; Gilsenon 1973; Nelson 1985; Waugh 1989) have focused more on the formal discourse of Islam. Studies of such local Islamic tradition as shrine visitation (Betteridge 1980; Campo 1983) describe a more quotidian discourse.

Abu Lughod's study of bedouin women of the Awlad Ali of northern Egypt explains that poetry is a privileged medium of communication for women, their own discourse outside of the mundane, humdrum interaction of everyday life. Abu Lughod notes that bedouin women "attach special weight to the messages conveyed in poetry and are moved, often to tears, by the sentiments expressed" (Abu Lughod 1986:177). The poetry itself is formulaic, but it leaves room for adaptation of the individual experience—the biographic, the specific—to the cultural generality. Poetry ultimately takes its meaning from the social contexts in which it is embedded; this poetry is the poetry of personal sentiment (Abu Lughod 1986:177–185). Most of this type of poetry was about negative, dysphoric sentiments, and the belief that when women get what they want, "they shut up." Much as bedouin women feel better after communicating their private sentiments through this privileged medium of poetry, so baladi women find emotional support through sympathetic interventions of listeners to their narratives. This kind of support is rarely given in the impersonal interaction with social service agency employees.

While the beduoin women's discourse is personally created within a shared format, Middle Eastern verbal performances can also draw on more formal text, as seen in two recent studies by Mills (Afghanistan) and Caton (Yemen). It is significant that Abu Lughod and I worked with women's text, while those dealing with more formal text, Mills and Caton, worked with men. Afghani tales of buffoonery, ethnic stereotypes, and sexual candor are a "window onto a complex vision of noninstitutional moral authority and autonomy intensely egalitarian . . . the bulk of this material . . . is saturated with overt and implicit Islamic ideology" (Mills 1991:345). Tribal poetry in north Yemen is "embedded in an extremely important political process—the dispute mediation—in which power, such as it exists in this system, must be achieved through persuasion" (Caton 1990:13). Poetry is not just communication, it is central to the tribal sociopolitical system. It is not mere text, as "most tribal verse genres include compositions created in a dance-like performance which comprise an aesthetic-semiotic ensemble along with words and music" (Caton 1990:19).

All three of these studies address the emergence of culture in a communicative act, whether personal sentiments about social expectations (Egyptian), stories as open texts which flow into and comment upon each other (Afghani), or the ideology of poetic practice (Yemeni). The issue of the relation of the cultural system to social practice is the crux of the discourse analysis. As I consider the folktales, the poetry, the epics, and other more formal texts of Middle Eastern society, I hesitate to place baladi women's utterances in the same genre. The only "formal, repeated" texts I ever heard in baladi women's society were frequently repeated, continually heard Quranic verses, and standard lines of insults hurled in street disputes or standard verses sung in life-event processions. Reputation was negotiated not via stereotypic insults, but rather via idiosyncratic, spontaneous texts presented here. These texts are not tales of tribal conquests or of folk heroes; nevertheless, each refers to cultural lore that forms the building blocks of baladi culture—whether a social maxim such as "Each neighbor should keep to herself" or a historical perception that "the days of the British (World War II) were days of glory and opulence."

Works on Egyptian women, as part of a general trend that emphasizes the wisdom of the personal and the idiosyncratic, are moving to understand these lives by *listening* to what the women have to say—by listening hard, one can catch coded references, the nuggets of cultural wisdom uttered in the cracks of ordinary discourse. Personal accounts both valorize the raconteur's struggles and also provide the teller with a personal catharsis. Andrea Rugh notes how the expressive autobiographies of Naiyre Attiya's *Khul Khaal* provide a gold mine of cultural information that is better than analytic models of kinship or decision-making. These women are philosophers who reduce all the tragedies and passions of their lives to a few themes, in stories carefully crafted so that the narrator acts in an exemplary fashion. The stories reflect "extraordinary natural perception about the world in which they live" (Attiya 1982:viii, x).

The search for the author's roots in her native Egypt, recorded by Wedad Zenie-Ziegler in *In Search of Shadows: Conversations with Egyptian Women*, is similar to Attiya's quest to understand the women who surrounded her in Egypt. "I went back in search of those who had been the shadows of my childhood, trying to penetrate their secret world, catch them in their everyday life. I went to find them in the working-class districts of Cairo and in the villages of the Nile Delta and Upper Egypt" (Zenie-Ziegler 1988:7). Unlike Attiya's autobiographical vignettes, this one is topical, with anecdotes on polygamy, marriage customs, and other themes related to women's rights.

Andrea Rugh, in *Family in Contemporary Egypt*, also pays attention to women but goes a step further, organizing data from interviews to provide biographic examples of family roles, marriage, culturally defined social relations (such as that of "obligation") and adjustment to such social trends as the population explosion. Rugh presents the family as stable and constant, providing "a useful instrument with which Egyptians can manipulate life's chances and respond to the requirements of contemporary life" (Rugh 1984:289).

Unni Wikan notes the "power of words" in stories that women tell about one another in *Life among the Poor in Cairo* (1980), a book that analyzes the life situation of seventeen poor families living in thirteen houses of the Cairo suburb of Giza. Wikan suggests that the constant struggle for scarce goods dominates childrearing and social alliances. For Giza baladi women, stories represent one method of self-realization in an economically marginal society; these stories "function as myths for the people. They are legitimizing versions of existing relationships—and their truth value is completely secondary or unimportant" (Wikan 1980:130). Words have power to help, and to harm. Wikan notes:

> All these different forms of interpretation, criticism, lying, and slander are summarized by the poor themselves in their concept of "people's talk" (*kalam innas*) as a social institution which threatens everyone in the same unpredictable fashion everywhere. It is "people's talk" which most thoroughly can destroy a woman's efforts at self-presentation, ? d it is "people's talk" which she must constantly do battle against (1980:144).

To combat "people's talk," baladi women spin narratives that present themselves in the best light and that seek audience opinions—What was the best medicine for the child? Who was the best groom? and so on. The audience may encourage with expressions of agreement and support, and the speaker is likely to finish her account exhilarated.

After some time in the field in Cairo, I found myself bringing my own tales to my friends, and spontaneously invoking the platform that is a narrator's prerogative. If I had been frustrated in an office, or stymied in springing a package from customs, I regaled my acquaintances with my account. As with baladi women, I always felt better after being allowed to tell my tale and to hear my interlocutors' unconditional support and their jeers for my bureaucratic enemies. A memorable day was when my boyfriend and I had parted company. I tailored my story for my baladi friends' consumption to "There was this man whom I met and found attractive but he never asks after me." My listeners' immediate response was: "What a fool! Doesn't this man know who your father is, and your standing in the community? He is an idiot who deserves not a second thought!"

Talk of my problems always intertwined with talk of Bulaqi women's problems. With time I anticipated certain kinds of discourse. Does that mean I could perceive what was true baladi culture? Not necessarily. I share my colleagues' concern over how to interpret discourse recorded while in the field—a concern that has led to analogical anthropology and its "replacement of one discourse with another" (Tedlock 1983:324). Nevertheless, on return visits to Bulaq I witnessed many more spontaneous performances of the types I present here, and I continued to hear self-descriptions of baladi people as "authentic and downtrodden" contrasted with afrangi people who were "superficial and privileged."

In the next two chapters I describe the baladi quarter of Bulaq Abu 'Ala and analyze what it means to be baladi. The baladi: afrangi dichotomy is an ideal rendition of a world in which baladi people are honorable, hospitable, nationalistic, devout, and authentic while afrangi people are corrupt, stingy, unpatriotic, irreligious, and artificial. While the model may err on the side of what we used to call an "etic" or "outsider" analysis in its pristine division of the two tendencies, the women themselves use such a distinction as they plot medical, business, household management, and other strategies.

The baladi:afrangi relation is one of the insider and the outsider, of the have-nots and the haves, of the pragmatic and the ideal. Baladi economic frustration, exacerbated by continuing inflation and consequent deterioration of their economic situation, may be couched in cultural critiques of the pompous, afrangi lifestyle. The most dramatic portrayals are parodies of afrangi indulgence and buffoonery, including self-critique by folk singers and newspaper cartoonists.

Baladi economic practices are most successful in the informal sector between the private household and the public market economy. It is here that women like Fatima, the cheese merchant, show their mettle. The pragmatic baladi woman is able to cross from informal private dealing to the massive bureaucracies that fund medical and social aid. Her narratives tie personal histories with the public bureaucratic and political scene. In some ways, this book is about the clash of the pragmatic and the ideal, which parallels the potential clash of baladi and afrangi culture.

While appreciating that baladi economic opportunities are limited, this is not a study of the so-called "culture of poverty," nor is it a materialist analysis of class relations. Rather, the work presents the world through baladi eyes. I leave it to other scholars to present the culture of afrangi Egypt, which I oversimplify in this text because I view it exclusively from baladi eyes.

There are several excellent studies of baladi, traditional Egyptian urban culture. Nawwal Nadim el-Messiri's study, *Relations between the Sexes in a Harah of Cairo* (1975), analyzes childrearing and gender roles in the baladi lane of Sukkariyya. Sawsan el-Messiri's "Self Images of Traditional Urban Women in Cairo," (1978a) and *Ibn al-Balad: A Concept of Egyptian Identity* (1978b) plumb historic references and contemporary interviews to characterize the concept "baladi." Judith Tucker's *Women in Nineteenth-Century Egypt*, while outside the realm of contemporary anthropological studies of Egyptian women, is a welcome addition to the picture of nineteenth-century Egyptian women's economic role in agricultural production and in merchanting—including work as door-to-door peddlers, a job still practiced by Bulaqi women.

These works, and numerous discussions with the authors as well as with Wafiq Hassouna, Sayyid Oweiss, and Assad el-Nadim, were invaluable to my discussion of the concept of "baladi" throughout my book. In many ways this book follows the pattern through which I learned about the baladi lifestyle and culture. I began my fieldwork with a background of intensive training in the symbolic anthropology of the University of Chicago; while I temporarily focused on migrant adjustment, I was ultimately prepared to see Cairo in symbolic terms. But I soon found out that such an approach would tell at most half the story of those I met. Only when the lives of my informants and their mundane narratives showed me that successful women must continually negotiate the extremes of symbolic ideal and everyday necessity did I feel that I was beginning to understand and, to some extent, to share the world view of baladi people.

This book is organized in such a way as to induce the reader to get to know baladi culture as I did, through a gradual surrender of an absolute world view, accompanied by a growth of understanding of individuals responding to daily dilemmas. Chapter 2, on Bulaq Abu 'Ala, describes the physical setting of the study and introduces a typical baladi woman, Fatima, who lived in a building I visited frequently. Fatima offers a gestalt of the baladi woman early in the study. A recent migrant from a northern village, Fatima's work as a cheese merchant is typical of baladi, informal economic sector activity. A devout Muslim who prays regularly and studies the Quran in local mosques, Fatima also practices the popular Islam of shrines and vows. In Chapter 3, we hone our understanding of the baladi:afrangi dichotomy that permeates daily life in Bulaq by considering examples in baladi household management, gender roles, and medicine. Chapter 4 presents popular religious life passages, feasts, and shrines in addition to contemplating what the new "Islamicism" means for a baladi woman. Chapter 5 offers social performances of conflict and restitution closely linked with such other social ritual occasions as information management. By Chapter 6, we are equipped to plunge into personal narratives of marriage, virginity, fertility, politics, and business to see the baladi worldview lived out in biographic instances. It is this emergence of culture in the communicative event of baladi women's stories that we mentioned in this opening chapter, and to which we return in the concluding Chapter 7. To become acquainted with the study site, we begin in Chapter 2 with an historic and demographic look at Cairo and at the quarter of Bulaq Abu 'Ala.

2

The Industrial Quarter of Bulaq Abu 'Ala: Mameluke Playground Turned Vulcan Proletarian Forge

Bulaq History: From River Port to Industrial Quarter

B ulaq Abu 'Ala lies outside the walled city of medieval Cairo, which was founded east of the Nile River in 969 A.D. by the Fatimids, who named it Al-Qahira, or "The Victor." Successive Islamic governments ruled Cairo until the late eighteenth century, when the Napoleonic invasion added Western forces to the series of outside occupiers that had included the Mamelukes and the Ottomans. After the French came the British protectorate, which ended nominally in 1936 and definitively shortly after the 1952 revolution deposing King Farouq. Despite the relatively long British presence, modern Cairo most clearly bears the architectural imprint of the French and Italian.

Throughout the years Cairo expanded beyond her medieval walls west to the Nile and eventually across the river to the foot of the famous Giza pyramids. At the expense of agricultural land, she has continued to spawn northern and southern suburbs, such as Heliopolis and Ma'adi (Abu Lughod 1971). Bulaq was founded after the Nile River receded in the thirteenth century. Bulaq Abu 'Ala takes its name from the local saint Sultan Abu 'Ala, whose mosque commands the vantage point of the Nile bridge at the edge of modern-day Bulaq Abu 'Ala. An Englishman working in Egypt reported in his book on the saints of Cairo:

> The popularity of the Sultan Abu el-Ela is largely due to his being a local saint. Abd el-Wahab el-Sharani in *El-Tabaqat el-Kubra* refers to the head of the sainted Abu el-Ela being enshrined in Cairo, at Bulaq near the Nile. Natives of the spot assure me that that is so, but that his *sir* [spirit] keeps watch in the Nile, much as the spirit of another Weli near Qoft . . .

prevents any crocodile passing north. If it runs the spiritual
blockade it is forced to turn belly upwards, becoming an easy
prey. I have been asked why steamers blow their syrens in
passing near Bulaq Bridge. I have little doubt that it is in
honour of Abu el-Ela (McPherson 1946:145–146).

Sultan Malik Nasr founded the elite suburb of Bulaq on the
banks of the Nile in the fourteenth century. A set of docks was built
along the newly formed alluvial plains of Bulaq, and a canal was
dug to drain the tract of land on which present-day Bulaq stands.
The sultan encouraged princes to buy land. Princes, soldiers,
merchants, and common folk built houses, and Bulaq "sprang into
being" (Oweiss 1955). The area along the river was completely built
up with markets, mills, schools, baths, palaces, and belvederes
(Hanna 1983:4). There were grand palaces with gardens, sugar cane
fields, and water wheels. Mamelukes practiced archery and enjoyed
the cool Nile breezes on the stretch of sandbars west of the medieval
walled city. Bulaq was an "upper class suburban area where princes
and wealthy government officials built winter palaces and the
orchards of their agricultural estates" (Abu Lughod 1971:44).
    With the siltation of the nearby port of Al-Maqs, Bulaq became
a convenient port for traffic from the north. For example, during
Sultan Bibar's reign (1259 to 1277), it is reported that three boats a
year brought ice from the Syrian mountains for the royal kitchens.
The ice was taken from the port of Bulaq to the citadel by royal
mules. By the fifteenth century, all Delta traffic stopped at Bulaq
customs houses for taxation (Hanna 1983:6). Warehouses and inns
were built to accommodate caravans. Bulaq became a major point for
dispatching navies and a "key link and break-in-bulk point" for the
East-West spice trade (Abu Lughod 1971:44). Modern Bulaq's
massive iron and lumber depots, and spare parts stores echo this
past. The Bulaq of the fifteenth century had nine warehouses;
numerous sugar presses and cereal mills; sugar, grain, and oil
merchants; and woodworking, leather, and dye workshops.
    In the early nineteenth century, Muhammad Ali pinpointed
Bulaq for industrial development; Bulaq's elites fled the churn and
chaos of industry to resettle in northern suburbs. By the late
nineteenth century, Bulaq lacked the charm of medieval Cairo and
its elite foundations had crumbled. Vestiges of the grandeur remain.
People who give directions still refer to street "gates" that have
long since disappeared. Traces of rococo stucco rosettes, colonnades,
and arches on houses long since subdivided are reminders of Bulaq's
elegant past.
    In the early nineteenth century, Bulaq's industry included "two

Bulaq el-Gadid Street with Sultan Abu 'Ala mosque in the background

lathe shops where eight bulls turned one machine, a tint and dye plant with eight ovens and a Syrian overseeing Egyptian workers, and eighty iron workshops for ship fittings. There was a mammoth amount of charcoal in the workshops" (Toussin 1928:187–188). In 1818, a wool factory was established, followed by textile and spinning factories, Egypt's first iron foundry and first printing press, the Amiriyya. Today the area hosts numerous small printing presses plus Cairo's two major newspapers, *Al-Ahram* and *Akhbar al-Yawm*.

The rugged soul of Bulaq has captured the hearts of travelers drawn to the area's busy industrial atmosphere and those who remember its historic role. Bulaq outshone many quarters in its opposition to Napoleon and to the British. The French felt so harassed by Bulaqis that they burned down some buildings in Bulaq at the end of the eighteenth century. British consular reports on the 1919 revolution repeatedly refer to resistance in Bulaq. A Cairo British police report mentions an "unprovoked attack . . . made on the police who were returning to their quarters" in northern Bulaq in which eight British were wounded (F.O. 141/335, 1919 Consular Report). A recent article in *Akhbar al-Yawm*, a major Egyptian daily, eulogized a humble Bulaqi carpenter member of the Secret Organization of the Muslim Brotherhood. The carpenter was executed in 1926 for killing an English soldier on a Bulaqi street.

As the elite deserted Bulaq, the area changed from an aristocratic to a popular, baladi quarter resembling those of walled, medieval Cairo. These areas are known for their "toughs"—young men (or women) who protect their turf from outsiders, maintain order, and curb arbitrary arrests and plundering (see El-Messiri 1977:239 ff.). Bulaq is still considered a "tough" quarter, and my afrangi Egyptian friends cautioned me against visiting it, hinting at drugs and black market traffic. I never asked about such activities, and as an outsider interested in the Egyptian family, I was neither a threat nor threatened.

Present-day Bulaq's image is dominated by work, noise, and disorder. In 1939, a commentator described Bulaq as "Vulcan's Empire."

> On the way down towards El-Khadra street, hundreds of small dark workshops echo with the noise of hammers on red hot iron and on copper pans. An urchin hangs on to the chain of a smith's bellows whilst others are engaged in filing and adjusting. Screws, bolts, nails, and norags [sic] are made here. Like a dark Discobelus an iron monger throws the fly wheel of a borer. The smell of soldering acid irritates the nostrils. Dealers in old iron offer you all sorts of objects for which you have no use: dented mud-guards, out of date engines, enormous rusty wheels and even boilers. . . .
>
> There are ten thousand inhabitants to the square mile in this old quarter. Bulaq is stifling in its alleys. Bulaq el Guedid, which serves as a ventilation, is like a torrent of dead water. It is a world in itself.
>
> I remember an artificial paradise. Sad irony of words! A dark, crumbling basement. No morphine nor cocaine, those are too expensive. But, heroin. The barber has, in his bag, a syringe which is used by everyone. All that, in the shade of the bright, new Fouad I hospital. Thus surrounded by beautiful modern districts, Bulaq grovels in its poverty.
>
> Nevertheless, should it feel inclined, Bulaq could command all communications, gas, electricity and drinkable water. Barricaded in its *rabs* [medieval buildings], elusive in its labyrinths, it could hold the capital in check. It already is conscious of its power and has several times set fire to trams and buses, plundered workshops, and raised the scare of strikes. Heedless of the river god, it hammers away, forging proletarians. Should the modern city wish to resume the old

colloquy with the sacred Nile, and, in the interests of hygiene and beauty, push the industries of Bulaq off to the outskirts, this quarter might undergo profound transformations but its soul would never be entirely changed (Leprette 1939:253, 255).

Just as Leprette's Bulaq lacked the niceties of the nearby modern hospital, so today's Bulaq often lacks the electricity and running water readily available in downtown hotels a ten-minute walk away. Present-day Bulaq Abu 'Ala is replete with results of Muhammad Ali's industrialization. While Cairo's major textile and steel factories are in north and south suburbs, Bulaq is crammed with small-scale industries and workshops for carpentry, lathing, and metal and plastic works. Public sector representatives stream into Bulaq to buy specialized fittings, molds, and machine parts as well as the raw materials (often sold on the unofficial market) of its storehouses. The only two shops in Cairo that still fashion metal fittings for horse carriages are located in Bulaq. Welders, bricklayers, and other skilled laborers frequent the coffeehouses in Bulaq where contractors go to hire workers.

While Muhammad Ali's industrialization nudged the elite out to Cairo's suburbs, the economic boom that began in the 1970s displaced low-income Bulaqis to make room for office buildings and posh hotels. When I began research in 1974, Bulaq was a mixed commercial and residential area. While predominately made up of low-income residents, well-heeled merchants still lived a baladi life-style in elegant, crumbling apartments deep in the back lanes, or in spacious apartments on Bulaq al-Jadid Street abutting the wholesale clothing and used car parts markets.

The gentrification of Bulaq was inevitable. Near the Cairo Nile Hilton, Bulaq occupies prime commercial and riverfront land, which had remained undeveloped because foreign investors had shied away from Gamal Abdul Nasser's socialistic regime. When Egypt embarked on its policy of economic liberalization in the 1970s, foreign investment boomed, and historic landmark villas in the fashionable Garden City south of the Nile Hilton hotel fell to the wrecker's ball. Bulaq's yellow-baked mud-brick houses, with no patrons to protect them, were even more vulnerable. In the early 1980s blocks and blocks of homes in the workshop areas of Turgoman, Shahnin, and lower Darb el-Nasr had been cleared, and residents relocated to hastily constructed popular housing on the urban periphery. Sometimes the demolition notice was posted just hours before the work began, barely allowing time to clear furniture and detach wood shutters and doors for use in buildings elsewhere. When I returned in 1989 to visit, no hotels had been built, and vacant lots doubled as parking areas and soccer fields. The grand buildings once planned for Bulaq's interior had sprung up on its riverbank periphery.

A Baladi Neighborhood:
Bulaq Quarter in Primatial City Cairo

A primatial city at least three times as large as any other Egyptian city, Cairo has continued to grow at 5 percent per year (Abu Lughod 1971:200), or double the countrywide population growth. This growth rate outstrips that of all major North African cities except Tripoli and Benghazi in Libya. Cairo houses major government, health, and educational facilities, and major industries such as the steel works of Helwan. Government efforts to decentralize have been only minimally successful. Medical school graduates must serve two years in the countryside, but rural Egyptians assume that biggest is best and so travel hours to use Cairo's clinics. Regional industry remains embryonic; Mohalla el-Kubra's textile industry, which thrived as a cottage industry before its nationalization, has been a rare example of successful regional industry.

Egypt is in the throes of the demographic revolution caused by continuing high birth rates combined with improved standards of living. Its population is compressed into 3.6 percent of the terrain, with a population density of over 2,200 people per square mile for the country as a whole. Family planning programs provide a safe technology for an established practice, but may have only modest influence on population growth itself. Whether fertility declines are due to economic deprivation or to affluence is debatable, but the inescapable truth, which the Egyptian Ministry of Health appreciates, is that fertility behavior cannot be separated from health care and economic development.

The population explosion has strained Cairo's services, designed for a population of 1.5 million—a level exceeded by the end of World War II. It is no secret that Cairo's water, sewage, electric, and telephone systems are pushed past the breaking point. High-rise buildings without roof storage tanks receive no water by day. Clogged sewers often back up. The anthropologist Nawwal el-Messiri reports that on some days friends would phone from her urban research site to say: "Do not visit today. It is a 'Venetian' day," although the sewage-clogged streets had none of the charm of Venice! Power brownouts are routine. The economic expansion and foreign aid of the 1970s and 1980s have meant improvements, but showcases such as the Cairo Center high-rise office building or the prefabricated airport hotels have not changed the face of baladi quarters, where crowding and services are worst. In the early 1980s, Cairo hosted nine million inhabitants by day, in a country whose entire population was around fifty million. The city offered hope to landless peasants who were as much "pushed" as "pulled" to the city; their large numbers have made Cairo a top-heavy city where most migrants find work in service and public sectors. Housing is a problem for all classes; many couples, abandoning hope of finding an apartment, marry and live with parents. Egyptian professionals and foreigners monopolize the best housing in the central business district and the fashionable afrangi neighborhoods of Zamalek, Heliopolis, and Ma'adi. Exacerbating the problem is that fact that Egyptians who travel prefer to leave their apartments empty rather than rent them to someone whom they may not be able to evict upon return. There are estimates of over one-half million empty apartments in Cairo. The predicament does not stop there. Both baladi sun-dried brick buildings and concrete apartment buildings collapse regularly in Cairo. The latter are theoretically more stable, but are often built by overeager developers not following proper technical controls.

A *sebil* constructed to provide drinking water in a Bulaq Abu 'Ala lane

Cairo absorbs rural migrants by cramming them into existing units. As early as 1973 the city's population density was higher than that of New York City. Unlike New Yorkers, however, Cairenes reside in buildings of not more than five floors, and these buildings are interspersed among factories, parks, cemeteries, and agricultural plots. Population density is thus not vertical, but horizontal; in baladi quarters, a family of six to eight often lives in a single room. The baladi quarter of Bab as-Sha'ariyya topped the list of population density with 135,901 persons per square kilometer, while Bulaq had a density of approximately 70,000 per square kilometer (Waterbury 1978: II.8. p. 4).

Cairo's hopelessly overloaded mass transit system of the 1970s has been somewhat decongested with the opening of the Cairo metro and the construction of overpasses, which divert traffic from crowded downtown areas. Taxis became effectively extinct in the late 1970s while I was conducting research. With time and demand, what had been "private" taxis became group taxis where anyone heading in approximately the same direction took a seat. This "proletarianization" of taxis was completed by the early 1980s; a driver packed his cab and charged each rider full fare, with adjustments for long detours. Import regulation changes in the 1980s that facilitated importation of cars to be used as taxis markedly increased the number of taxis, which often double as personal cars at night.

Baladi Egyptians rely on buses, and they pick routes and times carefully to gain optimal standing room. Rush-hour traffic in Cairo is compounded by animal-drawn vehicles as well as pushcarts, trucks, and private vehicles. Importation of new buses to cruise already-choked streets, whose width was rigidified in the late nineteenth century by stone and reinforced poured concrete buildings just as traffic was becoming more dense (Abu Lughod 1971:160), has proved an unsatisfactory stopgap measure.

Only horse carts and occasional courageous cars travel through baladi quarters, which are a maze of major market thoroughfares, crosscut by residential lanes with nooks and crannies curving back on themselves. One navigates via such major landmarks as mosques or shops to reach the neighborhood, and then by such idiosyncratic markers as a brick wall or a water pump. Two favorite landmarks in Bulaq are "Zaki the fish seller" and "the arch below Tel Nasr." Street names and numbers are little used, and I soon learned locations of lumber warehouses or popular restaurants to fix friends' homes in my mental maps.

With no land zoning, private, public, and production activities intermingle in baladi streets. Young boys play with yarn and rubber balls, wheels on sticks and scooter boards; groups of girls enjoy hopscotch, bottle-top tossing, and chalk drawing. Private lives spill into the streets. In the lane, barbers shave men, and women force-feed ducks with soaked bread. Children play, eat, and defecate. Life in crowded one-room apartments overflows into the lane, where baladi social decorum guides the mingling of private and public. Vehement quarrels swirl while bystanders try to arbitrate, women josh with merchants, and young people flirt.

To observe a baladi street is to read a newspaper of local events. Quranic recitation over loudspeakers signals a funeral. A lane blocked by a horse-drawn cart announces a household's move. A nearby peddler or a scrawled note tells of a family crisis forcing the absence of a shopkeeper. A walk through a lane demands interaction; one must be prepared to respond to another's predicament or to queries about one's own presence. A walk down an afrangi street, however, requires so little involvement that a baladi person asking directions may well feel rebuffed.

Every baladi lane tells a complex economic, political, and technological story. Some lanes have stone curbs, which double as footbridges when sewers back up. A welding shop with sparks flying stands next to a dry goods shop and an apartment building with goats sheltered in the courtyard. Horse carts loaded with bricks, scrap iron, wooden wardrobes, or clover wind their way through the lanes to workshops and storehouses. Goat herds graze lazily over garbage piles. Vendors rove with merchandise: basketball-size cabbages, pinches of spices, stacks of tea glasses. They sell bean sandwiches or tea and milk in the morning, and macaroni and ice cream (or in winter hot chickpeas) in the afternoon. Vendors move their carts and makeshift stands with charcoal grills and burners from place to place, but some claim the same spot on the street daily. They avoid shop rental costs, although they may have to pay an official to "ignore" their unlicensed street activity.

The cross-section of technology is striking. Not far from a printing business with computerized typesetting sits a woman dabbing her finger into a glue pot as she fashions sacks out of scrap paper. Rooms lighted by kerosene lamps abut others in which dazzling neon tubes spew garish colors. On major market streets, ground floors of dwelling units have been converted to fancy boutiques with flashy aluminum siding.

Brick buildings with one to five stories, stuccoed a mustard yellow, rise about the lanes. Chunky, wooden-railed cement balconies jut overhead; clothes flap from ropes on sticks skewed from the balconies. Wooden shutters admit cooling breezes and block out the sun, flies, and dust. Painted green and blue, the shutters provide a pleasing break from the drabness of the walls. Most baladi buildings have either an open courtyard or an air shaft; higher floors are reached via curving cement stairs, often crumbled to half their original width. Rickety wooden stairs lead to roofs.

Many dried-mud-brick buildings are not stable. During my research in Cairo, a private school in Bulaq fell into a heap (one child died), and several homes collapsed. The newspaper *Akhbar al-Yawm* is known for its attention to human suffering, carried descriptions of the refugees from fallen homes who lived in mosques and cemeteries. In addition to inherent structural problems, local customs, such as the one that forbids renovation for several years after a head-of-household death, contribute to the run-down appearance of many houses. Even in houses without deaths, more than simple furnishing is considered ostentatious and an invitation to envy. Baladi homes were rarely refurbished when I was working in Bulaq in the 1970s. The recent rise in more conspicuous consumption means that baladi families who would formerly have kept simple furnishings may now aspire to fill their homes with videotape players and gadgets, and order imported Scandinavian-designed furniture for their salon and chic aluminum facades for their wood frame macaroni stands.

Building exteriors and surrounding lanes are considered public space and are left crumbling and cluttered, but the indoor, private space of a baladi home is mopped several times a day. Furniture covers are kept spotless, and paper lace designs regularly trim shelves and tables. Once I saw a similar paper design on an Egypt Air plane—paper napkins festooning all the cracks of the galley.

In baladi geography, landmarks are more important than street names: so too, the baladi ethos is unstructured and personalized. A Bulaq resident once categorized grocery stores for me as follows:

> In a baladi grocery, there are a few things scattered about on the shelf, rather disordered, with a lot of dust. The proprietor knows his goods and prices piece by piece. He offers customized service, such as placing orders in baskets lowered from balconies. In an afrangi grocery everything is sorted neatly with price tags and there is a large stock of each item. One must go to the store and purchase in an orderly way.

While the baladi see themselves as informal and personal, and enjoy asking for directions to landmarks and houses in baladi back lanes, the afrangi person who has grown up in more modern, grid-structured neighborhoods may view baladi lanes as convoluted and confusing. In a similar manner, the baladi Cairene sees Cairo's new, distant suburbs, such as Medinat Nasr, as orderly, depersonalized square blocks. Faceless but functional, one navigates them not by landmarks, but by street names and numbers. Offering little chance for social interaction, their sterility bewilders baladi visitors. Urban afrangi quarters have wide streets with walled villas and high-rise apartment buildings complete with sleek elevators and marble staircases. There are few commercial establishments except for corner groceries and restaurants. Afrangis see their own neighborhoods as neater and quieter than baladi ones.

Differences between neighborhoods of the eastern city of Old Cairo, the city's administrative center since the twelfth century, and the western city, founded in the nineteenth century and developed during the British protectorate, were more pronounced in the past. Through time, the baladi medieval Old Cairo and the afrangi British cities began to change, and the transitional zone between the eastern medieval city and the western modern Gold Coast grew more homogenized:

> Today . . . the city grows more and more into one cultural unit. As the Gold Coast becomes increasingly "baladized" and the medieval city becomes more modernized, the belt between them— neither fish nor fowl—widens to mediate between the narrowing social contrast. . . . (The) transitional business district, the link between the Western shops and the Oriental *aswaq* . . . is an unattractive melange having neither the modernity of the Western zone, nor the exotic charm of the Eastern bazaars: a place of crudely fashioned but brightly colored imitations of Western products, of odd assortments of second-hand plumbing pipes, old containers or coiled rubber hoses in disorganized display on pushcarts (Abu Lughod 1971:208–209).

Since the 1952 revolution, economic leveling and building expansion has fostered a superficial sense of homogenization. The disparity in living quarters is not readily visible, because lavish apartments for a four-person family and single rooms housing a ten-member family do not appear so different when both are located in a deteriorating mustard-yellow building. All shops are filled with the same Egyptian public-sector tinned goods and, more recently, with imported Earl Grey tea and Kellogg's cornflakes. All kebab and butcher shops have the same formica-top tables and sawdust-covered floors. Vendors push flamboyantly painted baladi wagons through afrangi streets to sell lentil and macaroni hot dishes and fava bean sandwiches. Baladi women, most of them servants, frequent government food cooperatives in such afrangi districts as Garden City. Businessmen cruise baladi quarters in flashy cars—but only to seek the labor or goods most easily found in these multipurpose neighborhoods.

Since the wealthy afrangi have lost the privilege of geographic isolation, they distance themselves in other ways. Cognitive boundaries have become rigid as territorial lines have relaxed in response to the population crunch and Nasserist policies of nationalization and public sector development. Afrangi and baladi quarters may be contiguous, but in the minds of their residents a concrete barrier exists between them. In much the same way, U.S. street gangs establish the boundaries of their turf, which is known to all but cannot be seen.

Boundaries between neighborhoods may be suggested by dramatic markers such as the Abu 'Ala bridge between humble Bulaq and elegant Zamalek. But most divisions are less remarkable; an open market area or a cluster of multipurpose buildings with shops and dwellings may separate crumbling baladi buildings from fashionable villas and boutiques. Vertical separation is even more tenuous in high-rises, where parquet-floor apartments lie just below a veritable barnyard of animals raised by the doorman, who lives in a shack on the roof.

There is a thick overlay of rural life in baladi quarters. Women construct rural-style ovens on the roof, in the courtyard, and even in the front entryway. The clay and brick oven is fueled by scrap wood in the city, and by straw, corncobs or manure patties in the country. Livestock and poultry are crammed into every corner. Roofs host goats and sheep; balconies, chickens and pigeons.

Cairenes yearn for the countryside because they live in an oversized urban mass. Small wonder that baladis are eager to visit such a suburban bedroom community as Matar Imbaba despite its wide, unpaved thoroughfares and its faceless, sterile, blocks of housing. These peripheral quarters are attractive because they abut agricultural land so missed by downtown rural migrants. A water buffalo may turn a waterwheel next to a three-story mud-brick building; crops grow next to high rises. There is no hustle and bustle of downtown Cairo's specialty shops, cinemas, and parks, with casinos offering nothing more potent than lemonade. Center city dwellers praise the suburbs' wide open spaces with peace and quiet and see them as an ideal spot for rest and relaxation.

Baladi Business: A Merchant Woman of Shaykh Ali Lane

Bulaqi women regularly move about Cairo, between Cairo and their home village, and between Cairo and the Arab world. Although they do not sit on boards of directors of international corporations, baladi women do participate in international and national markets and labor migration. They work at the intersection of the informal and the formal economies, frequently bridging the two sectors to expedite bureaucratic snags in pensions or to sell imported goods.

Older, illiterate women may work in the shadow economy selling sweets, fruit, or roasted corn along the street. They may also operate fruit stands, coffeehouses, bread stands, or grocery stores. More ambitious older women of limited means may enter the international job market as domestics in the Levant or the Gulf; they may also travel to Libya to procure household and personal goods to sell door to door. Wealthier women run furniture and clothes businesses and lend money on the side. Young educated women work in businesses, as well as in government ministries and textile or pharmaceutical factories. Women also work as professionals; it is not unusual in Egypt to see a woman engineer supervising construction workers or a woman physician running a private clinic.

My friend Fatima exemplifies many of the Bulaqi women I knew who operate in the informal economic sector of marketing and credit. She returned weekly to her village market in northern Egypt to bring to Cairo and sell on credit the highly sought-after country fresh cheese and ghee (clarified butter). Her business is discussed in greater detail in Chapter 6.

I first met Fatima when I visited her neighbor Aniyat, whom I had met at the Behig clinic, at her home in Shaykh Ali Lane. We sat on the landing chatting about the beauty of Fatima's home village where "ducks swim in the irrigation ditch and cool breezes caress your cheeks." Aniyat and Fatima lived on the second floor of a four-story building behind a school-book printing press and the offices of *Akhbar al-Yawm* newspaper. Aniyat, who moved to Cairo from a village near Assyut sixteen years ago, pulled her kinky hair back in two braids anchored by a black knotted scarf. In her mid-thirties, her face was still smooth, with a few freckles matching the youth of her voice. Laughter gurgled up from the back of her throat, although when she disciplined a child, her voice turned sharp. Her right earlobe had a jagged tear where a heavy gold earring had pulled through. In addition to the gold bracelets worn on their arms, baladi women wear huge gold earrings shaped into hoops, love birds, curlicues, or calligraphic intricacies. Aniyat often wore a khaki army shirt over a *gellabeyya* of printed cotton. In public, she draped an oblong black chiffon scarf over her head and around her neck; if she ventured far from the immediate lane, she also donned a black southern Egypt-style gellabeyya over her house dress. In 1977 Aniyat had three girls: Badriyya, 13; Rida, 4; and Jihan, 4 months; and one three-year-old boy, Muhammad.

In the winter of 1977, Badriyya lagged in school, partly because of her rheumatic heart, and she quit. Her parents considered sending Badriyya to a Quranic school to learn rudimentary reading and writing. Aniyat felt that education is a matter of inclination. Mona, a girl who lives downstairs, left school early and is illiterate, whereas Mona's mother completed fourth grade and can read captions and headlines when she leafs through magazines. Badriyya reads better than Mona, but Badriyya's mother is illiterate.

Several migrants from Aniyat's village, her *baladiyat,* live in the Shaykh Ali building. This is common in a crowded urban area, where fellow villagers are privy to hot news about vacant apartments, and relay the information to newly arrived villagers doubled up with family. Urban mobility is surprisingly neighborhood-centric. A family may move several times within one house or one block to jockey for better sun exposure and ventilation; both items are at a premium in densely populated areas where windows (if available) face walls or other windows. Aniyat relocated three times since her move to Cairo two years after her marriage. She first settled in a house down the street from her mother-in-law (a distant cousin and a baladiyya) and close to several other fellow villagers. She moved to another house in 1973. I met her in 1974, when she lived in a room on the fourth floor of the Shaykh Ali four-story building. Before I left Egypt in 1977, she had moved to a larger room on the third floor. By 1980, she was back on the fourth floor in the only room with cross ventilation.

In 1977, Aniyat shared a landing with three other families, each in a single room. One family was my friend Fatima's; the other two were migrants from the Said, one Coptic woman named Miriam, and the other a Cairene woman "who sticks to herself, accepting nothing from anyone." Aniyat had met her floor-mates years before; when she moved next to them, their relationship changed little, although by force of proximity they saw more of each other. Miriam described earlier days, at the time Aniyat first arrived, in a glowing narrative she told while we drank tea to warm ourselves one winter day:

> Remember when the entire house would party and sun themselves on the roof? What days those were! We first met when

you were pregnant with Badriyya and came to visit your husband and mother-in-law in the house up the lane. We were married at the same time, but you became pregnant after two months, whereas it took me a year! In those days we would sit a whole winter's day on the roof and eat tangerines and sun ourselves. The new roof tenants are unsociable and have closed off the roof entrance to us.

When Aniyat settled in Cairo, her relative Um Adel introduced her to the city and to village migrants. Now Aniyat shows other baladiyat new to Cairo major attractions like the Sultan Abu 'Ala mosque and Wikalat el-Balah with its used clothes bargains and the best vegetable and meat merchants. Aniyat's social life pivots around the four blocks between her home and her mother-in-law's up the lane. When she bakes bread, she uses the oven built in the ground floor hallway at her mother-in-law's house, moving between the two houses carrying straw baskets with cooling bread and wearing a tattered house dress splotched with flour.

When her brother-in-law became engaged, Aniyat joined a procession of women that carried pans of wedding trousseau dresses, fruit, sugar, and rice from her mother-in-law's to the groom's house three lanes away. These processions, typical of rural Egypt, are a peculiar sight in the winding, vehicle-clogged streets of Cairo. In the village they are a colorful sight, with girls decked out in bright floral chiffon dresses, singing and happy to be away from chores. Urban processions are shorter and drabber, and not as lengthy a break from housework!

Several baladiyat live within a few blocks of Aniyat's. She is often summoned to attend their death observances or weddings. At night she frequents her mother-in-law's, where the children can watch television, or her old home next door to see her distant relative Um Ali the landlady or her friend and fellow villager Um Sadaq, who recently moved from the roof of Aniyat's house to Um Ali's. Um Sadaq is frequently morose; her eldest son died in the 1973 war. However, her next eldest son has just married, and now her daughter-in-law provides an extra set of hands to help with housework. The couple lives with Um Sadaq, having crammed all their dowry furniture into one of Um Sadaq's two bedrooms.

Fatima, the cheese merchant, grew up in a town in the Menoufiyya province north of Cairo and migrated to Cairo twenty-six years ago when her husband sold his land and took a job as an office clerk at the Ministry of Culture. When we met in 1974, she shared a landing with Aniyat. Fatima and her husband now live a few lanes from the house where they resided for their first twenty-four years in Cairo. Their one son, Muhammad, lives across the lane. None of their three married daughters or other kin live nearby. Some years ago, Fatima quarreled with her husband and returned with their son to her home town in Menoufiyya. Soon after I met her, she recounted a business narrative, framed by her heightened voice pitch and rendered as we peeled garlic on the landing. The tale was sparked when a neighbor dropped by to reserve two kilos of ghee from Fatima's market load the next week. Fatima spoke of how she started her business:

> Several years ago my husband Abu Muhammad and I quarreled because he gambled so much there was nothing left for household expenses. I returned to my village with my son and opened a bean and fried chickpea sandwich stand. I would never have made up with Abu Muhammad except for my son's sake. But I did return to Cairo and start to trade ghee and cheese with the money I saved from my sandwich stand. As my reputation grew, I had more orders than I could carry on the train even though I went to the village every week. When I go to the village I stay with Um Ahmad, the half-blind widow whose house is across from my old sandwich stand. It is more relaxed than at my sister's or my brother's, who would feel obliged to invite me for a meal. Um Ahmad fills me in on the latest news. . . .
>
> My neighbors here in Bulaq are happy to buy my fresher, better products and now I cannot carry back enough to satisfy them. . . . Why, I made enough money to marry off my son without even a piaster from his father! (Early 1985a:79)

The future of such baladi-sector merchants as Fatima is uncertain. The last few times I marketed in Menoufiyya with Fatima, I noted several well-groomed men leaning against Peugeot station wagons at the edge of the dairy section of the market; they were buying up ghee and cheese to take back to Cairo for sale. They were one notch up the merchant scale toward the afrangi marketing companies. Their station wagons could carry hundreds of kilos of produce, while Fatima strained her back to carry two baskets weighing around twenty kilos on the train.

Small-scale, local merchants may survive because these women provide not only valued fresh rural dairy products, but also informal credit—a critical service in the marginal economy of Bulaq, where a householder's budget barely covers food for the day. Meat is a special, occasional expense. Bulk food or home furnishings often require financing, and small merchants, such as Fatima, or larger creditors lend for a year's supply of cooking fat or for a new bedroom set. This informal credit enables a woman to save money through bulk purchase and to buy furniture she could not otherwise afford. Fatima allows customers to pay by installment, and her clientele has grown until she cannot carry enough produce in her two baskets to meet the demand.

On a typical market day, Fatima's husband waits for her train. Fatima tugs at her two straw baskets and slides them onto the platform at the provincial train station, which adjoins Bab el-Hadid, Cairo's main train station on Ramses street. Her husband takes one basket on the nape of his neck, she balances one on her head, and the two of them make their way through back streets. Fatima arrives on the one o'clock train, and the streets are soon clogged with rush-hour traffic, which will peak at two when government offices close. Luckily, Fatima lives only a mile away; no taxi will accept the produce-laden baskets, and buses are far too crowded at this hour. They descend from the train platform and join the melange in the street below. Crowds stream along: children in cotton pajamas, schoolgirls in modest navy-blue pants with tunic tops, young women in tight pants and knit tops, older women whose colorful house dresses show from under their black outer wrap, men in flowing robes and brown wool caps or in work garb of wrinkled shirts and pants. Fatima herself wears the traditional Menoufi black robe, free-falling from a tight yolk, and a black head scarf secured with a band.

Once home, Fatima sets up her scales. Neighbors have observed Fatima's return and send their children early before the cheese runs out; more distant customers may arrive too late. Neighborhood children wander in to order a quarter or half kilo of cheese or ghee. Fatima carefully weighs out pre-ordered parcels of ghee before she portions out small lots for last-minute customers. When her load is sold, Fatima fetches bread from a nearby shop; she and her husband sit on the straw mat between the four-post bed and narrow couch and eat fresh cheese, green hot peppers, tomatoes, and bread. Then Fatima primes and lights the single-burner, oil primus stove to boil thick, sweet tea. In her in-laws' village, only men and boys make tea. There they use a corncob fire rather than a primus stove, and serve a second round of reboiled, lighter tea. Here in Cairo, where women serve both men and women, tea drinking is not as leisurely an event. Fatima always serves the tea, and she steeps only one "round."

Fatima goes to sleep early. Tomorrow she will visit her daughter Nadia, who lives in Cairo's agricultural periphery of Matar Imbaba, where fields and water wheels adjoin dwellings. In contrast, Fatima lives amidst workshops and warehouses of Bulaq;

when she collects payments from customers, she passes the television tower and the Abu 'Ala mosque, and crosses the fashionable 26th of July Street, where shop windows are crammed with cassette recorders and platform-heel shoes. She likes to visit the National Museum on Tahrir Square, not to see Pharonic relics but to ogle the blond, broad-shouldered tourists with their hefty camera bags.

For Fatima, downtown opulence is something to observe, not experience. Although she lives a mere ten-minute walk from Cairo's air-conditioned downtown Hilton Hotel, Fatima fetches her water from a street tap and lights her windowless room with a kerosene lamp. She envies Nadia's "country" life; her daughter has the run of an entire, if humble, mud-brick one-story house with electricity, running water, and a private roof where Nadia suns in winter and enjoys evening breezes in summer. Fatima's windowless room is fetid, and she treasures fresh air. Egyptians open windows even in cold weather. One "smells the breeze" when one strolls.

In many ways Fatima is an outsider. Although she has lived in Bulaq for twenty-six years, urbanites still consider her a peasant and not a *bint al-balad* ("daughter of the city"). Fatima enjoys few urban comforts, and she supports herself by selling goods from village markets, although her customers and her friends are mostly urbanites. Fatima is unusual in other ways: she is better educated and more devout than many urban women. She has completed the fourth grade; she writes her own ledger of customer accounts, a detailed system of amount purchased and installments made. Fatima prays five times a day and attends mosque lessons regularly. One day at a village shrine, her daughter-in-law's mother inquired about a fertility amulet for her daughter. Fatima rebuked her in a ringing voice. Her pronouncement, a mundane performance played out at the shrine's door, resembled a liturgical statement:

> I place my faith in the saints; they are the source of all good. We learn about their lives from the imams of the mosque. We learn to pray and to tithe. All these amulets are not Islam; we hear nothing about them in Islam. But [turning to the woman guardian of the shrine who had offered an amulet] do not worry, for your intention is good and when my daughter-in-law has a child, you will receive your just share of our rejoicing.

Fatima's response demonstrates typical baladi blending of aspects of popular Islam (belief in holy people or saints who can mediate) with some of orthodox Islam (prayer and tithing). While Fatima distances herself from what she considers to be superstitions, such as amulets, she also expresses her sympathy for the shrine's guardian saying she does not wish to deprive the woman of her income.

Baladi women are equally eclectic in their curative practices. Fatima told me that she dressed her children in black aprons against the evil eye, but when her children were sick she took them to the best clinics. When she herself fell ill, she searched the cardiac clinics of Cairo for the most famous specialist, and eagerly displayed her cardiograms to visitors.

During my research, I passed many memorable hours with Fatima, especially when we traveled to her home town and her husband's home village for marketing trips and for her son Muhammad's engagement to Sabah, who lived in the village and was distantly related to Muhammad's father. On a 1981 return visit, four years after my formal research ended in Egypt, I found that Fatima had moved out of the Shaykh Ali house and lived several blocks away, across the street from her former room, which she and her husband had given her married son Muhammad. Fatima and her husband recently left that airy room. Its shuttered windows open onto the lane and its door onto a dirt courtyard. An adjacent room is occupied by a woman with a "long tongue" and rowdy children; Fatima regrets that she once recommended them to the landlord. The remainder of the building's three multiroom apartments house the landlord and two of his children's families. On the roof, reached by rickety stairs, residents hang clothes and raise ducks and chickens. The crippled landlord suns himself in the courtyard or watches the world from a chair at the front door. His family's presence made Fatima feel like an outsider when she lived there, so she entered the courtyard only to gain access to the common toilet or to the roof. Most baladi one-story buildings have a pit latrine, whereas multistory buildings hook one oriental (porcelain floor) toilet per floor to a central sewage pipe.

Muhammad and Sabah had a three-year-old son; during my visit the boy kept calling his mother Sabah a "peasant" and himself a "Cairene." Sabah scolded her son, saying that his parents and grandparents were all peasants and so was he! Such talk out of the mouth of a child merely reflects what other adults say and think. Our examination of the baladi identity in the next chapter highlights the disdain of urbanites for peasants. At the same time, many urbanites are in fact of recent rural origin.

Talk during my 1981 return visit also pointed to the tenuous, and ambivalent, baladi:afrangi and rural:urban contrasts. The latest news was that an urban renewal project had vacated houses for demolition within six blocks of Fatima's house. Bulaqis were being relocated to popular housing on the agricultural periphery of Cairo. Fatima's family answered my flustered inquiries with a calmness bred through years of suffering incorrigible landlords and a debilitating environment. Fatima, cynical in her wisdom, guessed it would be years before the project reached their house. Sabah, fresh from the village and cramped by urban quarters, figured matters could not be worse. Unlike some baladi urbanites, she had a window, but she warned me about leaning against a crumbling wall. She had no electricity and paid neighbors forty piasters a month to carry water from their tap.

When I visited Aniyat that day at the Shaykh Ali house, her Coptic neighbor Miriam was equally optimistic. When I bemoaned the relocation of Bulaq's residents to an area an hour's bus ride from the city's center, Miriam shrugged her shoulders and intoned a baladi commentary mixing recognition and resignation:

> We are day laborers; we work wherever we find ourselves. My husband will sell fruit there just as he does here. . . . They say that in Ain Shams every family will have its own bathroom and kitchen, and for every four members there will be a room; that means that my husband, five children, and I will have two rooms.

Miriam anticipated quarters relatively luxurious compared to her one room with its one four-poster bed and two baladi couches, which she pushes together in winter to allow people to cozy up. Her family shares a toilet with the floor's three other families and carries water from a downstairs hall tap.

Miriam's family is the only Coptic Christian one in the building. Coptic Christians are descendants of the original Christian church formed in Egypt and Ethiopia in the first century A.D. Egypt was largely Coptic Christian until Muslim forces arrived in the seventh century. Today at least 10 percent of the population of Egypt is Coptic Christian. Miriam's priest told her that the new housing area would have a church and would offer children's religious instruction. Miriam was optimistic, but Fatima was right. In my latest return visit in 1991, I found Miriam's family living in the same room in the Shaykh Ali house; urban renewal was arrested at a large parking lot a few blocks away.

Throughout my work in Bulaq I found relations between Coptic Egyptians (such as Miriam and her family) and their Muslim neighbors to be excellent. Even though they maintain their sectarian markers, they sometimes share rituals. From time to time, however, there is sectarian tension in Egypt and one day during my 1981 visit, the conversation among a group of women in Shaykh Ali house turned to the recent clashes between Copts and Muslims in the Zawiyya el-Hamra popular housing project on the outskirts of Cairo. Aniyat's daughter Badriyya claimed direct news of the event from a co-worker at the handkerchief factory; the co-worker lives in the district. Badriyya found a rapt audience as she framed her narrative in a thin, high voice with the formulaic "I can tell you how it happened. I know someone who was there."

> It all started when a Muslim bought land in Zawiyya to build a factory and a mosque. The Christians felt that if he were to build a mosque, they should have some of the land for a church. Last Wednesday two women began to quarrel because the washing of the Coptic woman was dripping on the balcony of the Muslim woman. A crowd gathered, and the Copts and the Muslims started hitting each other. The police came to break it up.
> The next day, Thursday, at sunset prayers, when the Muslims were at prayer in a mosque in Zawiyya, a group of Christians entered the mosque and gunned them down.

When Badriyya had finished her account, Miriam exclaimed: "Whoever did that was neither Christian nor Muslim. Prayer time is a sacred time when one does not anticipate attack. Here we live together in harmony."

But Miriam had more immediate concerns than a sectarian clash in another urban quarter, or a possible move to an even more distant quarter. Her sister across the Nile River in Giza had died last winter; the eldest daughter, who had come from Minya to look after the children during the school year, had returned home. Miriam planned to cook food today to take to her sister's children in Giza.

Bulaqi women move about Cairo, between Cairo and the countryside, and between Cairo and the world, with ease. Having situated them physically, we now turn to situate them culturally by examining the baladi ethos. The next chapter uses situated discourse to present the ambivalent relation of baladi women to the afrangi, more well-to-do world. Bulaqi women praise aspects of afrangi culture (such as medical technology) and critique other aspects (such as gullibility and a pampered life-style). By listening to women's narratives, we can start to appreciate the ambivalences of the baladi:afrangi opposition that allows the women's eclectic manipulation of alternatives within the rich, baladi culture.

3

To Be Baladi Is to Be Savvy: Playing with an Egg and a Stone Without Breaking the Egg

aladi is a rich cultural concept based on a series of
traditional:modern (baladi:afrangi) oppositions, which
contrast baladi people (who are resourceful, authentic, religious,
and honorable) with afrangi people (who are gullible, superficial,
nonreligious, and pampered). Popular cartoons and films valorize
the savvy baladi versus the more crass afrangi. Each concept is
defined by this opposition. There is the baladi society of the street
versus the afrangi society of isolated villas; there is the cottage-
industry, informal economy of baladi business versus the industrial,
professional sphere of afrangi work; and there is the colorful folk
religious devotion of shrines versus the pallid afrangi religion of
mosques. Although baladi people tend to live in low-income quarters
and afrangi people in middle- and upper-income areas, the two life-
styles are not strictly tied to economic class or consumption. Some
millionaire merchants live a simple life near their baladi quarter
warehouses; some low-income Egyptians struggle to emulate
consumption styles of the afrangi populations.

Bulaqi women constantly move between baladi and afrangi
cultural options, blurring the opposition, although they realize that
economically much of afrangi life is beyond their reach. A telling
example of this continual movement was a mother's reaction to my
joking suggestion that she name her baby after me. The mother
laughed and said:

> No one could ever pronounce your name. But we know how to say
> it because you are our friend! We could call her "Ev-leen" at
> home so she could be afrangi here, and her other name at school
> so she could be baladi there.

Baladi women continually move between hard reality and the

hoped-for, more comfortable afrangi life. Sakkina is such a woman. When I met her, she lived in Tel Nasr, a central neighborhood of Bulaq, off a courtyard filled with dust and with smoke from the oven. Sakkina rued her bad luck and romanticized her uncle's apartment in nearby Fransawi, named for the neighborhood French Catholic convent and school. The Fransawi neighborhood, near the major 26th of July Street, had spacious, well-maintained apartments. One day as we walked to her home from the Sharia Behig Street MCH clinic past Fransawi, Sakkina pointed out her uncle's lane with its grand buildings and spoke of her past with an introductory "Let me tell you about my condition of oppression":

> I used to live in an apartment near the clinic, but the building collapsed just after party officials arrived at two in the morning to evacuate us. We relocated to the hovel we now must call home. First we lived with the woman upstairs, and when it vacated, we moved to the two-room apartment downstairs. We are forced to live next to this dusty, filthy courtyard, but at least we do not have to share a toilet as the upper floors do. Whenever anyone upstairs wants water, they yell for me to turn mine off. The other day the women upstairs cooking called down so many times that finally I just turned off my water, even though I was in the midst of washing clothes, just to let them finish. I didn't even wash the fruit that I had brought for lunch.
>
> I have never stopped looking for a new apartment. I found one in Shoubra el-Khema, but I do not want to move there where all my husband's relatives live.

Every time I saw Sakkina, she complained about her neighbors and recounted her attempts to secure an apartment via her uncle and via "the party," where she had found a sympathetic official she hoped to bribe. Sakkina never asked her husband to help her find a better apartment; baladi men spend precious little time at home and take little interest in household conditions. Eventually Sakkina's uncle helped her to obtain an apartment on the periphery of Cairo. In the meantime she resented her close quarters, and yearned for an afrangi quarter where "people leave you alone."

One October day in 1974, while I was visiting Sakkina, she grabbed my arm and led me to her back room to escape the group of women baking bread in the courtyard outside her door. She announced, "You won't believe what happened to me today!" Such an expression of surprise is a typical baladi verbal formula used to introduce a narrative piece. Sakkina sputtered:

Everyone who lives in this building is a criminal. This morning I cursed the daughter of the first floor neighbors; she dates boys and besmirches our building's reputation. They are Christians. When my husband heard us arguing, he dragged me by the hair into the house and hit me across the face. Um Mona's family on the third floor just watched, pretending nothing was happening. One of my earrings fell out and they brought it to me, without a comment. At least Um Mona's household, whom I always greet, could have taken my side. I am left to fight the entire building. It's been that way ever since I arrived. I have not felt like wearing my good clothes, nor spreading my elegant coverlets on my furniture. Why should I? No one here would appreciate them.

This morning my husband told me not to go out, but I took my sons, bought some beans and bread, and went to the garden on the Nile Corniche. Then I visited my uncle, who told me to be patient about finding an apartment and that the lottery for flats would be tomorrow. I cannot wait to be rid of this building and the hypocrites living here, and live an afrangi life like my uncle.

As baladi people's fortunes fluctuate, their accounts weave the specific reality of the biographic "now" with the general ideal of the "hoped for." Sakkina's uncle, a telephone company employee, was the main link to her envisioned afrangi world of comfort. Finally Sakkina escaped to the newly constructed housing in Zawiyya el-Hamra. When I visited her in 1980, she was smugly closeted behind the doors of a two-bedroom flat. Nevertheless, she greeted all the neighbors as I departed—announcing loudly that I had come from the United States to visit. Such a high-status event was too good to risk going unnoticed.

Baladi and Afrangi:
The Have-Nots and the Haves

The baladi:afrangi opposition is the Egyptian cultural version of the social-economic oppositions developing:developed and have-nots:haves. Riddled with an ambivalence that signals pride at times, and self-deprecation at others, the concept "baladi" implicitly critiques the privileged, developed countries of the world at the same time that it explicitly pits itself against afrangi culture in Egypt. This study presents cultural understandings as they appeared in the late 1970s and early 1980s in Egypt without judging the socioeconomic validity of the categories. Indeed with changing economic and consumption patterns, baladi may have begun to lose its simple, nonflamboyant trademarks and be on its way to becoming something similar to the American concept of the "frontier." Witness, for example, the Ramadan television serial, *Liyali Hilmiyya* (*The Nights of Hilmiyya*—a baladi quarter) by Anwar Okasha. Two of the main protagonists are a Hilmiyya industrialist who survived Nasser's nationalization, and a village mayor who migrated to Hilmiyya leaving his agricultural concerns in the hands of a son. Television audiences have followed the fates of the families through four years of Ramadans at this writing. The generational changes are there, with the mothers running small shops and the daughters studying medicine and journalism. Through it all runs the theme of protecting the community from drug traffickers and from swindlers in the classic definition of "baladi" as the defender of the home turf.

Historically, "baladi" indicated the locals, the Egyptians, as versus the Turks, the Mamelukes, the French, or the British. To be *ibna' al-balad*, sons of the country, was to defend Egypt against French and British occupiers. *Balad*, a noun, means community—whether country, city, town, or village; in colloquial Egyptian it can mean "downtown" or village. *Baladi*, the adjective form, means local or indigenous. Through time, baladi has come to connote the residents and life of urban quarters such as Bulaq Abu 'Ala. It is a self-descriptive, emic term that can roughly be translated "traditional" but which also retains a rich infusion of the local and authentic.

The early nineteenth-century historian Abd al-Rahman al-Jabarti used *ibn al-balad* to mean urbanite (Cairene) Muslims who shared a dialect and a religion as opposed to foreign rulers who spoke stilted Arabic and violated Muslim norms. Jibarti detailed the mistreatment of these Cairene theologians, merchants, and artisans by ruling elites. The following Al-Jabarti references are quoted in El-Messiri (1970: 24–56): "Some of the troops used to buy sheep and slaughter them, then sell them at a high price. They would give short weight and *ibn al-balad* could do nothing to check them."

The pious ibna' al-balad were offended by the rude, irreligious Turkish soldiers who ate publicly during Ramadan, the month of fasting. The local residents ridiculed and harassed the occupiers whenever they could. Al-Jabarti reported that when a Bulaqi was killed, the people of the district "rose in revolt" (Al-Jabarti 1958: 637). This association of centralized authority with alien or corrupt powers in part explains the modern Bulaqi's resistance to government interference, especially when related to the black market. At the same time, Bulaqis hark back to World War II which they see as a time of abundance, when the British "arrived with wagon loads of provisions" and would hand out packets of meat and cigarettes to anyone who asked.

The baladi view of present-day afrangis is full of the ambivalence wrought by pride coupled with hardship. Aniyat's husband, a telephone company employee who worked at night as a coffeehouse waiter, spoke one day of the harshness of his life compared to that of former classmates "on afrangi schedules":

I was in the preparatory school in Shoubra (the quarter north of Bulaq) and was one of the top five in my class. One of my school friends, who had a French mother, invited me to lunch. I still remember that we ate lentils and rice. Afterwards we became fast friends and spent a lot of time together. But after I left preparatory school, I never saw him again. He must have gone on to take higher degrees and become an (afrangi) "employee." Look what happened to me. I find myself in this disgusting situation. . . . Sometimes I ride around on buses and trams just to have a change of scenery, and sometimes I meet old friends. Once a police officer I met by chance embraced me as an old classmate and said, "Come with me and visit my family." But I didn't accept his invitation; I am not going to enter the afrangi world via the lives of former classmates. . . .

I used to live the schedule of the foreigners who get up and go to their shop from nine to one and, even if they're going to lose one hundred pounds of profit, eat lunch and take a nap. Then they open their shop again from five to eight in the evening. Then from eight to midnight, they have four hours to play with their children or go to the cinema. But they get twelve hours of sleep. Some Egyptians also have this foreign schedule. I used to be a "foreigner" like this—coming home and sleeping and going to the British Library to read books, or to the cinema. Then the world turned upside down, and now I am in a baladi class and I have to earn as much as I can and work all the time to take care of my children.

Bulaqis both disdain and emulate afrangis. I compare the subtlety of the baladi love/hate relationship with afrangi culture with my own reactions to East Coast Americans' views of "Midwesterners" from states such as my native South Dakota. Afrangis view baladi Egyptians in much the same way East Coast

Americans view Midwesterners as "simple rustics," but of "solid, hardworking stock."

One day my Bulaqi friend Ibtisam extolled baladi life to a taxi driver as he drove us to Ras el Barra in northern Egypt to visit Ibtisam's relatives. The driver good-naturedly teased her: "What is a baladi woman such as yourself doing with this foreigner?" Ibtisam bristled, then laughed, saying "You had better watch out for us Bulaqis. We're baladi, tough, and resourceful. I could beat you up!" Ibtisam chuckled as she flexed her muscular bicep from beneath her sleeve. She had refined her plucky manners while supervising her deceased father's lathing workshop. Defensive with the cabby, Ibtisam at other times disparaged the filth and ill manners of baladi quarters. When she sewed, it was stylish afrangi clothes for work or parties.

Each arena of everyday life has its baladi and its afrangi alternatives, which often roughly correspond to inexpensive and expensive. Baladi businesswomen offer credit accounts to customers who would never receive credit in the formal economic sector. Baladi dress (such as the simple black sheet or *melaya liff*, which renders the most tattered house dress respectable) and baladi furnishings (dominated by the humble hard cushion of the baladi couch) are—as with baladi medicine or ceremonies—less costly than the afrangi alternative. Baladi medicine offers cheap home remedies and herbs available from the lane's herbal pharmacist and includes the use of amulets and exorcism. Afrangi medicine offers costlier cures from the more distant modern pharmacy.

While it is true that not everyone who lives a baladi life-style is economically marginal, the ethos of poverty and the cultural concept *gallaba* (downtrodden and destitute) are central to the definition of baladi. When baladi people are frustrated about food prices, housing shortages, or bureaucratic hassles, they intone: "What should we do in our wretched condition, at the mercy of greedy landlords, recalcitrant bureaucrats, and inflation?" A Saudi husband sent his Bulaqi wife's parents money when his wife gave birth. The wife's father remarked: "My daughter was destitute, but God gave her a great chance when she married."

Although everyone knows who is downtrodden, and who is not, baladi practices designed to avoid envy often obscure levels of wealth. One does not flaunt good fortune and tempt the evil eye. This is why children are dressed in black aprons, and a baby is never called pretty. Similarly, in the countryside one does not invite inspection of an abundant grape arbor or a pregnant cow. If others do not know one's wealth, they can not feel envious. A woman who sells onions in the lane may also own several apartment buildings, or land and water buffaloes in her home village.

Baladi life is simple and deemphasizes differences in income, so landlords may live like their neighbors. Thus, wealthy baladi people, or even those of modest means with a relative working abroad, add no more to the fundamental baladi furnishings than a refrigerator, a television, chairs, and a table. In the late 1980s, consumption patterns began to change, and baladi Egyptians began to emulate afrangi consumption with a new-found fervor, adding posh parlor furniture and accessories such as VCRs to simple baladi furnishings. This new consumerism may change measures of baladi status, demonstrated in the past by hosting hefty meals of roast sheep, and by wearing rows and rows of gold bracelets. Already Bulaqis are discussing who has which electronic gadget in the same way that some middle-class Americans compare their automobiles. It is no surprise that religious reformists decry the materialism wrought by "Western capitalism."

To date, ritual life has escaped the new-found ostentation of household furnishings. In baladi culture, one observes life passages according to the baladi cultural precept "each according to his means." Each rite of passage requires minimal acts that can increase, with status, in fanfare and calories. For example, the only prerequisites for the death observance are a Quranic reader and a microphone. Most baladi Egyptians receive condolences in their homes. The well-to-do add a magnificent tent in the middle of the street for male mourners and hire a famous reader. For a wedding or engagement party, a drum, a string of lights for decoration, punch, and cardboard boxes of pastries and sandwiches are enough, but the celebration can escalate to a party at a local club with hired musicians and a sumptuous buffet. The final proof of economic status is, of course, in the jewelry and trousseau.

Some rituals are reserved for the well-to-do. Only they can afford the pilgrimage to Mecca, and according to classical Islam, one should not borrow money to undertake this pilgrimage. The *zar*, or spiritual purging, which involves an expensive party, is held for a possessed woman. Baladi women say: "Only rich women are possessed by spirits. How could we poor gallaba baladi women afford to hire a shaykha and band and feed everybody?" In reality it is the well-to-do baladi women who usually hold zars. In the early twentieth century, many tracts attacking "superstitions" such as the zar or amulets were published in Egypt. As neo-Islamic movements increase their following among baladi Egyptians, such practices will be challenged as "un-Islamic." See the discussion of Islam in Chapter 4.

Other baladi or folk Islamic practices are inexpensive and accessible to all. Since a baladi woman can not "afford" to be possessed, she will cure any dysphoria by a combination of folk religion, folk medicine, and cosmopolitan medicine.

Since the lives of many baladis are a concatenation of baladi and afrangi, their celebrations mix the familial informality of the baladi with the ostentatiousness of afrangi observances. Such a family is Nadia's, who lives in a five-room apartment with a refrigerator and television on the top floor of a crumbling, yellow, sun-dried brick building in the heart of Bulaq Abu 'Ala. All Nadia's siblings study a trade or a profession. They approach life differently than traditional baladis; Nadia confided to me how her neighbors "hit their children as if the pain will make them learn."

Nadia's father works as a government surveyor during the day and as a private cartography consultant in the evening. Nadia's family chooses to live in baladi Bulaq, but they are relatively well-to-do and identify with many afrangi customs. Nevertheless, Nadia's wedding was not an afrangi hotel buffet party, but rather was held in a local club. Her family invited all the neighbors in the lane via engraved announcements addressed to husbands rather than the traditional oral invitation. It was, however, the women of the lane they knew and therefore the women of the lane who attended.

The wedding was a "woman's event," with some afrangi male guests, and the Bulaqi women enjoyed themselves as if at a home wedding. They chewed pumpkin seeds they had brought in their pockets and commented loudly on other guests and on the music as it poured through the scratchy loudspeakers. They wore afrangi maxi dresses, and some even sported wigs for the occasion. A few young people danced baladi solo dances, but there was none of the afrangi ballroom dancing so popular in hotel weddings. Nadia's father forbade his daughters to dance. Jewelry was displayed with a grand flourish, to baladi ululations. The guests ate sandwiches and cakes served in bakery cardboard boxes decorated with a red-inked sketch of a bride and groom. Nadia's family mingled with the guests, chatting familiarly with neighbors they had only met in the briefest of encounters in the lane. Families such as Nadia's might be able to afford to move to an afrangi quarter, but they prefer a baladi quarter because they are comfortable with its ways. With their modest furnishings and consumption habits, they do not stand out as different in Bulaq. If they did, other Bulaqis would not hesitate to satirize their pretension and moral, if not financial, corruption.

That is exactly what happened at another wedding attended by Aniyat and her neighbor Mahrusa from Shaykh Ali. Mahrusa's nephew was marrying a woman considered wealthy, and Mahrusa pointed out the two shops of the bride's family on our way to the wedding. We were all surprised to be asked to go to the roof rather than join the bride's family, and as we sat waiting for the wedding to start, Mahrusa bemoaned the lack of conviviality that usually marks baladi weddings:

> See that woman over there? She is the cousin of the bride. Now they will all gather around together and we will never meet them. Did you see how downstairs they even had to ask who was the mother of the groom? And now here she is sitting with us while the bride's family ignores her! Imagine that my nephew asked us to wait on the roof rather than in the house of the bride.

We had arrived at the customary time for a baladi wedding, but it was several hours before the musicians hired for the event began to arrive. Mahrusa, who clearly would have preferred the traditional drumming and dancing, announced that she was ready to leave, and we all departed without saying good-bye. Mahrusa's nephew came running after us to stop us, saying "This is not the custom." Mahrusa replied that her daughter's throat hurt from sitting on the cold roof. On the way home, Mahrusa sputtered:

> If they are going to put us on the roof where we freeze and the bride's comings and goings are a big secret, why should we stay? They are rich. People should not marry outside their level. These people are giving my nephew a hard time, but he asked for it by dealing with them.

At this point we met Mahrusa's husband, also leaving, and he added his disapproval of the event: "They are drinking beer and smoking hashish in the men's section. Let's be on our way. This is not our kind of place."

As baladis criticize pretension in weddings, so the Egyptian media celebrates baladi Egyptian resourcefulness, and critiques upper-class hypocrisy using a popularized caricature of a baladi personality. El-Messiri's interview of Rakha, the cartoonist who introduced the image of ibn al-balad to Egyptian magazines, provides a unique insight:

> In the year 1929 the caricature of al-Misri Effendi was born in the magazine *Ruz al-Yuussuf*. This caricature symbolized the good and submissive person, who is passive and fatalistic, and who, in the face of calamity, calls for God's help saying, "Damn

Reprinted with permission from *Sabah el-Khayr* (Cairo, 1976).

Jehan Sadat: "Happy Feast! Take some feast cookies."

Onlooker: "See how she is touched by the plight of the poor? Isn't it wonderful?"

Reprinted with permission from *Sabah el-Khayr* (Cairo, 1976).

Government inspector: "Madam, these cookies are less than the legal weight for feast cookies. That is exploitation of your husband, and the ministry does not allow exploitation."

those who have done me injustice." In the year 1941, the chief editor of the magazine held a meeting with the editorial staff of Dar al-Hilal (the publishing house), where it was decided that the caricature of al-Misri Effendi did not, and should not, symbolize the Egyptian, because it represented the lowest class of government official, that is the effendi class, or petty bureaucrats. They decided that the personality of *ibn al-balad* represented a more independent and emancipated personality and one which really represented the Egyptian (El-Messiri 1976:67).

The media has remained resplendent with baladi images. A particularly vivid series of cartoons that highlighted the down-trodden:spoiled dichotomy appeared at Ramadan feast time in 1976, when Jehan Sadat distributed feast biscuits to the poor. As the accompanying cartoon portraying photographers surrounding Mrs. Sadat as she gives cookies to one beggar shows, the president's wife's generosity was seen as a "Let them eat cake" media event. During the same period, another series of cartoons lampooned government economic policies. In the one here, the inspector of rations (seen as responsible for sugar and flour shortages) criticizes the baladi woman for not having made the right weight of cookies—a reference to government reduction of subsidized bread weights.

Critiques of afrangi and elites alike are a familiar thread in Egyptian film and music. Films of the late 1970s pilloried sleazy contractors and government officials who took bribes and constructed unsafe buildings. One particularly biting social commentary portrayed a garbage collector who rose to riches as a realtor, and clumsily attempted to adopt afrangi accoutrements. A popular singer, Shaykh Imam, from the baladi Darb al-Ahmar quarter poked fun at the government's overtures to France in 1976:

> Instead of naming our children Muhammad, we will name them
>   Jean
> And all of our cars will run on perfume,
> And savings societies will be formed all over,
> And all our televisions will be colored,
> And we will all become like the elite. . . (Nejm 1976)

Cartoons, films, and songs are not the Bulaqi woman's usual text, but they are Egyptian cultural texts that reflect local perceptions. As the baladi:afrangi counterpoint is replete with ambivalence, so praise and criticism flow both ways in the media.

It is baladi spunk that wins afrangi Egyptian admiration. In the stereotypical film portrayal of baladi life, women flail their cheeks and wail at calamity. Neighbors crack jokes from balconies. The baladi personality has been well documented by the Egyptian novelist Naguib Mahfouz in novels such as *As-Sukhariyya* and *Zuqaq al-Midaq*. There are many classic films about savvy survivors who fashion a ploy and a joke for every obstacle. The beloved singer Um Kathsum and the famed actress Leila Murad starred in these films as a baladi damsel distraught by the choice between an authentic lad of the back streets of Cairo and a rich, corrupt businessman. *Al-Usta Hassan* contrasts the life of a rich woman living in Zamalek with that of her lover, an auto mechanic living in Bulaq Abu 'Ala. The bridge that spans the Nile river dividing the two quarters symbolically links the two lovers and the two life styles (Gaffney 1987).

Afrangi Egyptians are as ambivalent as the baladi about the baladi:afrangi opposition—a theory neat only in the hands of a symbolic anthropologist. Afrangis will extol the virtues of the "simple, authentic" baladi folk as if they were Rousseau's noble savage, embellished with baladi "light-blooded" good humor and cleverness—the ability to make something out of nothing.

The very savvy that afrangi Egyptians praise can change, in the blink of an afrangi eye, to uppity cunningness, which afrangi Egyptians denounce. Baladi Egyptians are also often lampooned as stupid and simple by the very media that glorifies baladi drama and humor. Afrangi ambivalence shines through in cartoons of "simple ibn al-balad" whose lack of family planning has resulted in a giant, hungry family next to a cartoon of "oppressed ibn al-balad" struck low by bureaucratic woes.

Afrangi vacillation percolates up in social contacts. Within two hours, an afrangi friend of mine both lauded the resourcefulness of baladi shoppers and castigated a woman selling Pepsi on her street as a "baladi woman spreading trash up and down the street, and disgustingly nursing her baby in public." (In the 1970s, middle-class Egyptians almost entirely used baby bottles, while lower-class, baladi, Egyptians—and Westerners favoring natural breast feeding—did not.) My friend's revulsion at first shocked me, but I realized it was an afrangi reaction to the "creeping baladization" of Cairo. By the late 1970s, divisions between baladi and afrangi quarters were breaking down and the "homogenized" zones referred to by Abu Lughod in her 1971 study of Cairo (see Chapter 2) were getting larger and larger. Baladis had invaded afrangi space much as the homeless had assaulted the dignified downtown park sites of American cities in the 1980s.

Baladi ambivalence toward afrangi outsiders had an impact on my status as an "outside researcher." As a foreign student researcher at the Ministry of Health clinic, speaking Arabic with a foreign accent, I was clearly not an Egyptian afrangi. Had I been, Bulaqi women might not have invited me to homes considered by afrangis to be spartan and unkempt. Baladi homes are often cleaner than afrangi ones (since baladi women mop floors of garbage from cooking and street mud tracked in several times a day), but afrangis tend to stereotype the cramped baladi houses as dirty nonetheless, reacting to the filth of the streets surrounding the homes. One day, at the clinic, the afrangi social worker asked me whether Um Ahmad's house was filthy when I visited her. Caught in a classic quandary, I answered "It was spotless," since I wanted to ally myself with baladi Egyptians—at the price of aggravating the social worker.

It was my distance as foreigner and outsider that allowed me to ask questions, but the same distance made me appear to have access to endless goods. To avoid false expectations, which I could not have met on my student stipend, and to avoid commercializing my research, I brought only consumable gifts. I wore modest "fieldwork" clothes, which my friends clearly found inappropriate for weddings and parties we attended together. My constraint here was not money but my concept of modesty, which governed shopping and packing in the United States. Clearly, I had not anticipated baladi women's occasional flashy, modern attire. The result was confirmation that I was a weird foreigner, not a dress-conscious afrangi.

My friends had seen pictures and heard stories of my family; as a single woman, I had carefully constructed my social identity. The final blow to my possible identity as an afrangi Egyptian fell when my visiting parents, retired professor and kindergarten teacher, accompanied me to Bulaq. Finally, I do not wish to suggest by the above that Egyptian researchers who divest themselves of "afrangi baggage" cannot do research in baladi quarters.

To Dupe or Be Duped

Bulaqi women see themselves as destitute, but also as dexterous in their dealings with afrangi Egyptians. They relish duping the less-astute afrangi. One day, as we consoled a neighbor who despaired of receiving her widow's pension, her friend spontaneously recounted an incident that occurred to her because its content would instruct the widow on possible courses of action to circumvent bureaucracy. She set off her narrative from ordinary discourse with the typical baladi frame, "That reminds me of the time. . . ."

My friends and I were on our way to visit my daughter Amal. As we stood by the side of the road a well-dressed afrangi man offered us a ride in his car. Since we were a group, we were not afraid to ride with him. Maybe he wanted some money to help with gas, maybe he was being nice, maybe he wanted some fun. But we were old women! My neighbor started to chat and discovered the man was in the army. Straightaway she asked how she could secure her son's early release from the army. He gave her the name of a person to see and advised her what to say. We arrived at our destination and got out of the car, thanking the man nicely. We never paid for our ride, and in addition, we received some good advice!

This narrative both consoled the neighbor and celebrated the savvy of baladi women who use their wits to compensate for limited resources in dealings with "pampered" afrangis spoiled by their soft life. A lively conversation ensued in which the neighbor tested out ideas for a personal approach to bureaucracy. The account by Amal's mother is an example of the "naturally occurring discursive forms through which emotion . . . (is) articulated, communicated, and experienced" (DelVecchio-Good, Good, Fisher, et al. 1988:4).

Baladi people see office employees as prototypical afrangis who lack independence and work for a pittance. Although baladi workers range from occasional laborers to wealthy merchants, the baladi self-image of baladi work is that it is informal, individualized, and encourages workers to show initiative, whereas afrangi work, in formal bureaucratic and industrial sectors, is boring and provides little opportunity for freedom. Baladi people— historically artisans, service providers, or piecework and day laborers—resist the factory production lines of Helwan's steel works or Shoubra's pharmaceutical concerns. Bulaq's workshop sector provides the "fine arts" support for industry: molds from foundries and small parts from its lathes. An afrangi businessman who orders parts in a baladi workshop conducts his business quickly in the unfamiliar baladi quarter; baladis consider him aloof, ignorant of baladi life, credulous, and easily fooled (El-Messiri 1976:105).

Baladis prefer free-wheeling trade or skilled labor, although such work may involve long hours. An afrangi office worker goes home for lunch and a nap, whereas a baladi woman street vendor goes to the wholesale market before dawn and works until dusk. Proud of her freedom, a baladi woman merchant sees herself as

a character-type associated with the nature of the job—selling fruits, vegetables, butter, fish, and so on. Such work requires foresight and intelligence; it is said, "One *bint al-balad* equals twenty men in trading." In contrast, a woman employee in the government is "bound" to her desk and hence lacks experience and is unaware of the world about her (El-Messiri 1978b:532).

As afrangis work in impersonal offices, so they also have a lesser sense of honor and loyalty to friends. As one baladi put it, "Afrangi people don't rally to help a neighbor in distress; baladi people do. Here, if there is a problem, the whole house turns out."

Baladis are extremely honorable, unlike the afrangis who have shed many moral standards and emulate such Western practices as premarital dating. A woman whose family had lived in Bulaq "forever" volunteered the following historical narrative as we discussed the shops lining the lanes of Bulaq's Tel Nasr area. Her account neatly tied poverty and honor to the Bulaqi self-image, and was set off from our routine musings on types of stores in Tel Nasr with the comment, "You know, this area was not always so full of shops."

> One of my ancestors worked for Muhammad Ali [who ruled Egypt in the early nineteenth century] in his castle tutoring his children. The ruler's secretary offered my relative the hilly area of Tel Nasr for free, but my ancestor was not interested. Nowadays Tel Nasr is not just a hill, which is why this relative rejected it, but an urbanized area dense with buildings and small shops. Think how rich we would have been! Instead we are poor baladi people, but at least we are honorable and don't let our daughters go out with men until they marry. Some people imitate the West and its afrangi style; they allow their daughters to go out with their fiancées before they are married.

Traditional moral obligations include protection of family and neighbors, obedience to parents, and respect for the elderly. In her study of ibn al-balad, Sawsan El-Messiri's informants singled out gallantry—which they defined as a mixture of nobility, audacity, boldness, respectability, generosity, vigor, and manliness—as the most significant baladi trait. "Ibn al-balad is the one who interferes in settling a quarrel without knowing the persons who are involved in it" (El-Messiri 1976:88). Indeed, there are degrees of honor and cleverness that distinguish baladi from the two peasant groups: *fellahin* (northern rural) and *Saidi* (southern rural). Baladi women view peasants as a noncosmopolitan group who live a routine, mindless existence, and rural women as inept and dull. El-Messiri notes:

One can take advantage of the *fellaha* and can make a fool of her, but not so with *bint al-balad*, who is more likely to be the one fooling others. A popular description of *bint al-balad* is one who is "capable of playing with an egg and a stone at the same time"—and without breaking an egg. She sees herself as alert and inquiring—attributes emanating from a style of life that brings her into contact with a wide variety of people and situations (El-Messiri 1978a:530).

Not all peasants are country bumpkins. First, many baladi people were themselves peasants not so long ago. Second, certain rural groups, such as Menoufiyyans from northern Egypt, are famed for shrewdness and are feared, if not respected. A folk proverb says it best: "Beware of a Menoufiyyan. He will offer you the worst cut of meat but lead you to believe that it is the best." While criticizing rural backwardness, baladis also idealize the tranquil countryside life of fresh air and open space. One woman in a windowless Cairo room without water or electricity remarked: "Why do I live here? In the village they have electricity and a T.V." Another contrasted the typical diet in the two settings: "We come here to the countryside for a week. It is a change. We don't eat the chickpeas and beans of Cairo, but enjoy the fresh cheese and butter of the village."

On the other side of the coin, rural women see urban women as superficial and fickle, wearing risqué, low-cut dresses. Yet, rural women may hold urban women in awe. One day as I walked with a peasant friend in her family's fields in Menoufiyya, she paused in the midst of talking about clover for their "three handsome water buffalo in the stable" to say: "But my life here is not like that of an urban woman who lives 'with her eyes open' and moves about and 'sees the world.'" My friend's admiration of the urban women's worldliness was mixed; to be worldly is to be both savvy and crass.

The southern, Saidi, view of self and other mirrors that of the northern peasant. The currency of honor, the attention to religious and social duty, figures heavily in the baladi:Saidi opposition. The Saidi view of urban contagion is summed up in the maxim: "The farther south the train station [the farther from Cairo], the more honorable the person." Just as baladi Cairenes fault afrangi for lack of respect for people and traditions, so Saidis criticize Cairenes for lack of respect for the dead. "Cairenes make a quick trip to the cemetery in a car and do not revisit the grave."

A Woman's Home Is Her Castle:
Baladi Gender Roles

The term "baladi" defines a total life-style. There are baladi ways to run a household, to relate to a spouse, and to raise children. There are baladi ways to greet, to socialize, to marry, to worship, to do business, to cure, and to negotiate life. There are also specific roles in baladi culture defined by gender.

Marriage is an expected stage in both women's and men's life, but for a woman the more important event is to give birth to a son. Mother-son relations are affectionate, and a mother pampers her son, who in turn defends her in old age from the empire-building of the son's wife. In an extended family with daughters-in-law to assist, a mother manages a household while performing only such tasks as she chooses. As an older woman, she has considerable freedom of movement and may sit with men, smoke water pipes, and argue vociferously. She is served first in groups of young men and relatives. Her virtue is assured; she is postmenopausal and has a high status derived from grown children. While extended families are much more common in rural Egypt than urban, still the mother-son relationship remains important and tempers husband-wife relations.

Even Vivian Gornick, who in her confessions of her tourist life in Egypt saw the country only from the perspective of a certain brand of male Egyptian tourist leech, commented on the special mother-son relationship. Visiting a family in Shoubra, the next quarter over from Bulaq, she empathized with the mother making pastries in the small kitchen:

> Suddenly, here in this scullery in Shoubra, one can see the whole Egyptian mother-son life for what it bare-bones really is. Here, in the ghetto, the quality that infuses the power of this national family love becomes crystal clear: loving each other is all we've got. The son is the treasure, the mother, the only giver of value. . . . She does not nag, she does not reprove, she does not demand. She guards, she serves, she consoles. "You are the sun in the heavens," she whispers fiercely, day in, year out. . . . "You must take for your wife one who was trained to be your servant, even as I—unhappily, oh my son—was trained to serve your father. And that, my Egyptian son, is your inheritance" (Gornick 1973:189).

A baladi woman is first and foremost a household manager and a mother. Women drop by to borrow or return goods, to trade information, or just to visit. Friends and neighbors swap food or utensils as well as information on the market, medical treatment, and neighborhood events. A woman's main obligations to her husband are to feed him, meet his sexual demands, and raise their children. Although a woman will defer to her husband and serve tea and meals to anyone he invites to visit, a wise baladi man asks for little more than lunch and a quiet afternoon. After he retires, he may still leave home each morning to frequent coffee shops or in some cases his old work place, safely out of his wife's way.

The fact that the home is the woman's castle was dramatized for me one morning when a husband returned home unexpectedly from work to find his wife and her friends cooking. He paused to knock, not daring to enter without alerting the women within. A woman whose husband moonlights as a night watchman and comes home only to eat and change clothes spends free time with women neighbors and feels content, not neglected. "It's better this way," she says. "He has a long tongue and all he does at home is quarrel." Nevertheless, image counts, and a baladi man must always appear to be in charge. A wise wife never challenges her husband in public, and she consults him about such major expenses as trips, medical treatment, or weddings. The man supports the house, and the woman keeps her income, including money saved from prudent shopping, in a special cache for trips to her parents, feast clothes for the children, and other treats.

Baladi women devise many ways to save from their household budget. Miriam, the Coptic woman in Shaykh Ali, told me in confidence one day how her Muslim neighbors saved, while at the same time revealing a sectarian stereotype—Muslim women live in fear of divorce.

> My Muslim neighbor saves from the forty piasters her husband
> gives her for expenses every day. She might buy potatoes and a
> couple of liters of gas, and save at least half of her purchase and
> send it to her family in the village. Then if she is ever divorced,
> she can go to her village and spend her money [made selling the
> things she sends there]. You know that Muslims are afraid
> because their husbands can remarry. . . . When my neighbor's
> husband brings her bread for one and one-half piasters, she
> resells it to the neighbors for one piaster. She also sells her rice.
> She also buys things on installment and forces her husband to
> cover her payments. I too save from my daily expense allowance,
> but I buy everything with cash and do not sell things my

husband brings. By buying frugally I was able to save to buy the new dresses my daughters are wearing.

Although the home is the center of their social life, Egyptian women are hardly the cloistered Middle Eastern women of media stereotypes. To crack this image, one needs to understand Islam's stand on modesty, and the relation between class and gender. In particular, the use of the term "veil" confuses discussions of Middle Eastern women. The first entry under "veil" in the Random House Dictionary is "a piece of opaque or transparent material worn over the face, especially by women." The third entry is "something that covers or conceals." A pious Muslim woman should cover her arms, legs, and hair while at prayer, but even in the mosque she is never requested to cover her face. Contemporary women who cover their face generally do so out of personal choice, not religious dictate. "The choice to wear Islamic dress is one that [women] make themselves, and it must come 'from inner religious conviction'" (Fernea 1993:5). Elizabeth Warnock Fernea notes that Western stories of organized Muslim groups paying women to wear Islamic dress appear to be unfounded.

In nineteenth- and early twentieth-century Cairo, the division of male and female space—dramatized by face covering and female seclusion in the *haramlik* portion of the house—was a sign of affluence; the family did not need the woman's labor. In the haramlik, women could watch the activities in the men's reception rooms unseen from behind their latticework windows. The word "haramlik" is derived from the verb *harama,* to forbid or protect: *harim* is a word used for "protected women." Women transferred the household management skills they gained in the haramlik to work with benevolent societies or in the professional labor force once gender division broke down in the 1920s (Marsot 1978).

Most Egyptian women abandoned the face veil in 1919, after the feminist Huda Sha'arawi returned from a women's federation conference in Europe and tore off her face covering (by then little more than a symbolic net hanging from an ornament, sometimes made of gold, balanced on the nose) to participate in anti-British demonstrations. Peasant women, whose labor was needed in the fields, had almost never covered their faces. In nineteenth-century Egypt, the

> peasant woman was first and foremost a producing member of the family; her activities in agricultural and craft production were performed in the context of the family. . . . That women were thought perfectly fit for heavy manual labor was made

abundantly clear by the early nineteenth century policy of subjecting them to corvée labor (Tucker 1985:18, 40).

The labor of urban lower-class women was also needed—whether in cottage industry or petty street trade. Some wore the black loose-holed netting, more for fashion than decorum, as they sold their wares on Cairo's streets. Historic photos show women vendors casually retying their nets in full view of the public. At home, these women lived in tiny hovels which could ill support the life of the haramlik. Tucker's archival study of nineteenth-century Egyptian women confirms that rural and urban women participated in petty trade, with some owning small shops and a few of the more wealthy women investing in the spice and caravan slave trade. Their commerce followed logically from their work in textile and craft production (Tucker 1985:81–83).

In baladi quarters today, physical separation of people in general or of sexes in particular is nearly impossible. Most families live in one or two rooms and share a bathroom with several other families. Much socializing occurs on stairs and door stoops, and although members of each sex gravitate toward their own, women and men inevitably know each other well in the cheek-by-jowl domestic space of baladi quarters. In a public space, a woman may talk with any man while she markets, runs an errand, or visits a religious shrine; she would not risk besmirching her family's honor, however, by entertaining unrelated males in her home. In like manner, in the work place women and men interact as engineers, physicians, or assembly line workers rather than as women and men. It is this cultural definition of space that cushions what would otherwise be unacceptably close contact for nonrelated women and men.

Traditional baladi dress is a *melaya liff*, literally "wrapped cloth," which can be draped sari-like over a house dress to cover the hair and the entire body; the ends of the long wrap are tucked under the arm. From underneath, a tightly knotted scarf covers the hair. Andrea Rugh remarks that the melaya liff of Cairo and Alexandria was originally introduced in urban areas from Turkey during Ottoman times and was supposed to protect women's modesty (Rugh 1986:13). Both El-Messiri and Rugh point to the provocative potential of the melaya liff. In films, a typical baladi maiden banters with lads while her melaya liff slips from her shoulders to reveal a bright, low-cut robe underneath. Her head kerchief, theoretically secured with a knot, likewise slips to reveal her hair, as she stops mid-street to readjust her garments. Sawsan El-Messiri remarks on how the typical bint al-balad performs:

a series of alluring gestures . . . walk(ing) coquettishly in a
manner that makes her hips seem to roll to the rhythm of her
clicking slippers, tinkling bracelets, and the little bursting
noises of chewing gum bubbles. . . . Both glamor and modesty are
combined in the bint al-balad's wearing apparel, the melaya
liff, which reveals the graceful bodily curves (particularly of
the midriff), yet covers what should not be revealed or what is
shameful (El-Messiri 1978a:526, 529).

Rugh also notes how young women make use of the garment's
seductive potential:

To wear this wrap is to be continually occupied with its slippery
and voluminous folds. . . . The melaya is a slinky large rectangle
of shiny nylon, silk, or other thin, clinging material. . . .
Commonly when walking, a woman gathers up the bottom half,
pulls it tightly around her and lets the ends hang over one arm;
in back view, the shape and movements of her buttocks are
clearly visible under the cloak (Rugh 1986:109).

As the melaya liff is a baladi trademark and makes a woman
respectable and unassailable even when alone, a woman may wear
one when shopping to identify herself as local so as to obtain the
best bargains. The garment is also practical to throw quickly over a
house dress; many younger women wear it for short errands near
home. On visits they remove the melaya liff at the door and lounge
in a comfortable house dress. The wrap can be drawn over the head
to offer anonymity to a woman wishing to avoid recognition. Once
their bodies mature, young girls must don a melaya liff over their
cotton pajamas whenever they leave the house.

Although older women always wear the melaya liff or the more
rural robe, younger women vary their dress with place and activity.
A young woman I knew wrapped a melaya liff over the latest style
of trousers to go to market, but she wore a pants suit to supervise
workers in the family workshop and a black robe to visit the
cemetery. Women from provincial towns often wear a black dress and
coat reaching to mid-calf with black nylons and shoes rather than
the traditional dress; these women have also adopted a black pants
suit or a long skirt for cemetery visits.

Many baladi women who are originally from the village
complain that the urban wrap slips and slides, and they continue to
wear the black flowing robe that they wore in the village. In rural
Egypt, unmarried women wear bright patterned cotton or chiffon
dresses. Once married, they never appear in public without a black

A southern gellabaya

Woman dressed in moda, or modern, dress passes a traditional water seller in the marketplace

flowing robe worn over layers of chiffon dresses, cotton house dresses, and slips from their trousseau. Northern Egyptian dresses have a felt-trimmed square yoke from which the garment falls loosely. Slits at each side accommodate nursing babies. Black velvet marks special occasions. In the south, the robes have a looser, round yoke sewn from lighter, often translucent, cotton. Village women drape a black chiffon-like scarf over their hair. Some northern village women secure the scarf with a black band, giving the impression of Roman headgear. Although veiling of the face was practically nonexistent in Egypt during the 1970s, an occasional older urban Delta woman might drape a translucent, black chiffon scarf over her face when venturing outside her neighborhood. With the rise of neo-Islamic movements in Egypt in the late 1970s and 1980s, one began to see the new form of veil—a head scarf wrapped so as to leave only eyes, nose, and mouth (some times only eyes) showing.

Fashion reveals religion. A baladi Coptic Christian tattoos a blue cross on her inner wrist. Unmarried Coptic women wear bright print house dresses with black chiffon scarves, ignoring the baladi preference for black garments; married Coptic women avoid the melaya liff, which is considered a Muslim garment. This belief is shared by Muslim women, who remark that Coptic churches prohibit a melaya liff except for ecumenical events, such as funerals and weddings, when Muslim friends and neighbors join Copts to grieve or celebrate. In Chapter 4 I discuss each sect's tendency to share in the more social aspects of the celebration of the other sect's rituals in baladi quarters. Neighbors advised a Muslim woman en route to Easter Eve services against wearing not only a melaya liff, but also her house dress, lest she be "stopped at the door for wearing a nightgown." She changed to a bright house dress, flung a black chiffon scarf over her hair, and practiced walking "like a Copt"—strutting with her stomach thrust forward and one hand placed on the bulge. Her performance brought howls of laughter from the Muslim women in one of the few ethnic satires I witnessed in Bulaq.

The traditional male garment is a long cotton or woolen robe flowing to the ground with ample side pockets and a buttoned shirt top. A pocketed satin vest, often striped, with tiny covered buttons, is worn underneath. What we call pajamas are an accepted daytime dress for young boys and for men who are at home, but once again activity dictates dress; a young man may wear pajamas or a robe while in his lane, but tailored sport pants or tight blue jeans and fancy suits away from home.

Baladi Egyptians carry any commodity, dead or alive, wrapped in newspapers or stuffed in plastic bags or reed baskets. A common all-purpose container is the ample circular basket, often laden with

Two variations of draping the melaya liff

A northern gellabaya, on the right

bundles of clothes, bread, fruit, and primus stoves for a village trip or a day at the cemetery. Women carry baskets on their heads; men, on their shoulders or on the napes of their necks. Although women will carry anything, including cement at construction sites, men will not fetch water. Female neighbors supply water for bachelors.

One cannot judge a life style by dress, since baladi wardrobes are extremely versatile. In addition to traditional dress, "moda" has become widespread. This style includes A-line dresses (which conveniently flare to hide ample hips), tight slacks, knit tops, and pants suits. Girls' school uniforms have changed from skirts to pants with long, square-bottomed jackets—an example of modern dress being less risqué than traditional.

Destination also determines dress. A young woman who dons a black robe to visit a mosque will wear pants and a knit top to attend a picnic at the Agricultural Museum. At home she greets her fiancé in a house dress, which she wears while laundering clothes, and on an errand up the lane she wraps herself in a melaya liff. This versatility is the stock and trade of baladi savvy.

Cooking and Crises: Baladi Households

Egyptian women both manage a household and participate in the labor force at all skill levels. Their work outside the home has little effect, however, on the division of labor within the house. It is the women who cook, clean, and raise children. Minimal furnishings for a baladi home, often only a single room, are a bed layered with several mattresses, a cupboard, a low round table (diners sit around the table on the floor), and a straw mat. There may also be a wardrobe, a kitchen cabinet, a table, chairs, couches with hard cushions that double as beds, a refrigerator, a television, a two-burner bottled gas stove, and perhaps even a wringer washer stashed out of the way in the bathroom. Families with larger apartments may have sideboards, dressing tables, and Louis XVth gold-leafed parlor sets. These are standard dowry items, although they are usually covered with white sheets except when distinguished guests visit. Bridal furniture is used according to space and need. Tools or food, not clothing, may fill dressing table drawers. When newlyweds are forced to live with parents, an entire dining room set may be stacked in the bedroom for lack of space.

Major redecorations generally occur only at the time of a joyous event such as pilgrimage or marriage. The favored apartment wall color is turquoise blue, which is thought to ward off the evil eye. Strawberry pink, lemon yellow, and clover green are also common.

Ceilings are white and may have a hand-painted border swirl of flowers and vines. Some walls are "wallpapered" with roller-painted designs. All walls display family photos; magazine pictures of movie stars, singers, and soccer teams; and religious items, such as a rug with a design of Mecca pilgrimage sites or a Coptic saint. A popular wall item is a cheery baby promoting milk formula. Beds, preferably four-posters placed high on cinder blocks, dominate one-room dwellings. Under the bed, the family stores bundles of clothes and wicker crates holding everything from pans to live birds.

Bulaqis refurbish a bed or couch cushions just like they dress up children for feasts or holidays. One woman adorned her bed with a pink satin coverlet and canopy made from a wedding dress when she left town to spend the feast in her village, saying: "Let the house observe the feast by itself while I am away." At Coptic Easter and the national holiday Sham an-Nasim, Copts signal spring by sewing new slipcovers and rearranging furniture, since sleeping close to one another to keep warm is no longer necessary.

A pear-shaped water jar stands in the corner of every living area that lacks piped water. When I conducted research in the 1970s, women carried water in square tins from a downstairs or public tap. When I visited Cairo in the late 1980s, I found that all the women had abandoned the rusty square tins for a circular aluminum pot designed and made locally by an enterprising Egyptian company. Women may siphon water from a nearby house, using a hose passed through a hole bored in the wall for this purpose.

More and more baladi homes have electricity, which requires an initial installation fee for stringing a wire and installing a meter. Sometimes two families will share a line. Electricity is popular because of television. Just as a refrigerator attracts neighbors begging ice or storage space, so too a television draws a crowd of children who sit shoulder to shoulder on the floor, motionless and speechless, lest their hosts revoke the privilege of watching. Children's education is another, but secondary, incentive to install electricity. One mother said: "I myself wouldn't have thought of installing electricity, but my daughter wanted it to study by." Without electricity, a child must find a corner in a neighbor's house or use a gas lamp at home.

If a baladi woman works outside the home, she dovetails household management with her job as well as possible—preparing breakfast before leaving for work, or washing clothes and cooking lunch late in the evening. A baladi housewife balances routine housework, special tasks such as restuffing flat mattresses or cushions, and unpredictable crises such as sickness.

A baladi woman rises before dawn to light the primus stove and boil the tea and milk, which, with biscuits, comprise an initial breakfast. Her family carries sandwiches in satchels to work or school to eat later in the morning. A woman's day is hectic until she finishes cooking lunch in time for her husband's return, around two P.M. If passing produce carts have inferior vegetables, she walks to a main market. If children of errand-running age are scarce, she cajoles older children into helping or lowers a basket from the balcony to vendors passing in the street below. Cooking is multistaged, with separate preparation of sauces, vegetables, rice, and occasionally meat. Morning visitors help to pick gravel out of the rice or to clean and chop vegetables. The last morning task is to mop the floor of dirt, vegetable peels, and papers; frequent mopping enhances the room's coolness and makes wastebaskets unnecessary. A woman's morning work is continually interrupted: a child must be dressed, a school apron mended, lunch expenses disbursed, a friend's request to borrow sugar answered, a vendor's wares examined. If a door-to-door saleswoman, or *dallala,* drops by, one seizes the chance to view cheap tea glasses from the Gulf or dress shoes from Libyan markets.

A major project such as baking bread or visiting the pediatric clinic will modify cooking and cleaning projects and may mean the family will have to eat bean sandwiches rather than a cooked dish for lunch. Baking and washing require cooperation. Even those without ovens bake special breads (such as the round loaves customarily given to the poor on feast days or the thin lefsa-like bread for the Feast of Sacrifice) in the ovens of neighbors or friends. Two or three women work together to mix, roll out, cook, and cool bread. One reserves an oven ahead of time, as one reserves lines on the roof to dry clothes.

Clothes are subjected to a more thorough cleaning than most automatic washers can perform. Washing has five distinct steps: boiling, scrubbing, soaking, rinsing, and bleaching. A woman boils white clothes in a square tin on a primus stove; she scrubs and soaks clothes in two flat round pans between rinsings, wrings and stacks high mounds of clothes in casserole pans or, should pans fill up, on her head.

Special social occasions can obliterate plans. A feast requires special breads, elaborate cooking, new clothes, and room refurbishing. A woman arranges fresh bedspreads and perhaps a flounce on a four-poster bed plus other special touches such as newly cut paper "snowflake" liners on cabinet shelves. Certain "women's rituals" occur in the morning: death condolences with Quranic readings (men attend a similar event at night); the marriage "morning after" ceremony, when women bring gifts and examine the bride's sheets for virginal blood; and the *subu'a* ceremony held a week after birth. These special rituals interrupt a day's work.

The household chores take precedence over more perfunctory rituals such as calls to congratulate or condole relatives and friends, and more frivolous excursions to shrines, parks, and museums. But women adjust schedules for invitations deemed "too good to be rejected," such as a dinner to celebrate an engagement or a shopping spree when bargain shipments arrive. During these larks an older daughter or neighbor watches the house and young children. Baladi women are reluctant to leave their house totally unattended; padlocks are flimsy at best, and one's life's savings may be stuffed under the mattress. Also, because her husband may return unexpectedly, a woman wants to avoid criticism for "roaming about."

Emergencies are, of course, unavoidable, but they vary in urgency. If the death observance is not for a close relative or friend, one can make a perfunctory appearance. Major crises at home—sickness, death, or feuding—take precedence, as do special domestic occasions like weddings and births. Social obligations to close friends or patrons also take priority. If fulfillment of an obligation appears problematic, a woman may simply become inaccessible; to do so she absents herself from home and joins friends in an undisclosed place. Sometimes a woman must excuse herself from social obligations because it is difficult, for example, to leave washing in midstream; the stove is lit to boil water, the floor is swishing with water, and clothes must be hung to dry before sunset. Baking is an even more compelling excuse, since rising dough cannot cook itself.

Neighborhood stores supply all household essentials except stylish clothes and accessories. Grocery and dry goods stores, modern and herbal pharmacies, and even gold merchants are found in every neighborhood. Vendors roll carts loaded with underwear, combs, and sponges through the street. There are butchers in every lane, and a fish market is located near the vegetable market. This proliferation of shops facilitates the day-to-day purchases that are necessary in a society of few refrigerators. Even those lucky few households with refrigerators prefer to cook daily; dishes stored overnight are considered unappetizing and are fed to the chickens. A leanly stocked kitchen provides a ready excuse to aspiring borrowers: "I just cooked my last cup of rice." Thus, even nonperishable staples are bought in small quantities or tucked away safe from view. Women who lend tea swear the borrower to secrecy "lest the neighbors think we have plenty of tea to lend."

The gold merchant is often located among the bakeries and butcheries. He functions much like a branch bank, since women wear their savings on their arms, in gold bracelets. He also caps teeth with gold. When women have extra money, they cap a tooth or trade a gold bracelet for a heavier one. Services such as grinding coffee (or sugar, to dust on feast cookies), ironing, baking, repairing shoes, and sewing are located within a lane or two. Women can walk to the large cloth market, located just before the car workshops of Wikalat al-Balah, to buy material and used clothing. The used clothing market attracts people from all over Cairo to buy bargain European clothes from foreign charity shipments, often resold rather than distributed to the needy. Nearby Bulaq al-Jadid street offers furniture and appliance shops and cotton mattress stuffers, in addition to a panorama of sweets, juices, notions, and gold.

A baladi woman more often plays with the barren stone than the fertile egg as she works to stretch lean resources. She commissions as many clothes and household furnishings as possible from local, inexpensive seamstresses, mattress stuffers, and so on. She arranges credit through a local woman merchant for larger items. Another source of credit is the savings association, a monthly pooling of money by ten to twelve people. Participants agree beforehand on the order of collection. Often the founder, who may have established the association to finance a wedding or substantial investment, such as a television, collects first. Some prefer a final collection when they have completed payments. One may take two shares, pay double, and collect twice. A woman may time her savings association "cash in" to coincide with other income, such as an inheritance, in order to make a substantial purchase.

Both installment payments and savings associations are strategies to stretch the budget and to avoid frittering away money on snacks or trinkets. Money assigned to monthly payments cannot be given to a child to "waste" on candy. This commitment helps a woman justify asking her husband for money, which of course is exactly why men vehemently oppose installment plans and savings associations—they know that their wives will appeal to them to meet the obligations.

While creditor merchants finance large purchases, baladi women also lend small sums of money to each other. Accounts are unwritten, but they are recited at each payment and may be transferred from person to person. For example, if Fatima owes Karima one-half kilo of sugar and Suad borrows a kilo from Fatima, Suad can owe one-half kilo to Karima and one-half to Fatima. Personal loans carry no interest. Only with a large loan, or if the borrower is leaving town, would a written agreement or other guarantee be conceivable. For example, a woman who borrowed forty pounds to visit her husband in Libya signed nothing but left the lender the key to her room. When she decided to vacate the room, she instructed the lender to keep some of her furniture as collateral until she returned from Libya.

A woman works hard to obtain health services and education for her children. If she is too poor to pay for a private clinic, or if she feels the symptom is minor, a woman will endure long waits at public and benevolent society clinics to gain free care and medicine. Sometimes the woman seeks not the medicine, but the rations of milk or flour being distributed that day. If her child has severe or unremitting symptoms, a woman will pay several days' wages for private clinic consultations. As for education, a baladi mother may circumvent enrollment regulations and register a failing child in a school reported to more easily pass students. If she wants to enter her child in school a year early, a baladi woman locates schools that accept younger children because of lower enrollment demands or more sympathetic school mistresses. With a few days of paperwork, the mother can transfer her child back to the home district the next year.

Banks, government offices, clinics, and schools are just a few of the bureaucratic systems with which baladi women cope. Husbands sometimes help, but since a day laborer does not have time and an office worker's schedule conflicts with government office hours, a woman is usually more likely than her husband to deal with bureaucracy. At the same time, she is prudent in what she mixes and matches from baladi and afrangi systems to enhance her family's position.

To Test Is to Control:
Maximizing Baladi and Afrangi Medicines

Bulaqi women's narratives about business, housekeeping, marriage, religion, and health were the building blocks for my understanding the entire culture. In health matters, baladi women maximize from the traditional and the modern. Not only do they conserve scant resources by using cheaper baladi medicine when possible, but by mixing baladi and afrangi medicine, they retain the known and comforting traditions while benefitting from "more powerful" modern medicine.

An example of this melding of medical options is Laila's handling of her Rh-negative blood condition, which results in jaundiced children by the third birth. Laila, the wife of a school teacher, bridges baladi and afrangi worlds. Raised in a merchant family that has lived in Bulaq for several generations, Laila finished two years of secondary school and reads some English. Although she uses baladi home remedies, she is well acquainted with afrangi remedies and seeks out prominent doctors, including a gynecologist whose position as hospital director makes him, in Laila's eyes, a superior choice to treat her jaundiced babies.

Laila delivered her first two children normally. She then gave birth to two sons, both of whom died within a few days of birth. Laila has an Rh-negative blood factor and her husband is Rh-positive; in these cases the first child is usually normal, and subsequent babies, if Rh-positive, are born jaundiced if the mother does not receive proper treatment. Despite the two deaths, Laila continued to trust afrangi medicine and felt her problem stemmed from poorly performed lab tests. To hedge her bets, however, she left no afrangi or baladi path to a healthy delivery unexplored. Although Laila would have been content with two daughters, her husband wanted a son so badly that he pressed for continued pregnancies despite the complications. Laila considered adopting a son, but she dared not suggest it to her husband. When I visited her in December 1974 shortly after the death of her second son, she hardly let me sit down before she rushed into the typical baladi verbal formula for a personal narrative of distress: "Where have you been? I need to tell you what happened while you were away!" Laila then began the long, sad story of the death of her second son, and her visit with her husband to the clinic after the forty-day mourning period to inform the doctor. Since I was her only interlocutor I interjected questions (indicated by italics) from time to time, and I grant that these may be more motivated by medical anthropological research than by an attempt to interject what a typical baladi interlocutor might have added. Nonetheless, Laila's account deviated little from vignettes I heard from her later.

> We went to the same doctor in Babaluk who had examined our baby earlier. He told us the same thing that other doctors have—that the blood transfusion should have been made right away; that the child's A, B, or O [blood type] could be different from ours and needed changing right away. . . . So it is another "thing"—the A, B, or O; and not the Rh. . . . Here at the local clinic the doctor told me that I bore no responsibility for the child's death: "It was not your fault." The doctor told me that before I delivered my fourth child I should go to have a blood test at a private clinic and not here in the hospital. My husband and I both went (we had already been tested at Farouq Hospital) and the results were the same and I brought the paper

to the doctor at the local clinic. He said: "The baby will live this time."

Did you ask anyone about the death of the first son [third child] who was jaundiced?

No, we took the first boy to a hospital, and we decided that we'd never do that again, but that we'd go to a specialist this time. We took the first boy to Abu Reich Hospital; either the local clinic or Farouq Hospital referred us—I don't remember, as I was here [i.e., gave birth at home]. My mother-in-law and husband took the baby to the doctor at Abu Reich Hospital; my mother-in-law cried more this time with the second boy than I did; I was too tired to cry. . . . That time [with the first son] we took him on the third day; he had a fever of 40 degrees [centigrade] when he got there in the morning, so they waited for the fever to subside before making the blood transfusion. "You cannot mix fever and transfusion." He was such a young thing that he had no veins in his arms, and they gave him the transfusion in his forehead. By the time they'd finished the transfusion he had died.

Didn't you wonder why your first son died?

We had all the tests after the first baby died to check our blood and our Wassermann results. The tests were all normal. But this time we wanted to find out what was the cause of the death; and I have discovered that it was not the Rh factor, but something else—the A, B, O factor. So the next time I will deliver the baby in a hospital, so we can have the transfusion right away. The doctor in Babaluk also works at Abu Reich Hospital and said we could contact him for the transfusion. But we will find even better contacts than this doctor. My husband now teaches at Cairo University so he will talk to people in the medical school (Early 1988:68–69).

The next September I found Laila four months pregnant. She had taken medication to prevent miscarriage plus tonics and vitamins. She had changed from her clinic doctor to a gynecologist who was the former director of Farouq Hospital, who her sister-in-law had recommended. It was Ramadan and she was fasting so that "God will let me have this baby." She planned to give birth in the hospital, she said, and then paused to frame a narrative piece with a "Let me tell you what else I have done."

They [her sister-in-law] told me that when I am in my seventh month of pregnancy I should wear a white *gellabeyya* [house dress] . . . and slaughter a pigeon and put its blood on my gellabeyya and on a small gellabeyya in which I will dress the newborn. . . . Then I should sleep alone in a room with a candle burning, having bought different kinds of beans, with the small gellabeyya under my head. In the morning I should bring children and feed them the beans and candies as well as the pigeon.

Why?

So that the children will enjoy themselves. I do not do this for myself, but so that my brother "under the ground" will be satisfied.

You mean your qarin [spiritual double]?

Yes (Early 1988:69).

The food given to the children symbolizes life, as does the blood of the pigeon. The import for the life of the baby to be born is clear.

Laila, literate and economically comfortable, often separates herself from baladi customs in the same way that Nadia, whose family hosted a hybrid "baladi/afrangi" wedding, remarked more than once to me how her neighbors did not have "broad minds" capable of understanding. After Laila told me her plans for killing pigeons, she drifted to other topics, including how she did not like to spend time mixing with her neighbors who were baladi and spent hours gossiping about one another. Laila is baladi because she lives in Bulaq and because her father is an urban merchant, but she picks and chooses its elements. Although she was desperate enough to perform the gellabeyya ceremony, she refuses to visit saints' tombs or cemeteries on feast days, as many of her neighbors do. She never dons the traditional melaya liff, but wears a modern mid-calf skirt with a roomy jacket. At home, she dresses in pajamas rather than the customary gellabeyya. When she offers condolences at a traditional ceremony, Laila borrows the requisite black gellabeyya from a neighbor. Laila dissociates herself from back lane society, saying that it only leads to idle chatter and malice, and that it is better to keep to one's self.

Despite Laila's claims of avoiding baladi Islamic practices, when she was pushed to the limit she turned to popular Islam, already part of her curative repertoire, and found it a familiar prop to relieve her anxiety. Maximizing both systems as best she understood, she simultaneously sought doctors of influence and rituals of power. Laila felt that afrangi medicine would "deliver" and that if only enough lab tests were taken and if the results were accurate, all matter of maladies could be righted. She focused on new details (like blood types) without necessarily understanding them. An afrangi paradigm of medicine stipulates specific treatment at the first two births of an Rh factor mother, as well as subsequent transfusions. A baladi paradigm accords afrangi treatments and lab tests miraculous powers, similar to those attributed to injections and antibiotics by baladi clients. Laila planned to deliver at a clinic next to that of a pediatrician, so he could assume responsibility immediately after the birth. She pondered the possibility of a complete blood transfusion, which had been suggested by one of her doctors, and planned to discuss this with the pediatrician. She arranged to have the most powerful mediating forces at her disposal. A relative arranged a bed at the famous Cairo hospital Qasr el-Aini. Laila simultaneously planned the seven-month pigeon sacrifice and a hospital stay for her last month of pregnancy.

Laila's melding of baladi and afrangi medical strategies mixes the comfort of familiar rituals with the power of cosmopolitan medicine. The important thing for Laila was to have a renowned specialist who could best dispense the miracles of modern medicine—much as the afrangi British of apocryphal tales dispensed nonending packets of meat. In Chapter 6 we continue to explore health and politics and the body as template of society. But in the next chapter, we consider baladi devotional life and the praxis of Islam.

4

Popular Baladi Islam: Processions and Vows

Saints' Days: Passage to Personhood

B aladi Islam (a cultural and not a theological category) draws from both orthodoxy and praxis. Throughout this study I refer to the Islam practiced in baladi quarters such as Bulaq Abu 'Ala as "popular Islam" in the conventional anthropological use to indicate everyday religious practice, which mixes scriptural and local traditions. It does not mean that "more formal" or "more orthodox" Islam is "unpopular." Nor should it be forgotten that many baladi Egyptians follow many devotional conventions stipulated by "orthodox Islam." A dynamic mix of textual and local practice is exemplified by the processions during the *mawlid*, or saint's day, of Sultan Abu 'Ala, whose mosque and tomb lie on the edge of Bulaq. A mawlid is baladi, popular Islam at its best: processions, circumcisions, vow fulfillment, and shrine visitation. Each saint has his or her annual day of celebration, which is the most propitious, as well as exciting, time to visit the shrine. Mawlids are religious carnivals, complete with outdoor restaurants and vendors hawking everything from socks to incense over microphones. A battery of pinball machines clatters discreetly out of view of the mosque. Peasants and Sufis camp on the sidewalk in makeshift tents of sheets and rugs.

Theologians barely tolerate saints' days. During the 1970s in Egypt numerous newspaper articles by religious scholars criticized mawlids as noisy and superstitious events, elevating a mere person to the status of intermediary between believer and God. Probably the best-attended mawlid is that of the beloved Sayyid al-Badawi in Tanta, a delta city halfway between Cairo and Alexandria. His mawlid is solar, not lunar, and it always falls after the autumn harvest—thereby encouraging attendance and spending by peasants who have just harvested their crops. (Most saints' days, including

85

the minor ones in Bulaq, occur during the lunar calendar months of Ragab and Sha'aban, which means that their date, like those of the two major Muslim feasts, shifts back thirteen days each year in the solar calendar.) Originally from Morocco, Sayyid al-Badawi died and was buried in Tanta. His annual mawlid ends with a procession in which the mosque guardian dresses in red robes and a white padded hat and rides a camel, flanked by a tympani-drum honor guard. Army units, Sufi orders displaying banners, and labor groups portraying their skills (iron workers clanging their anvils, for example) complete the parade. In a 1940s account, an Englishman chronicles this mawlid parade;

> Several years ago, I think 1933, I witnessed a queer sight at dawn of the last day. . . . It was a procession of gaily decorated carts bearing the prostitutes of the town with their admirers, with much music and song. At that date the secular side of mawlids had become rather too much like ancient Greek and Roman feasts. . . . These have been properly suppressed, but it would be a disaster if the pendulum were forced to swing too much the other way (McPherson 1946:286).

Mawlid visitors, Muslim and Copt alike, bring back gifts imbued with the saint's *baraka* (grace) for friends and neighbors. These gifts may be plastic amulet hands or crosses to ward off the evil eye, cheap costume jewelry, baby rattles, scarves, or nuts and sweets.

Mawlids of major Cairo mosques, like Hussain or Sayyidna Zainab, are thronged with Sufi mystic orders and peasants. Those of smaller mosques, such as Sultan Abu 'Ala or Sidi Nasr in the heart of Bulaq, are attended mainly by area residents. J. W. McPherson's historic account just cited follows the Bulaq Sultan Abu 'Ala mawlid, the one at which all my friends at various times circumcised their sons:

> I enjoyed the fine mawlid of Sultan Abu el-Ela repeatedly, early in this century, well before the war of 1914–18. It was very big and popular, and extended not only all around and about the mosque, but far into the little Bulaq lanes on the other side of the main street. There was a sober brilliance about it; not many secular shows but many singing sheikhs in the shops and houses, and people were allowed to collect and listen and enjoy in peace, not irritated and hustled, and even beaten, as of recent years when they were goaded to a sort of perpetual motion.
>
> Then came tragedy! A part of the mosque collapsed with tragic results. It was taken deeply to heart: not so much the loss

of life and the expense of repairs, but the shock that so holy a place should fall down. "Why did not Sultan Abu el-Ela intervene?" asked some pious simple souls (McPherson 1946:145–147).

By the time I conducted research in the mid-1970s, the Sultan Abu 'Ala mosque had slipped from public view, figuratively and literally: it was under the exit ramp of a newly constructed overpass, and its saint's day was purely local except for a few Sufi groups who camped out on the saints' days circuit. On the eve of the saint's day in April 1976, eager to see the boys' circumcision processions scheduled that auspicious day, I arrived at Suad's house in Tel Nasr in the early afternoon. Suad told me that the wagon for her son Yassir's procession would arrive any minute. Yassir was dressed in a white gellabeyya and a gold-embroidered and braided white head scarf. His sisters clamored for a drum, but Suad said she could not afford the twenty-five piasters and did not want to bother the neighbor woman upstairs with requests to borrow hers.

While waiting for the popular ritual to begin, I overheard tidbits of social talk concerning which neighbors had given Yassir his *nuqta*, or money gift. The talk summarized the social relations of the short, dead-end lane. By 4:30 in the afternoon, Yassir's procession had not begun and I left to go up Tel Nasr to Bulaq el-Jadid street to watch other processions. As I left Tel Nasr, I ran into a procession led by a long-haired dervish hired for the occasion, shimmying his green skirt up his waist to his shoulders and back down again. His body continually gyrated. A half dozen tambourine players followed him, stepping and kicking their feet in synchrony. Next came men carrying two banners, one green and one red, with such white-lettered phrases as "God is Great" and with names of Muslim leaders. They were followed by two young boys on horseback dressed as Yassir was, held on by their fathers. The horses were festooned with blue-embroidered white saddle covers, and the bright scarves that baladi women normally wore on their heads tied through the bridle loops. Next came a horse-drawn cart filled with several dozen women and children drumming and chanting the standard refrains of "Pray to God," "Pray for the circumcised (boy)," "Where is the mother of the circumcised (boy)? We are coming to congratulate her! Here she is!" The procession snaked past sweets and paper-hat carts in the main road, the cheese and household utensil carts at the entrance to Tel Nasr, and the coffee vendors slowly turning their roasting coffee in drums over charcoal fires along Tel Nasr. The procession paused in front of the boys' home and, oblivious to the blocked traffic on both sides, paused for several minutes while well-wishers clapped the boys into the house. I

Circumsicion kiosk set up at mawlid time next to Sultan Abu 'Ala mosque

continued up Bulaq el-Jadid street, meeting other processions as I made my way toward Abu 'Ala mosque. I began to notice the same dervishes, banners, and horses being recycled in new processions. An arch of lighted arabesque tenting framed Abu 'Ala mosque at the dead-end of Bulaq el-Jadid at 26th of July Street—which connected Bulaq with afrangi Zamalek one way over the Nile Bridge and with downtown Cairo the other way.

Near the mosque, I met Zahra from the Shaykh Ali house. She carried a pail of bean sandwiches which she planned to distribute to fulfill a vow to feed the poor if her son recovered from an illness. A mawlid is an auspicious time for such donations, customarily made at the Thursday sunset prayer, which is also the time for the procession of the mosque guardian. Beggars were gathered by the mosque door in anticipation. After she gave away her sandwiches, Zahra and I strolled over to the circumcision kiosk, set up by an itinerant barber at the side of the mosque. Painted green with red minaret-like decorations on each side, it sported a mural of a white-coated doctor bending over a child. The modern medical image of this baladi barber kiosk was completed by the Ministry of Health license number scrawled in black across the mural's bottom. About ten mothers holding boys one to five years of age waited to have them circumcised behind the kiosk's flapping green curtains. We next visited the barber shop across the street. The barber swabbed with alcohol, cut with a sharp razor, doused with Mercurochrome, and bandaged with swabs of cotton the private parts of boy after boy.

Zahra and I moved into position to watch the mosque guardian proceed on horseback behind a troop of dervishes, drummers, and elegant banner carriers. The guardian carried the new tomb vestments: a white conical turban and a green cloth embroidered in white with Quranic sayings. In the distance I saw Yassir's family drumming their way down the street. The guardian's procession left the mosque and returned to the mosque, while the processions of the young circumcised boys started at the mosque and ended at the boys' homes. The boys' processions replicated the guardian's. The boys' white gowns and head covers made them look simultaneously like pilgrims to Mecca (who dress in white, although they do not cover their head) and like Saudis.

Mesmerized by the dervish, who had grown enthusiastic and had mounted a city bus attempting to negotiate the one lane of traffic left on the busy street, I wondered idly if he would reach the other end of the bus rooftop without falling off. As I watched, I remembered a sight I had witnessed early in the afternoon on my way to Suad's. As I had turned into Tel Nasr Lane, I met a procession. This one had no horses, no carts, and no chanting. Everyone walked. Men carried a wooden box covered with a white cloth. Women followed—emotional, but this time screaming and tearing their hair. It was a funeral procession! It had started at the deceased's house, and was winding out of the narrow lanes to the wider streets to the Abu 'Ala mosque. This was the very corner where several hours later I saw a procession heading the opposite direction. I wrote in my field notes: "A funeral starts at the person's house and takes him/her out to the main wide street and then the mosque. A circumcision procession starts near the mosque in the main wide street and takes a boy back through narrow streets to his home. Note the two opposite directions."

When I later contemplated baladi ideas on fertility, infertility, and circumcision, I was struck by how the drama of the two processions and their directions reinforced the cluster of symbols expressed by the baladi concept of *mushahara* (infertility or insufficient lactation). In Chapter 6, fertility is discussed further, but here I want to briefly explain mushahara, an important baladi cultural theme.

A woman's ability to bear children is a critical resource and she expends much energy to regain it if infertile. According to baladi tradition, the condition of mushahara is caused by incorrect juxtapositions of a vulnerable woman (one newly married or recently having delivered) with other people considered potent (and dangerous) because they are passing through certain life crises (birth, circumcision, death) or because of their condition (recently shaven, recently weaned a baby, or carrying such objects as eggplant or raw meat). Mushahara results when a potent person is careless— if not maliciously purposeful—in relating to a vulnerable woman. For example, if someone who has just lost a family member enters a room where a young bride is sitting, the bride may be "struck" infertile. Powerful substances, such as virginal or circumcision blood, are used in vaginal suppositories to combat mushahara.

Both circumcision rituals and funerals organize potentially disruptive forces related to fertility and to infertility into ritual processions of well-wishers and condolers. One procession delivers a boy from the mosque where he was circumcised to his home and family. Having fulfilled a baladi Islamic ritual of circumcision, he returns to his family, where he has years of coddling ahead; he returns as a pilgrim, as a Muslim, as a *person* now worthy of a funeral. The second procession delivers the deceased from his/her home to the mosque to be prayed over.

Baladis do not consider very young infants to be real "persons" deserving of a full funeral. If they die, they are quietly buried in a family grave or under a stone. In a society whose infant mortality remains high, this belief somewhat eases grief. Baladi women reference all the heady symbolism we have just discussed in such exclamations as "The baby was too young to be counted" (infants are not yet people) or "Don't you let your excised girl turn in front of me" (excision, the female version of circumcision, makes one ritually dangerous). We will return to a discussion of mushahara in Chapter 6.

The Islamic Ritual Calendar

While the saints' days of today may not be as elaborate as those of the past, these baladi Islamic events attract many residents of the surrounding quarter. We need to remember that the same person chanting circumcision verses on the horse-drawn cart may have just prayed at the mosque, may have traveled to Mecca on the pilgrimage, and may have memorized the Quran. Baladi Egyptians pick and choose from popular and orthodox traditions just as they meld baladi and afrangi social customs, business, or medicine. A woman who assiduously follows Quranic instruction at the local mosque and criticizes popular beliefs as "non-Islamic" may occasionally join women friends visiting shrines. By the same token, afrangi Egyptians who go on pilgrimage and fast during Ramadan, may pin a traditional gold amulet in their babies' hair.

There are, however, some typically baladi practices (such as picnics at shrines, and overnights in cemeteries) that draw fire from afrangis. These resemble the demographic "baladization" of Cairo discussed in Chapter 2; afrangi Egyptians dislike arriving for a quick prayer at a shrine or cemetery, only to find a carnival atmosphere created by baladis who boil tea and chat while their children run about. Theologically there is no "afrangi" or "baladi" Islam, but afrangi Egyptians tend to be more orthodox (although not necessarily more strict) than baladi Egyptians. At the same time, Islamic revival movements offer a personal piety embraced by baladis and afrangis alike.

Bulaq Abu 'Ala, predominantly Muslim, has a high proportion of migrants from the heavily Coptic south, or Said. Fourteen neighborhood mosques, five shrines, and four Coptic churches are located in Bulaq. Greek Orthodox and Maronite churches on its periphery serve the multinational population of nearby downtown Cairo. While I speak here for simplicity's sake as if all baladis were Muslim, this is of course not the case (some 10 percent are Coptic Christian). However, Islam colors baladi culture at the same time that Muslims may share in baladi Coptic ritual practice.

A baladi person's life cycle is set to an Islamic beat. At birth, the call to prayer is whispered in the baby's right ear, and parents are congratulated with the phrase "May God grant you a good life." At the naming ceremony held seven days after birth, the midwife recites the *Fatiha*, the opening verse of the Quran. There are customary Muslim names, such as Muhammad or Fatima, and Coptic ones, such as Butros or Miriam. Grateful parents distribute alms to the poor around the mosque.

Learning to recite the Quran is an integral part of a child's early education. Pupils study the Quran in mosque schools; some have failed public school and this is their only recourse, while others have sought out religious education. Young children are expected to learn to say "in the name of God"—"that great Muslim invocation which initiates any significant activity" (Denny 1983:48). Quranic recitation punctuates secular life.

You may hear a beggar, sitting with palm outstretched on a corner in a residential neighborhood, reciting [the Quran] in full voice. . . . Halfway up the block, a group of men, sitting formally on small stools which spill out of the store onto the sidewalk,

are listening to a recording of a recitation. They are there to
honor the memory of a deceased colleague. . . . Radio and television stations program recitations regularly during the course of
the day (Nelson 1993:8).

A Westerner's day is punctuated with the alarm clock, clattering
dishes, traffic, phones, and typewriters. Westerners hear no sound
equivalent to the majesty of the Quran, and indeed to hear "a Bach
cantata in your local delicatessen . . . would be a rare occasion"
(Nelson 1993:8–9). It is true, however, that westerners now hear
opera music advertising luxury items like BMW cars, and that
religious radio stations broadcast popular songs with Biblical
verses.

The mosque is a ritual center both for prayer and for life
passages. The processions of popular Islam move to the mosque to
fete circumcised boys; newly married couples celebrate with a spin
around Hussain mosque in a taxi; pilgrims return from Mecca to pray
in the local mosque. Those who can afford the pilgrimage to Mecca
may defer it until they have sown their wild oats and feel
spiritually mature; upon their return, pilgrims are addressed as
hajj(a) and expected to behave as devout Muslims. At death, the
body is washed according to Muslim custom and wrapped in a white
shroud symbolizing the white, seamless garment of a pilgrim; final
prayers are said over the body at the mosque.

There are myriad studies of Islam, including Islamic theology
and Islam in praxis (for example, Denny 1983; Nelson 1985).
Orthodox and popular Islam differ on the status of saints; official
Islam rejects any mediation between people and God and any
bargaining over destiny, but the shrines of the saints elevate a holy
person to the status of intercessor to whom baladis vow to bring
certain gifts if their wish is granted. Piety is personal, and Bulaqis
practice unique mixes of formal and local Islam; for example, a
baladi merchant woman had faith in the unorthodox saints but
rejected amulets, which were considered even more unorthodox.
Baladi religious ritual, not always approved by Muslim
theologians, epitomizes baladi values. Baladi social duty, for
example, is expressed in such popular rituals as processions of food
exchange.

Some baladi rituals, such as prayer and pilgrimage, deviate
little from orthodox Islam. The five prayer times structure the day
for all. One hears: "Pass by my house after the sunset prayer," or "I
woke at the dawn prayer and have been working ever since." The
prescribed Thursday, forty-day, and yearly observances of death
mark the passing of loved ones for years to come. The feasts

celebrating the end of Ramadan and the Mecca pilgrimage punctuate the year.

While baladi men tend to gather at the coffeehouses, baladi women's one acceptable public meeting place is in the mosques, where they not only pray but also sit in the quiet coolness, a welcome respite from the dusty streets outside. When I accompanied my friends to the market, we might slip into a mosque for a few minutes to rest. Following the lead of Coptic women, I visited Muslim shrines but did not join in prayer. At formal prayer time, women pray behind a curtain, to the side, or in a balcony; at other times they move freely throughout the mosque. Women pray in the work place in a special room or other niche; men, on temporary mats outside—sometimes expropriating hallways. At the obligatory community mosque prayer on Friday at noon, crowds of men spill over onto the sidewalks. Some baladi women pray five times a day and attend the morning religious instruction, which rotates among six mosques in Bulaq. A scholar trained at Al-Azhar in Cairo, the Muslim world's premier seminary, instructs and leads recitations. Afterwards, he takes questions on such topics as voluntary prayer and social principles of Islam. Some men meet regularly in mosque groups to perfect their Quranic recitation; like the women, they follow a noted reciter from mosque to mosque.

Baladi women prefer companionship in rituals and they mobilize their associates to enhance the experience. One day Fatima encouraged her former neighbor Mahrusa to join her at these mosque sessions; her soliloquy lauded the companionship and social side of piety.

> Remember when we lived in the same house how I used to call out for you as I went down the stairs to mosque class? We would go and sit together and listen to the *imam* (prayer leader) explain the Quran. I liked the times where we all recited together the best. Even before our teacher arrived we would chant with one of the women who had made the pilgrimage and who knew the Quran leading us. The imam would answer such questions as how to be moral in business.

Women attending such classes recognize their own hierarchy of religious learning, and urge forward the woman most suited to lead the prayers.

Neighborhood mosques sponsor benevolent societies, which distribute charity from tithes and operate clinics, youth clubs, and Quranic schools. Coptic churches hold classes on Sunday for children and on Tuesday night for women. The Caritas Catholic mission in

Bulaq provides a clinic for all residents. The clinic distributes religious pictures and gifts at Christian feasts. Churches do not encourage the informal sociability of mosques.

Muslim feasts break routine and—with their festive foods, clothes, and visits—mark time's passing. Muslims follow a *hijriyya* calendar, so called because it figures time from the Prophet's migration (*hijra*) to Medina. The two major feasts are 'Aid el-Futr ("The Small Feast" or "Feast of Breaking the [Ramadan] Fast") and 'Aid el-Adha ("The Great Feast" or "The Feast of Sacrifice").

'Aid el-Futr takes its name from the verb *fatara*, which means "to break the fast," and celebrates the end of the month-long Ramadan prohibition of food and drink during daylight hours. Fasting is obligatory for all Muslims except travelers, children, the sick, and menstruating women (who are ritually impure and barred from mosques as well). A Muslim fasts extra days after Ramadan to compensate for any missed days. During Ramadan, newspaper columns debate fasting's medical benefits (e.g., the digestive tract takes a rest) and the allowed exceptions to fasting (e.g., during which trimesters pregnant women should break the fast).

Children learn to fast gradually, starting with a few hours a day and increasing until they can tolerate an entire day. Even if only one household member is fasting, the family maintains a Ramadan schedule. At sundown they break the fast with a heavy meal of lentil soup, meats, vegetables, and sweets. During Ramadan in Egypt, television carries a special quiz program and serials (such as "Liyali Hilmiyya" noted in Chapter 2 as epitomizing baladi life) directly after the evening meal. These are so popular that Cairo streets remain almost deserted during showtime. Families visit until the wee hours of the morning, with some not bothering to sleep until after the predawn meal.

In the early morning, a drummer strolls through the streets calling out names to rouse late sleepers for the predawn meal composed of heavy, sweet foods to help fasters last the day without food and drink. Sweets stalls decorated with arabesque embroidered cloth and festooned with lights spring up in every lane to offer either the dough to bake at home or the freshly fried tarts filled with raisins and doused in thick cinnamon syrup to eat. Under a tent, a man dribbles strings of dough onto sizzling griddles, stirring them into mounds of shredded wheat. Delicious smells of hot sugary syrup, spices, and incense from open bags at the spice shop mix with the acrid smoke of water pipes from the neighborhood coffeehouses as people buy their sweets to eat before dawn. Small rich cookies, *kak*, are the "cuisine" for this feast, during which a hostess offers formal guests tea and kak, and casual visitors tea and lighter biscuits but not necessarily the heavy kak. If dear friends do not pass by at feast time, a hostess stores "their share" for their next visit.

The other major feast is 'Aid al-Adha, "The Feast of Sacrifice," celebrated on the tenth day of the month of pilgrimage. Pilgrimage to Mecca, the holy city of Islam, is one of the five main tenets (pillars) of Islam, and every devout Muslim aspires to once in his or her life to circumambulate the sacred *Ka'aba* stone. Muslims fortunate enough to make the pilgrimage are sent off by neighbors with a night of drumming and chanting. Some give money to the pilgrim, who in turn brings back trinkets endowed, as with those from Tanta, with a grace derived from the place of acquisition, the holy spot of Mecca. More traditional gifts include water from the sacred spring of Zemzem and dates.

On the tenth day after visits to Mecca, Medina, and other holy sites, pilgrims gather at Mount Arafat to sacrifice sheep in memory of Abraham's (Ibrahim's) sacrifice. Even for Muslims not on pilgrimage, the feast is ideally observed by slaughtering a sheep and distributing the meat to the poor. Baladi Egyptians who cannot afford to sacrifice a sheep buy a kilo or so of meat and cook it layered with the feast special bread *ruqaq*, which is wafer-thin. Weeks before the feast women sit at low tables in the street rolling out the dough with long wooden rods.

There are five minor Muslim feasts, including the Prophet's Birthday, that are marked by other special foods. These seven feasts pace the year, as rites of passage pace a lifetime.

Rites of Passage: The Glue of Life

Birth

Life passages, a kind of "social and ritual glue," move a person along his or her life course. Childbirth is a joyous occasion for a baladi woman because it confirms her fertility and adult status, and assures her support in her old age. Observance of one life passage evokes memories of others. One day Mahrusa, several women neighbors, and I admired pictures of her daughter Mona's first child, Sana, dressed in a white embroidered coverlet and surrounded by smiling relatives. Clucking over the cute child, we naturally thought of other babies, including those of Sherifa, a former resident of the Shaykh Ali building originally from Nubia in the south. Admiring pictures of Mona's baby sparked discussion of an old neighbor, Sherifa. Mahrusa opened her story with a typical verbal formula: "Remember Sherifa next door and the time she had that difficult birth?" The expressions in italics are questions asked by the neighborhood women listening to Mahrusa.

> When Sherifa lived next door, she would say to me "Come visit," and I would go in and sit with her in her room inside. . . . But I never ate any of her food, because I don't like Nubian food.
> *Don't they have dishes like yours?*
> I don't know why I don't like their food, but I don't, and I can't drink their water. I used to sit with Sherifa and say, "I think I hear my husband calling me," and come drink water here, although Sherifa would have a cup set in front of me. When I returned, she would ask: "You went to drink water, didn't you?" I would respond: "No, why would I do that when there is water here in front of me?" Then she would say, "You don't like Nubian things, and I won't force you to drink my water. What if you fell sick? You are a parent after all." When she made tea I would send for my glasses, tea, and sugar, and she would complain.
> After Sherifa's daughter was born, she took her to the family home in Nubia when she was four months so that she would learn to speak the Nubian language. Sherifa's husband said that if they stayed in the house she would speak Nubian in the room, and then go out and speak Egyptian with all the other children and forget Nubian. So Sherifa took her to Nubia. When she returned after eighteen months, the family lived in the Sarkis district. I visited them and found the daughter speaking Nubian. I told her, "You naughty child!"
> You should have seen Sherifa's birth! There was another time like this when a Nubian in the house across the street gave birth, and another Nubian came and asked her, "Are you like us, do you circumcise?" She said yes, and they brought a Nubian midwife who cut the part which must be cut for delivery. [Nubians practice infibulation, which is radical excision followed by stitching of the labia majora. A woman's stitches must be cut open before each birth.] When Sherifa was in labor for her first birth, she said that she had pain in her back and stomach, and I told her we would bring the clinic midwife. The rest of the house was reluctant but I stood firm. The car came and I told Um Khaysha (who was an old Nubian) to ride with them. When the clinic midwife asked me to go with them, I said that I had three children—Hussein was on my arm at the time—and that I had to see to them first and then I would come to the clinic, and God willing, by the time I came she would have given birth. . . . The whole house went down and sat outside by the

clinic, and we found that she had delivered while the nurse went to the next room to get the instruments to open her circumcised part.

All the neighbors went again when it was time to bring her home, and we tipped the clinic taxi to bring her to the door. When we were coming back the first time, we met her husband and told him we had taken her to the clinic. He said, all right.

Why did you not want to ride in the clinic car?

If she delivered on the way, I would not have known how to deliver her, since she was infibulated.

The above account aptly presents baladi views, not only of a clinic-assisted birth, but also of ethnicity and neighborly responsibility. Sherifa's experience was fairly typical of a baladi birth: neighbors gathered around to assist and they sent for the clinic midwife at the last minute. Baladi women know that if they call the clinic midwife too early, she will check the mother's dilation, complain that they have wasted her time, and return to the clinic. The comment that Sherifa gave birth while the midwife was in the next room is a jab at a bureaucracy seen by baladi women as offering little. Even the clinic driver expects a tip. The clinic midwife expects a tip at the birth and during the newborn check up. Some with strong personal ties may participate in the *subu'a* (naming ceremony) and be handsomely tipped. If an unofficial midwife attends a birth or subu'a, she is careful not to draw attention to herself to avoid confrontation with the afrangi world of bureaucracy. She, too, will be tipped. In fact, baladi and afrangi midwives have developed a "cooperative and symbiotic relationship" (El-Hamamsy 1973:4), with the afrangi providing medicine and protection, and the baladi, traditional midwife helping to find houses and win mothers' confidence.

Mahrusa gave us a detailed background of Sherifa before discussing her birth, and Mahrusa's narrative stimulated talk of Nubia, its language, its food, and its people. Mahrusa said Sherifa was "different" because she was infibulated, but this is common knowledge and no more amazing to listeners than remarks on Nubian food. Mahrusa used the verb that means "to talk incoherently" when she described the Nubian language. She added, with a twinkle in her eye, "that is what our American friend does when she speaks her own language."

Most baladi births are at home, and women who have recently arrived from the village miss the warm, cozy atmosphere of village births, which customarily occur on top of the large brick and sod oven, where the family sleeps to keep warm in winter. On a visit to

a Menoufiyya village with my friend Fatima, I witnessed
Zakiyya's birth. One morning I awoke to hear the mother-in-law
dispatching one of the daughters-in-law to buy chickens for
Zakiyya to eat once she gave birth. About a half hour later, at
7:30 A.M., Zakiyya's water burst. We all thought her husband had
gone to bring the midwife on his bike (the daughter-in-law had
taken the sole donkey to buy the chicken) but he was sitting in the
front room. He left post haste, after Zakiyya crouched doubled over
in pain. Zakiyya asked for two old women of the area who assist at
births to join us, and finally the certified midwife, Atimad, also
arrived.

Atimad marched in saying her hands were already clean, but
Zakiyya was more interested in their being warm and Atimad
warmed them over a corncob fire. Zakiyya lay on her back on a
cloth, and her mother-in-law fished a child's gown out of the
clothes storage. The midwife encouraged Zakiyya to sit up and
warm her back over the fire, and to drink fenugreek to encourage her
labor. Atimad was calm and said all was in order and there was no
reason to call a doctor, even when Zakiyya said that her labor pains
had stopped and she couldn't tell when the birth would happen.

> *Zakiyya:* It has never been like this.
>
> *Atimad:* What could a doctor do? He would only move the baby
> about and change its appointed time of birth. What good would
> a shot do? It would only change God's will for it is God who sets
> the time of birth. There is no use in taking pills for pain; I don't
> believe in them. All is in order.
>
> [Throughout labor Zakiyya repeats "I am thinking of God,"
> "I call on the saints, on our lady saint Zainab," and similar
> invocations. At one point she asked her cousin to recite some
> Quran. Atimad explores the birth canal of Zakiyya, who
> complains bitterly.]
>
> *Atimad:* I *have* to put my hand in to position the baby.
>
> [At this point everyone realized it was a breech birth. There
> was a cry and the baby appeared.]

Atimad massaged Zakiyya's stomach to expel the afterbirth,
and asked for a knife, saying "Is it clean?" She tied the cord and cut
it. The afterbirth was saved for the sister-in-law, who wanted it to
step over seven times to help her get pregnant. The baby was dressed
in a gown and put in a sieve (see below). Atimad crossed her hands
and patted Zakiyya's body up and down, saying that this was to
prevent postpartum fever.

Atimad washed her hands and drank a cup of tea. She

regaled the woman with stories extolling her competence and questioning that of doctors. "One woman who screamed for a doctor gave birth before he arrived. I had already put an onion in her womb and given her eggs and fenugreek to encourage her labor and the woman delivered a breech birth without complications."

The senior women of the house sat on either side of Zakiyya as she gave birth, quoted Quranic verses for her, and rubbed her stomach. Children were allowed to stay in the room, unlike at urban births.

The message of the midwife is clear: she is in control of the birth and will brook no interference in its normal God-willed progression from doctors. She provides constant verbal assurance that all is well. In truth, her handling of the breech birth was remarkable.

Naming Ceremony

The first ritual in a baby's life is the ceremony seven days after birth, the *subu'a*, derived from the Arabic root for "seven." To celebrate a birth, afrangi Egyptians may host a tea party, which, while expensive, will be less complex a ritual and exchange event than for baladi Egyptians, for whom a subu'a expresses the state of social affairs and provides economic support at a time of increased family expense. The night before the party, the mother places a water jug in a pan of water with "seven grains" (*sab'a habub*). The "gender-linked imagery reflected in the ceremonial clay pot" (El-Guindi 1990) is clear, for a baby girl's jug has a round top whereas a baby boy's has a spigot. Fertility is clearly symbolized by the "seven grains," which include barley and wheat (grains that germinate); women sew the "seven grains" into amulets to protect children and give them to guests along with food packets of popcorn and nuts. The morning of the subu'a women gather to witness an older, knowledgeable woman (sometimes the midwife) shake the baby in a large sieve—suggesting the domesticity and purification associated with sifting flour. The mother then steps over the baby and sieve on the floor seven times—the same number of times that a pilgrim circumambulates the Ka'aba—while the midwife beats a mortar and pestle and admonishes the child to obey its parents. The children of the house process with candles to "bring down" the angels protecting the newborn. Well wishers offer money tips (nuqta) and eat pudding and *kos kossi* (steamed wheat sweetened with powdered sugar).

The ceremony is a time for visits and for exchanges of ideas on births, names, family conduct, infant deaths, and good or bad luck. When I accompanied Mahrusa to the subu'a of her relative Suad, we found that Suad's sister had cooked for her the last seven days so that Suad could rest in bed. The sister complained that their stepmother had traveled to Mecca on pilgrimage knowing full well that Suad would deliver before the stepmother's return. Later in the day as the woman sat and drank tea, talk turned to relatives on pilgrimage. Suad remarked "I do not know where my stepmother is; let me tell you what I dreamed the other night," and having caught everyone's attention, continued to narrate a dream clearly conveying her resentment at her stepmother for leaving Suad to give birth alone:

> I dreamed that I was sitting with all my women friends like you who are with me today. Suddenly someone came to tell me that my father's wife had returned early from pilgrimage. When I asked why, the messenger explained that my stepmother had taken a bag from someone who had asked her to carry it through customs and the police had seized her because the bag contained contraband. The police then deported her to Egypt.

Suad expressed moral judgment by directing a tale at someone (K. Basso 1984). Visions and dreams can comment on the past and predict the future. At the same subu'a, the women compared notes on name selection. Suad had a perfect forum for her personal narrative about her baby's name:

> My husband was at prayer in Hussein mosque one day when he saw a vision. In that vision he carried a child. A man came and tapped him on the back and said: "The name of this child is Ibrahim." My husband is a follower of the Ibrahim Desouqi Sufi order, so Ibrahim was an appropriate name!

Although a subu'a is a happy event, its focus on birth, newborns, and children may also evoke discussions of babies' deaths. More than once this subject arose as I sat with women cooking puddings and kos kossi for a subu'a. Baladi women speak of babies "dying just like that—by themselves." This is not an etiological truth, but a cultural belief that infants are not yet "real people," and that the very sick should be "allowed" to die. This is why a boy's circumcision is seen as a ritualized entry to "personhood," for the boy has survived the first few years of life when infant mortality is high. In the early 1980s when I returned to visit my Shaykh Ali house friend Aniyat, I asked after her baby girl Maha, whom I had met the year before. Aniyat related her daughter Maha's death:

> She was ill and I took her to Gala' hospital. They told me there that I should take her to Abu Risch hospital, but when I came home, my husband Ahmad told me not to take her because she was too sick to survive the long trip across town. Then I gave the baby to Rida who lives downstairs next to Mahrusa, because I knew the baby was ready to die, but its spirit cannot leave its body while the mother watches. The spirit gets stuck in the baby's throat that way. So I gave her to Rida, and she brought my baby back wrapped up dead. We buried her in my mother-in-law's cemetery plot because they had just had a funeral and it was "open." We did not even bring a Quranic reader, for the baby was not yet forty days.

Aniyat's account reflects the baladi views that a dying infant should not suffer unduly (as with a trip across town), that a child cannot die under its mother's protective gaze, and that an infant is not yet a person. Aniyat only surrendered her baby girl when she was clearly dying. Certain baladi cultural explanations may appear heartless, but in reality allow women to channel heavy sentiments. Often when I asked a baladi woman about a child who had "disappeared" since my last trip, she would respond curtly with a "we buried her" or sometimes with an anomalistic "*fi dahiyya,*" literally "she went to hell."

The baladi concept of fate (*nasib*) is used as an a posteriori explanation for death, often in tandem with the Quranic concept of death or fate as "written," as in "her time to die was written." The concept of fate or destiny never justifies inaction, and every woman I met during my three years in Bulaq had numerous tales to tell of desperate trips to clinics with deathly sick children.

At the Shaykh Ali house, there were different opinions about Maha's death—each a constructed social reality, a mirror of social relations. The Coptic neighbor Miriam said: "The baby died from neglect. They did not want a girl, so they paid little attention to an already-weak baby, and she died. They did not want to kill her, but they did not take care of her either." Another neighbor, Mahrusa, remarked: "The baby died 'by herself.' She was sickly and just died like that." "By itself" is a common baladi expression for matters vague or uncontrollable. People become angry by themselves, buildings collapse by themselves, and so on. Mahrusa's explanation steered clear of the issue of causation, while Miriam was willing to take it up head-on.

Circumcision

Babies who survive the first few years of life are feted in excision or circumcision rituals, privately for girls and publicly for boys. Excision/circumcision is a milestone, but not the rite of passage to adulthood it is in some African societies. Nevertheless, it serves an important, but different, function for each gender. Baladi Arabic refers to both female excision and male circumcision as *tahara*, from the verb "to purify." Baladi women explain excision both as local custom and religious (albeit not formal Islam) custom. It marks social maturity and occurs when the girl is at least six or seven (otherwise there is little to excise), but before puberty. In Egypt, when a girl's breasts begin to develop, it is shameful for her to wear pajamas that reveal her new curves, and she starts to wear the fuller cloak of the melaya liff. Kennedy notes similar explanations of the more radical infibulation practiced in Nubia, adding the explanation that infibulation—which literally sews up the woman—protects virginity (Kennedy 1970:146).

Excision of girls is a controversial practice that has been forbidden in Egypt since 1952 but which probably occurs in over 90 percent of baladi families. Afrangis and educated families have largely abandoned the practice, and baladi women realize that afrangis don't do it. Excisions vary in severity according to the practitioner, who may remove as little as a superficial strip of the labia minora or the entire labia minora and clitoris. In a special supplement on excision, the Arabic magazine *El-Doctor* published testimonies by medical doctors against excision including:

> I do not support excision. People believe that removing the clitoris at an early age will remove a girl's strong sexual drive. But experiments proved that this operation results in nothing except to deny the woman what is natural. . . .
>
> To get rid of hemorrhaging and infection and other dangerous side effects of excisions it must be forbidden, and health awareness classes must stress it (*El-Doktor* 1952:2, 4).

The continuation of excision is due to incredible peer pressure, buoyed by social expectations that an unexcised woman is not marriageable.

My baladi women friends answered my queries about excision much as they answered my queries "Why do you use amulets?" or "Why do you go to the cemetery on a feast day?": "Why? Because that's what we do." When I pressed, they said that excision made a woman "look nice"—a cosmetic measure. No man would accept an unexcised woman for marriage. The few women who escaped this practice, according to baladi lore, grew long and ugly labia minora.

Travelers' accounts, such as that of Aonnini in the eighteenth century, report that excision was for aesthetic considerations (Winkler 1936:196). A popular Bulaqi tale relates how a woman, raised as an orphan and never excised, is operated on a few nights before her marriage and thus saved from certain rejection by her husband. Another recounts a Christian woman seen delivering a baby in the hospital with "that part" hanging down. Excision is not the only cosmetic measure to signal maturity; a girl first plucks her eyebrows when she is engaged and first removes her body hair upon marriage. Once excised, a girl is expected to cast off childish behavior and act responsibly. She becomes an adult behaviorally, and physiologically.

Excision is a custom that some women consider *sunna,* or religious custom, and for which they cite versions of the following (unverified) religious tradition:

> A woman servant of Fatima's [the Prophet Muhammad's daughter] ran an errand, but she dallied and upon her return the Prophet said: "We must remove part of her to always remind her to obey and not tarry." So they removed that part that is to this day excised from all women.

This local belief is unsupported by Muslim texts or official Islam. Indeed, most Muslims around the world do not practice female excision, with the exception of Sudan's more drastic infibulation.

As I grew to know women better, some told me that excision heightens sexual pleasures because "it exposes the clitoris," although I also heard that Egyptian men take hashish to prolong sexual relations to satisfy an excised, less excitable wife. As an unmarried woman, I was not necessarily privy to all "woman talk" about sex, and when I assisted at births I was positioned with unmarried girls at the mother's head.

Westerners who cannot understand why any woman would let her daughters be "mutilated" by excision may be surprised to learn that similar practices occurred in nineteenth century Europe and the United States.

> Clitoridectomy was performed for indications of masturbation and the duplicity associated with it . . . in the United States from 1867 (or earlier) until at least 1904. . . . Circumcision of both girls and adult women continued to be performed in the United States at least until 1937, its fundamental rationale the curbing of woman's masturbation and the unappeasable erethism induced by unsatisfactory intercourse (Barker-Benfield 1978:353).

Excision is a low-visibility ritual and rarely announced in advance. A girl is excised when a midwife is available, when a grandmother visits, when there is a saint's day in full swing, or simply when it occurs to the mother. Usually the midwife comes to the house. At one saint's day celebration, I saw a family pass their girl into the circumcision kiosk used for boys; the barber obliged, but the onlookers all tisk-tisked the impropriety of this "public," albeit behind the curtains, excision.

After excision, a girl stays indoors and wears a white dress, which signals the event to the neighbors if they missed the midwife's visit. Close friends and family give the girl money gifts. She wraps the excised tissue in a cloth that she ties on her left arm. At the beginning of the next lunar month, she visits the river to bathe, then tosses the cloth and a handful of salt into the river. In rural areas, excised girls go together daily to the irrigation ditch to bathe "until they are healed." In Cairo, girls may omit a literal bath in the polluted Nile; however, they still visit the river at the new moon to ritually discard their excised tissue. It should be swept far away by the current so no one can employ it in black magic to render a woman infertile. Similarly, after birth, a woman's placenta is carefully buried to avoid black magic. Both of these body parts are intimately connected with fertility and by extension, infertility. The salt tossed into the river enhances life and fertility, as does the salt sewn into amulets. Salt symbolizes life; people who eat "bread and salt" together become fast friends.

My friend from the Shaykh Ali house, Aniyat, excised her daughter Badriyya in 1976. I had hinted that I wished to attend any circumcisions during Sultan Abu 'Ala's festival, but stopped short of requesting an invitation to this private event. Despite my friendship with Aniyat, I was not surprised to learn that her daughter was excised a day after I had dropped by to "check on things." A neighbor and the daughter volunteered their interpretation of the event.

Miriam, the Coptic neighbor, recounted her version spontaneously in the midst of her report on recent household events, framing it with "Guess what happened! We wished you were there!"

> Aniyat decided to excise Badriyya. We went to Abu 'Ala mosque, but found it crowded, so Badriyya's grandmother brought a midwife and she did it upstairs at about eight in the morning. The midwife took fifty piasters.
>
> It is shameful to make a fuss over a girl's circumcision, so nothing else has happened. But for boys, they organize a procession the night before. For our son Karam, we brought a pan

of henna [an herb used to redden hands and feet] with candles in it, and he rode a horse in the procession, and we slaughtered a sheep. We will wait to circumcise Nabil till we can afford another sheep and then fatten it; we tie it in the entryway by day, and on the balcony at nights. The children cried that they wanted henna when they saw Badriyya and her sister with henna on their hands after Badriyya's excision. Badriyya's family sent my children some food.

As with most baladi ritual, Badriyya was excised "when the time was right" and with little planning. One proof that excision for young girls is a local, not an Islamic, custom is the fact that most baladi Copts also excise their young girls, in addition to circumcising their boys. Miriam's sister-in-law once reminisced about going down to bathe in the irrigation ditch every night with the girls of her "excision group."

Even if Miriam had not alerted me, when Badriyya met me at the door in a frilly white dress, I knew she had been excised. With appropriate self-importance, she recounted the events that were important for her:

> See, this is my circumcision dress, and this is the handkerchief
> [a small square of gold-silver netting] with which I wiped my
> tears away. This is the one [a large white one] I put the money in
> that people brought, and then I gave the money to my mother. I
> tied "the thing" with some salt in this cloth on my arm.

When I asked why Badriyya's handkerchief was tied on the right arm (since I had been told one ties it on the left, "unclean" arm), neither she nor her mother had any idea. That was where the midwife put it. Aniyat told me on a return visit that Badriyya had gone to the river Nile the previous Thursday and thrown it in at the time of the afternoon prayer time.

A baladi girl is excised upon leaving childhood, when she is expected to act maturely; a baladi boy is circumcised upon entering childhood in the saint's day procession, affirming his family's fertility. Afrangi Egyptians circumcise their boys at birth, with no fanfare, in the hospital. In the village, circumcision is celebrated by a procession of women—walking and chanting along the irrigation ditch, carrying gifts of fruit and food cascading from trays for the mother of the boy of the moment. To rejoice too loudly at birth is to tempt fate too much; to circumcise more than one son at a time is also to flaunt luck too openly. Thus, a family who can afford only one circumcision celebration (which requires an animal sacrifice in the countryside) may fete several children at once, but actually circumcise them on different days.

Growing Up

Another ritual in early childhood is the first haircut. A boy's first haircut is traditionally performed at the shrine Sayyid al-Badawi. It is said that one should donate enough gold to equal the weight of the hair that has been cut off. Pilgrims converge on the shrine daily to make vows, pray, and buy the shrine's famous chickpeas to distribute to neighbors and relatives back home. One merchant can always be seen in the Tanta market, perched atop a mound of dried chickpeas, with colorful baskets into which he distributes the chickpeas strewn around him.

For Copts, the first haircut takes place at one of the popular Coptic shrines in Cairo—Zaytoun in Old Cairo with its Hanging Church, or Shubra's Saint Theresa's cathedral. Coptic boys are usually circumcised at the mawlid of Sidi Arayan, near Helwan south of Cairo. Like Miriam's son, they wear a white gellabeyya embroidered with their name, Coptic crosses, and floral designs, and they are paraded on a horse.

Childhood is freewheeling, and children are generally indulged, although by age four or five they begin to take on some tasks, particularly caring for younger siblings. A young child carrying a baby half its length is a common sight. When a baladi girl is excised, she is expected to act more maturely, to give up her childish ways of romping and screaming, and to begin serious apprenticeship at household tasks. Boys exit from childhood many years after their circumcision.

In rural areas girls pat out flour-laden loaves of bread on their mother's board by the time they are eight, and by ten or twelve are full-fledged household assistants. They also harvest clover and fruits and herd animals; however, they do not cultivate or irrigate. In urban areas girls do housework and run errands. In rural areas boys stay in the company of women until they are old enough to help herd, drive the water buffalo around the water wheel, carry manure, and harvest. In urban areas boys are conscripted for errands until they are twelve to fourteen years old; then they roam the streets or are apprenticed in a workshop.

Urban boys' patterns of geographic movement and task performance signal the end of indulged infancy and the start of responsible roles. The older a child becomes, the farther he moves from home, working his way into other lanes of the quarter and eventually into main market streets. The older the child, the more of the city he "conquers." This expanded movement occurs at first as a game, when he buys himself sweets. As the child becomes older, he assumes more complicated errands. Initially trusted with buying bread and beans, he is later expected to select vegetables and fruit and to find more distant shops. A boy or girl is no longer considered a child when he or she can run major errands and (in the girl's case) assist with chores. This competency is called *odeyan* (El-Messiri 1975).

A girl continues to run errands until she is engaged—at which time it is considered improper for her to be in the streets. She is not allowed to roam as far from home as the boys. Her entrance to adolescence is marked not by new jobs (although her home chores increase in sophistication) but by new dress, the melaya liff. When boys become a bit older, they refuse to run petty errands. They hold out for such prestige missions as delivering food gifts (they may be fed by the recipient) and shrink from trips to borrow items or to deliver bad news (that their mother will not come to help bake bread, for example). Errand abstinence is a kind of rite of passage to adolescence for boys, who then are apprenticed in a workshop, where such tasks as bringing tea and sandwiches replicate in his new work sphere the duties recently abandoned at home. Boys ride buses and trams—often for free, clutching to the rear bumpers—all over the city. Male adolescents frequent coffeehouses. The next ritual event for both girls and boys is marriage.

Marriage

Marriage affirms the adulthood hinted at by gradual behavioral changes in dress and household and street activity. Baladi women search for spouses for their children from the known, the near, or the encountered. Opportunities for chance meetings or exchange of information about potential matches abound on forays to market, fittings at the seamstress, and a host of other social errands. For example, a woman with a marriageable daughter eyes the son of a woman friend; the match is attractive from both sides because the boy will inherit a share in a mechanic shop and because the girl's acumen in household management has been demonstrated at close range to the future mother-in-law on informal visits.

Anthropologists report that the ideal match in Middle Eastern culture is parallel cousin marriage, based on interviews with informants who prefer marriage to a "known person" whom they describe euphemistically as the child of a "paternal uncle." In actuality, "paternal uncle" means any relative from the father's side of the family. Ideally, marriage is an alliance of interests with known folk—paternally related or not. For urbanites, business replaces land consolidation as a primary interest. Relatives are less available in a fluid urban setting, and shared business interests or neighborhood familiarity replace land ownership as a motive for marriage.

The first step in marriage negotiations is performed by relatives who provisionally agree on the bride price and on furnishing the household. The two matters are inextricable. For example, the groom may agree to buy all the furniture if his father-in-law will provide copper kitchenware. Next is the engagement, when rings are exchanged; this ceremony is often combined with the wedding contract among traditional Egyptians to free the couple to spend time alone together. To preserve his daughter's honor, the father may sign the contract even though the stipulated bride price will not be paid until the marriage is consummated after the wedding party. The wedding may occur several years later when the couple has found and furnished an apartment; some abandon hope and move their furnishings to the family flat and begin nuptial bliss crammed with their belongings into one room, sharing a bath with an entire floor of families.

Reading the Fatiha (the opening verse of the Quran) is the first seal on marriage negotiations. Muslims recite this verse to validate important agreements and to give courage at times of uncertainty, such as the start of a journey. Its opening words, "In the name of God," are recited to lend auspiciousness to countless daily events: to begin a meal, to indicate gratitude, to admire a baby, to deflect possible envy, and to introduce a public address. Devout Muslims may write this same phrase at the top of letters (and even school papers).

The bride's family hosts the engagement party, while the groom's family hosts the wedding. Both events are similar socially, but the first marks the contract and the second consummation and establishment of joint housekeeping. Baladi celebrations such as Nadia's (which we read about in Chapter 3), are at home or in a baladi club that provides tables and an open space with some grass, while afrangi weddings are in posh hotels. Women and children drum and dance in one room and men sip tea in another. Younger men exploit their borderline status and drift between the two rooms. Close kin and friends are served a hot meal in a side room. The bride's father or male relative and the groom sign a contract at the engagement. At the wedding, the dowry is flashed for all to see, and the couple departs for a hotel with much clapping and ululation. In more traditional families, the women pay a visit the next morning to inspect the sheets for virginal blood. In Chapter 6 we return to the importance of virginity and a baladi woman's memories of her wedding night.

Death

One day when I visited Mahrusa, I found her holding her neighbor baby, and looking very sad. As I walked in the door, she greeted me with a typical lead-in to a baladi personal narrative of tragedy: "Didn't my sister Karima die?"

> This Friday it will have been two weeks since my sister died after being burned by the primus stove. We will visit her children. One of the girls cooks for them now; the husband burned his hands trying to put out the flames. The day she died, her son came to tell me that his mother was "under observation" in the hospital and that no visitors were allowed. There was a curfew [imposed after the February 1977 food riots in Cairo] so I waited until the next morning when Um Abasiyya and I went to the Italian hospital. Even if we couldn't see her, "under observation" is serious and we wanted to try. When we arrived at the hospital, we saw people crying outside the hospital.
>
> We went in and asked ward by ward for Karima. They sent us one place but there was no one named Karima. Then they sent us somewhere else, several times, until they told us to go to the reception. There they told us: "Those people crying are here for Karima."
>
> I came back to tell my husband so that we could take my sister to the cemetery, leaving Um Abasiyya at the hospital telling them: "Be sure not to bury her before her sister returns." In the meantime my sister's son had come to our house with the news, so my husband had already left to tell another relative, and I found him there and we all went to the hospital and took her to the cemetery by taxis.
>
> For the next three days we went to the Quranic readings in Adawiyya. The "whole house" went with me. My sister never uttered a word after she was burned that Thursday night and by Friday she was dead. Her husband was asleep when she caught fire, and by the time he awoke it was too late. If only she had cried out "Save me!" She did not say anything. It's God's will. The world is hard and unfair. She was the youngest of us all and a good person.

She was still a bride. But didn't the old woman in Saudi Arabia die? No sooner had one died than the other followed her. We had not yet sent condolences to answer the cable from our daughter Mona that her mother-in-law had died, then we were sending a cable about my sister.

Mahrusa told a dramatic story of a sad and quick death. As she remarked on the people crying outside the hospital, her listeners sighed, anticipating that they were the mourners of Mahrusa's sister. She tied the death to that of her daughter's mother-in-law. Baladis say "If you open the ground of a family grave, after a short time more bodies will follow," and orthodox Islam prescribes burial before sundown. Indeed Mahrusa was afraid they would bury her sister so quickly that she would not have returned with her husband. In a proper baladi funeral, a procession of silent men and wailing women accompanies the body on foot the entire way to the cemetery. But this was a "taxi" funeral. During baladi rituals, men usually remain reserved, while women ululate for happy events such as marriage, and wail and tear their hair for sad events such as death. At death, women may wear a house dress, with hair uncovered and uncombed, and walk barefoot to demonstrate their grief. This gender role is so well established that it is often said that a man who does not have female child will have no one to lament properly at his death (El-Messiri 1975:60–62).

In Coptic funerals a hearse with a silver grille and cross carries the coffin to the cemetery. In afrangi Muslim funerals, a black limousine replaces the human procession. At funerals of rich and important persons (such as army and political officers) held in the downtown Omar Makrem mosque, men walk a token block in a human cortege. Death is a great equalizer because everyone who dies must be buried before sundown in a white shroud, and because black coffee is the only refreshment permitted at a death observance. There is variation in settings for condolences, from massive tents with gilded chairs downtown to mats spread in a baladi lane.

Custom prescribes a formal grieving period and decorum of sobriety and women in black. No one in a bereaved family can marry or attend a wedding for a year. One woman helping to sew a wedding dress asked me to carry it when we walked in the streets, because it would have been shameful for her to be seen even *carrying* a wedding dress a few weeks after her father's death. The bereaved family does not bake biscuits for 'Aid el-Futr for five years; neighbors send cookies "for the children." On feast days, one greets the bereaved with, "May God give you strength" rather than with the customary "Happy feast." Neighbors are also constrained; for example, a subu'a procession of children and candles does not leave the house if there has been death in the lane. When I was taking farewell photos, we could not pose in the courtyard out of respect for the landlord, whose relative had died that week.

The first three days after death, condolences are offered in the deceased's home or in a funeral tent of arabesque-quilted cloth in the street below. Women visit in the morning and sit on mats in the lane; men pay respects in the evening, in a funeral tent if available. A Quranic reader recites passages over a loudspeaker at both times. After the first three days, Quranic readings are held every Thursday night until the fortieth-day observance. Thereafter, the death is commemorated each year with a Quranic reading.

Feasts and Hospitality: Water, Tea, and Bread

In all life passages, food and drink are served, except at death where hospitality is restricted to the soberness of black coffee. Likewise, each Muslim feast has its special foods. Middle Easterners are famed for their generosity. They readily offer guests water, coffee, and tea. Bedouin lore exalts the generous person. Wilfred Thesiger recounts Glubb Pasha's tale of the bedouin shaykh known as "The Host of the Wolves." The shaykh was famed for slaughtering his camels for guests, until he had nothing. Dressed in rags, he roamed from camp to camp. At each campfire in the Saudi desert he was received as an honored guest, a man made holy by his generosity (Thesiger 1959). Bedouin poetry and contemporary baladi lore alike exalt generosity.

In traditional Bedouin society, water does not belong to an individual; in fact, outsiders are allowed first turn to water their animals at a well because they have farther to go. Apocryphal and other stories confirm the centrality of water in Islam and castigate anyone who withholds water. In a rural area of Menoufiyya neighbors stopped visiting Jamila after she refused to let them use her pump when theirs was broken. Their explanation carried a moral injunction aimed at Jamila (K. Basso 1984).

> We are furious that we cannot use Jamila's pump while ours— which everyone in the area uses—is broken. One is lucky to have water, and if one forbids others from using the water, then something bad will happen. Why, have you heard how once there was a man who would not let others use his water, and soon it became very blue as if a black robe had been washed in it.

Stories of pain and suffering meted out to bad Muslims who are afflicted by boils when they charge interest, see their children die when they steal, and so on, abound in the baladi morality-tale repertoire. Providing water is a classic good deed. Ornate, stuccoed water fountains in medieval cities show the charity of well-to-do Muslims. Ordinary believers may also provide a water source, either to fulfill a vow or to perform an act of charity. The water source may be as simple as a clay water jar with a cup placed on a street corner and filled regularly, or as elaborate as a wooden stand painted green and blue with flowers and curlicues and further enhanced with live plants.

Ideally, drinking water is available to all; practically, on a long walk, one tries to stop at a friend's for water if one cannot find a water source or willing merchant on the street. Water carriers who sell by the cup from skin bags still roam Cairo streets. Since water should not be denied, neighbors blessed with refrigerators are continually asked for ice or ice water. Tea and other drinks made from water are a form of generalized hospitality for which one does not anticipate reciprocation. In a low-income, traditional quarter of Cairo or most other Middle Eastern cities, one never says: "I drank tea with Fatima, and so we are good friends." In contrast, sharing food supports the baladi social ritual system and symbolizes mutuality, as demonstrated by the popular saying: "We have eaten bread and salt together, so I must ask after you [i.e., be concerned about your welfare]."

To share food is to demonstrate friendship. If unexpected distant acquaintances arrive to visit, one delays eating, offers them tea, and waits for them to leave before eating. If close friends arrive, one serves lunch sooner and invites them, or (if the meal is finished) assembles leftover trappings and presses them to eat. The fact that food symbolizes mutuality is not surprising. Food is intimate; it is chewed and then digested in interior parts; in some ways, it is more intimate than sex because food is both physically intimate and socially reciprocal. In traditional Egyptian society, sex is the prerogative of the man, practiced when and how he wants, with little thought to social interaction or to the woman's enjoyment. By contrast, the social mutuality of food is more a woman's prerogative than a man's.

Baladi Egyptians offer various combinations of drink and food at home or in the coffeehouse, while afrangi Egyptians make equivalent ritual statements by distinguishing among people they invite for lunch at home, for lunch at the club, for dinner at a restaurant, for afternoon tea at home, and so on. Particularly important times of sharing are feast times, life passages, and trips to the home village. Each Muslim feast has its special breads, pastas, sweets, and meat casseroles. Each passage has its characteristic food, such as the sweetened kos kossi eaten at the subu'a ceremony.

Food invitations and gifts are a social calibrator in baladi society, and so feasts are a flamboyant social display. Kak is served to a variety of guests, but meat with *ruqaq* (thin bread) and the casseroles of minor feasts are usually reserved for family. Ramadan kak is neither "bread and salt" nor meat; it is a tea snack and, like tea, is served widely, making Aid el-Futr a more open social event. The ruqaq and meat of Aid el-Adha are the bread and salt that symbolize mutuality, and thus that feast is more private, more family oriented.

Muslim charity stipulates food distribution at feasts. Any Muslim is assured of finding a sundown meal every night during Ramadan and receiving special dishes during the feast. Afrangi families feed their servants and guards and beggars; baladi benevolent societies set out plates of food for any passer by at the sunset *iftar*. Distribution of bread and fruit to the poor during feast-time cemetery visits is a controversial popular Islamic practice. Egyptians spend more time at cemeteries than most Middle Easterners. Some baladi women sleep at the cemetery to pray the dawn prayer at the family grave. They then spend the day picnicking and distributing food gifts (*rahma*) to the poor. Some afrangis build fancy shelters in the cemetery where they sit for an hour or so when they visit their dead, but they never stay the night or picnic. Other afrangis, as well as some orthodox Muslim baladis, oppose cemetery visitation altogether and criticize picnickers who desecrate the cemetery with their immodest dress, loud talk, and toilet habits.

I found cemetery outings pleasant picnic excursions. Typically we rose about four in the morning and walked through dark Bulaq lanes to the workshop street Shinin with its horse carts for rent. After bargaining good-naturedly, we mounted the flat cart behind the horse and rode, giggling, through the empty streets. When a policeman stopped us, each woman contributed a piaster to the driver to bribe the police to let us pass on a street normally closed to animal traffic. The horse-drawn cart is a baladi female mode of transportation used for group trips to the urban periphery. The male driver is called *arabagi niswan*, or "driver for women."

At the cemetery, we alighted with our baskets of primus stoves and tea pots to find obliging fruit merchants ringing the cemetery, offering dates and plums for those still needing rahma to distribute to beggars. The women went straight to the family graves to recite the opening verse of the Quran, while holding their palms open in prayer. Then we spread our straw mats nearby and ate breakfast. At such outings, the women of a recently bereaved family bring copious supplies of tea and sugar. One woman so poor that she rarely served me in her house, offered me several glasses of tea at the cemetery in memory of her deceased son. Children scampered up asking for rahma, and we freely gave until our dates and homemade flat bread were gone.

As the morning wore on, afrangi Egyptians started arriving; the baladi women remarked on these "people of leisure who can not be bothered to get up in time to see the sun rise at the cemetery." They commented on the afrangis' extravagant meat and mango rahma, and sent their children who had just distributed their own rahma to zero in on the newcomers. The afrangis hired a Quranic reciter, gave away rahma, sat a few minutes, and left. We stayed until midafternoon, long after the afrangis had gone, but easily found a horse cart in the large group that awaited their special women passengers. Going home, there was little to indicate that we happy, joking women had been to the cemetery—except the dust on our faces.

At home on feast days there is a flurry of visits to exchange greetings and to sample each other's feast foods. But in addition to religious duties and special foods, feasts are a time to dress up, decorate the house and lane, go out, and visit. Children promenade in new pant suits, pajamas, and maxi dresses. At the zoo, keepers sequester the animals for fear the crush of crowds will harm or unnerve them.

Decoration and Definition: Murals, Dress, and Ethnicity

Families fete returned Mecca pilgrims with a refurbished apartment (newly painted with new couch covers and bed canopies) as well as street-wall or stair-wall murals of pilgrimage ritual and travel scenes. The scenes depict the Mecca Ka'aba, Medina mosque, ships in blue waves, planes in white clouds, and trains on curved tracks. Bird and floral motifs connoting paradise intermingle with secular figures of gentlemen serving tea or women greeting guests. Current events and geography influence pilgrimage paintings. After the 1967 war, army officers appear incongruously painted as pilgrims shooting at Israelis. Campo notes the merging of epic figures in pilgrimage paintings:

Pilgrimage house painting in Bulaq

Egyptian perceptions of the Arab-Israeli war and the
pilgrimage are given mythic significance by the utilization of
the imagery of the warrior-saint. Like 'Antar and other heroes,
the pilgrim is portrayed defending his people and religion
(Campo 1983: 51).

The women serving tea in murals typically lack scarves, which are
customarily worn during prayers. Campo (1983) suggests that this is
a product of the "virgin:whore" complex in Egyptian society in
which women's family portraits routinely share a living room wall
with photos of scantily clad movie stars. An interesting local
influence is the appearance of the small *shawbti* statues (placed in
a Pharaoh's tomb to serve him each day of the year) in the
pilgrimage house paintings near Pharonic sites.

The inscriptions on pilgrimage murals are the only part of the
design actually permitted by orthodox Islam, which bans human
images in order to avoid idolatry. Indeed, the most famous Islamic
art is calligraphy and its geometric designs. The inscriptions on
pilgrimage murals are usually a formulaic expression adopted from

tradition or liturgy. Campo notes five semantic categories of epigraphic formulae in baladi house murals: God ("God is most great"; "Remember your Lord, O Negligent One"); the Prophet ("We have not sent you except as mercy for sentient beings"); pilgrimage and holy places ("A pilgrimage accepted by God, sin forgiven, a worthy effort"); divine blessing ("Enter it securely, in peace"); and victory over adversity ("To the envious: no") (Campo 1983:12–13). Lengthy verses, such those from the "Verse of Light" are shortened to a few words, in this case "light upon light." One often sees "God is great" scrawled in paint over a baladi door.

Another popular baladi mural motif is hand prints on the wall. These murals represent ritual in action, as they are made with the blood of a sacrificed animal. The hand is a rich image in popular Islam; its five fingers represent "the Holy Family of Five," meaning Muhammad the Prophet, his daughter Fatima, his son-in-law Ali, and Hassan and Hussain, his grandsons. Ali, Hassan, and Hussain are also the first three imams in Shi'a Islam. Images of hands are also popular amulets and are hung both on children and on animals. A horse may have a hand amulet tied in his mane, and a sweets cart or taxi may sport a neon-colored decal of the protective hand.

Five and seven are the two most auspicious numbers in Islam. *Khamaysa* is any amulet with five (*khamsa*) objects; baladi mothers often decorate their child's hair or apron with a khamaysa with objects such as peppers, hands, circles, or stars hanging from the five hooks. The amulet may also be pinned to a black apron— another device used to ward off the evil eye. Another way to protect a young child from envy or the evil eye is to repeat "What God wills" after any compliment is paid to a child.

Ephemeral art, that is, art created to enhance sense but not last permanently, marks major feasts. During Ramadan, celluloid mosques and Ramadan lamps swing above lane passageways. Lamp models range from crudely cut metal lamps for candles to fashionable fixtures with glass bowls holding electric bulbs. There are also tourist versions replete with Nefertiti's head on the base. The lamp symbolizes the season, and there are songs about "Ramadan lamps, children light."

The Prophet Muhammad's birthday is a particularly colorful celebration in Egypt. Sugar dolls, first made under the Fatamids, are sold in crepe-papered stalls set up on the streets for the occasion. The standard design is a sugar cone doll with a paper flounced dress, but there are stereotypical variations on dolls: horses with riders reminiscent of such heroic figures as Antar; mosques; and even war paraphernalia, such as cannons. All are decorated with bright paper and dribbles of frosting. A young man traditionally gives his fiancée a sugar doll, and adults, of course, treat children who happily eat the doll up after the feast. These dolls resemble the sugar doves made for the Holy Ghost Feast in the Azores (Salvador 1986); the sugar skulls made for the Mexican Day of the Dead; and the bread and sugar figurines of body parts made to mark popular religious events around the Mediterranean. All are potentially life-giving food crafted to symbolize life, death, and healing. As with Ramadan lamps, prophet dolls appear everywhere as a popular symbol; they sprout up talking in newspaper cartoons, or as human-sized cardboard dolls in Cairo's main square.

Pictures on the wall in a Coptic home in Bulaq

Coptic observances are marked by food and fasting. The major two feasts are Christmas and Easter, observed on the orthodox dates of the seventh of January and in mid-April, respectively. Coptic fasts occur periodically, in contrast to the Muslim one-month period of Ramadan. The Fast of the Virgin Mary, which precedes her saint day in August, is the most popular Coptic fast, sometimes shared by Muslim neighbors for a few days of solidarity. Copts fast from all meat products around the clock, whereas the Muslim fast prohibits all ingestion during sunlight hours. Sham an-Nasim—"to inhale the breeze," originally a Coptic feast marking spring's advent—is today a national holiday. Egyptians picnic on cured raw fish and onions early in the morning to "greet" the spring.

Muslims and Copts in Bulaq exchange social calls during each other's feasts, and visit and fulfill vows at each other's shrines. This sharing is most common in low-income quarters where personal life is mutual; elite groups, by contrast, know little of others' religious practices. One Easter eve, I met a Muslim woman bringing candles to a church to fulfill a vow; her son had been arrested for selling black-market sugar and had been released, she felt, in answer to her vow. Miracles of both faiths form a common lore. All Bulaq residents talk of the thief who stole from the coffers of St. Theresa's shrine and whose hand became crippled, or of the dead Sufi mystic who left his name written on a visitor's card at his tomb.

Despite ritual mutuality, each religion maintains sectarian boundaries. Mothers may leave children somewhat disheveled on the other faith's feast day so there will be no mistaking their identity. Although they maintain cordial relations with the neighbors they know, each group stereotypes the other group behind its back. Coptic women cluck over the fate of Muslim women, whom they perceive as continually threatened by divorce. Muslim women remark on the greed of Coptic merchants, "although those in our neighborhood are generous."

The Islamic Revival: A New Personal Piety

Baladi Islam is one system encompassing "standard Islam," revival of the "true Islam" (so-called "neo-Islam"), and local, so-called popular Islam. Piety is personal, and baladi women oscillate between following the orthodox dictates, such as prayers and fasting, and practicing popular Islam, with its visits and vows. Local practices such as cemetery visitation and saints' day processions are regarded by afrangis and even by some orthodox baladis as too superstitious, and they refuse to participate. At the same time, afrangis enjoy some festive elements of such folk practices as the mawlid as they pass by the mosque.

By the late 1980s, the new Islamic influence had significantly touched both baladi and afrangi religious life. Among the putative causes of the rise of the movement was the peoples' re-establishment of Egyptian, Muslim identity to counter the influence of Western mass culture, whether "Dallas" on TV or video games. Another cause was reaction to inflation and the widening income gap in the days of Sadat's economic liberalization, or *infitah*. El-

Guindi's discussion of the Egyptian Islamic movement that developed after the 1973 war notes:

On the one hand there is the *infitah*, intended as economic policy but which has consequences at the socio-moral level. . . . Along with consumer goods there is also importation of ideas. A new form of inequality has emerged—wealth for the entrepreneur, unemployment for the college-educated. The new materialism is leading to corruption, the increasing poverty to immorality (El-Guindi 1981:481).

On my return to Bulaq in 1980, after an absence of more than three years, I noted mundane but significant changes: more electric fans (actually I had never seen fans in Bulaq in 1974–1977), more refrigerators, more televisions. Many were in the homes of families whose daughters married in Saudi Arabia or whose husbands worked in Libya or the Arab peninsula. I did not note better nutrition; everyone still ate many meals of beans. People held two or three jobs to make ends meet. In every third or fourth house a son had migrated temporarily to another Arab country for work. More women sought visas to work abroad because, as men were deported from Libya because of political squabbles, Lebanese upper-class families needed domestics, and women became the ones to work abroad.

Some Bulaqis had wrangled better hours or working conditions. For example, in 1977 Badriyya's father worked at the telephone company by day and at the coffeehouse until midnight. By 1980 he had constructed a cart to rent for ten pounds a month, to ice cream vendors in the summer and hot-chickpea-drink vendors in the winter. Rent income and profits from sweet rolls he sold at his coffee shop allowed him to go home at 6 P.M. rather than at midnight. But Badriyya's father, along with most of Cairo's baladi people, lived no better. I summed up my impressions of Bulaq in my 1980 notes: "Life continues to be fraught with the same problems of making ends meet, but people have more refrigerators." Another side effect of Sadat's economic liberalization was gaudier shop displays. At the corner where I always turned for Aniyat's house, the old *kucheri* stand sported new aluminum front siding with trendy bright orange framed oval windows. Accustomed to the former tacky shop with plain glass in wooden frames, I asked a man drinking coffee where Shaykh Ali lane was. Like baladi people, I depended on landmarks, and this one had changed! He and his companion coffee drinker nodded and pointed (without my prompting) toward Aniyat's house; they recognized me, undoubtedly the only foreigner

except the French nuns to walk that street in the last three years!
The new boutique face of Cairo forms a thin facade for economic
desperation; brightly colored marquees may be glued to a crumbling
building. Outside one finds the bright face; inside one finds a paltry
selection.

By 1980 the religious conservatism was more apparent than it
had been in the mid-1970s. One marker was dress. I saw a few women
at the extreme end of the dress spectrum with floor-length capelike
coats, their gloved hands sometimes appearing through slits in the
side. Head coverings left only their eyes uncovered. When I left
Egypt in 1977, even the first stage of Islamic dress, a head scarf
and long sleeves, appeared mostly among afrangi Egyptians, but
by 1980 it had emerged in the baladi quarters as well. In
Bulaq, baladi women still shed their religious dress at the door,
just as their mothers and sisters had shed the traditional
melaya liff. In contrast, middle-class women tended to wear
religious garb at any time outside their bedroom, in case unrelated
men came to visit. Baladi women treat all males in their building as
"kin-like," and as they shed melaya liffs to wear house dresses
without embarrassment, so they shed their head scarf and long
sleeves.

My inability to "spot" the new conservatism in 1980 was
confirmed when, at the Shaykh Ali house, Mahrusa's youngest
daughter, Azza, bursting with pride, volunteered her news while we
sipped the lemonade she squeezed. She had assumed Islamic dress
just last week and realized that I wouldn't notice since she wore her
house dress in the home. I was fascinated by her narrative of
"conversion," which she framed with a "You haven't noticed, have
you?" Since I was her sole interlocutor, I interrupted with questions
for clarification.

> I grew convinced that this is the right way to dress and that it is
> obligatory. Those who do not yet dress conservatively are not
> yet convinced or they may be persuaded but ignore the fact that
> such dress is obligatory. I immediately assumed the *muhaggaba*
> stage. In this stage, married women cover the mouth, revealing
> only the eyes, whereas unmarried women can leave their whole
> face showing. Gloves are optional. The first stage of religious
> dress, which I bypassed, is the stage *mithashima* where a
> woman wears only a scarf over her head and also covers her
> legs and arms. A religious man has a mustache and beard
> and wears a white tunic to his mid-leg over pants. He is
> *mutaburgil*.

What besides clothes is the difference between a religiously dressed woman and a normally dressed woman?

A *muhaggaba* woman follows injunctions such as that she should obey her husband over her father. The Quran tells of a woman whose husband was traveling and had told her not to leave the house. People came to tell the woman her father was dying; she went to the Prophet and said she needed to see her father, but the Prophet advised her: "Follow the words of your husband." People approached the woman when her father was in his last throes of death. She went to the Prophet again. He told her: "Follow the orders of your husband." The woman's father died and she still stayed at home, following her husband's orders; and because of her obedience, the woman's father went straight to heaven.

Women dressed like that avoid talk with those who have not yet followed all the obligations of religion.

But can you actually ignore someone who is speaking with you?

Not really, but you just try not to.

Where do you pray on Friday?

At the Athim mosque in Bahith area with my aunt's children. I enjoy the Athim mosque because many young, conservative women pray there.

As we talked, Azza mentioned that her fiancé wore religious garb. Azza appeared sincere in her new expression of piety. I could not tell whether she had actually "joined" the Islamic community, where membership is gained through individual, internal transformation.

> Once an individual by volition and analytic thought has reached a state of *iqtina'* (conviction) he or she is then a member in this community. As one of the mitdayyinin (religious), this individual adheres to ritual rigidity, behavioral, verbal and dress prescriptions, and to the avoidance taboo between the sexes (El-Guindi 1981:474).

It was clear that Azza had absorbed the basic tenets of the "Islamic community" and that she enjoyed attending community prayers with her cousins. Her mother, always religious, prayed five times a day, but she was less conservative than Azza had become. Azza, the quiet youngest daughter who failed in school, did not go to work like her older sister Suad, a seamstress. Effectively "parked" at home waiting to marry and not exposed to intellectual currents at school, she is someone I was surprised to see adopt religiously conservative beliefs or dress. Her fiancé or her cousins had undoubtedly introduced her to this new style of religion, but she had probably made her own decision, as she seemed fairly strong-willed. For example, earlier she had rejected the overtures of a tailor interested in marriage. While her theological pinnings may not have been as deep as those of some, she had definitely, like many young Egyptian women who have grown tired of being hassled in the streets of Cairo, chosen Islamic dress as a practical, simple way of stating publicly, "I am a respectable woman. Leave me alone" (Fernea 1993:6). Azza had abandoned the respectable melaya liff of her mother's generation for the respectable dress of Islam.

For both baladi and afrangi Egyptians, wearing Islamic garb and participating in a religious awakening means more earnest discussion of the Quran and its meaning for life. As with many other religious revivals, they are reacting in part to the decadence of "Western, materialist society." For a young baladi women like Azza, who already lives a simple life at home, a return to the true Islam means Friday prayers with people of her persuasion, and a distinctive style of dress outside the house. In contrast, afrangi Egyptians who assume an Islamic life-style not only enhanced personal piety but also shed social habits such as drinking and dancing. They have more non-Muslim social habits to cast off than someone like Azza; they start to avoid gatherings with alcoholic drinks and substitute Quranic readings for family parties during religious holidays.

Azza's religiosity was different from that found among baladi women in the mid-1970s, when my friends gathered at the mosque to pray and to study; some followed a certain shaikh but they were not a self-defined "group" as Azza's seemed to be. While many of my friends still mixed the classical prayer of the mosque with the popular Islam of shrines and vows, adherents of the new orthodoxy, who, like Azza, disdained all folk Islam including shrine visitation, were growing in number.

Shrine Visitation: The Baladi Remedy

Shrine visitation remained an important part of local Islam as I saw in 1980 and in my last trip to Bulaq in 1991. Although orthodox Islam frowns on the mediation of holy people, they are popularly thought to intercede between the individual and God. The guardian of the famous Tanta Sayyid el Badawi mosque once told me that religious leaders were not against shrine visitation per se. The guardian of Tanta's mosque of Sayyid al-Bedawi (renowned for curing children) remarked: "We do not discourage such local practices as visiting our mosque for a child's first haircut or for the annual saint's day festival. Anything that makes people think of God and encourages them to visit the mosque to pray is a good thing." The guardian was less enthusiastic, however, about vow making. Afrangi Egyptians will often pay a quick visit to a famous shrine like Sayyid el-Badawi or el-Hussain to pray, but they are critical of the throngs of baladi women they find at the doors of the mosque, enjoying a day's outing. Much as the afrangis disdain the baladi picnics at the cemeteries, so they critique similar "carnival-like" atmospheres at what an afrangi, and an orthodox Muslim, consider to be a holy place and not a party place. Nevertheless, most afrangis would not criticize the Sufi orders who sometimes camp for days at the side of a mosque during the saint's day; this may be because Sufis tend to be men, because they tend to be quieter, or because they are viewed as religious mendicants. Ultimately, the difference between afrangi and baladi approaches to shrines is one of style of celebration. Afrangis are uncomfortable with the mess and clamor of baladi gatherings; baladis find afrangis sterile and cold in their approach to religion and to other social obligations.

Shrines are usually tombstones of holy men or women, often buried in a side room of a mosque. Shrines are imbued with the saint's grace (*baraka*), which is thought to be transmitted by touch—thus the repeated rubbing of the grillework, and the subsequent kissing of the hand that was used to touch the shrine. Baraka also inheres in objects purchased in the shrine's locale, so pilgrims return laden with trinkets for friends. Women find it calming to visit the cool, quiet shrines in the middle of a hectic day. They speak of "lightened" souls after confiding in saints. Sometimes they intercalate shrine visits in a busy schedule; sometimes they plan a special outing to expose their children to the shrine's auspicious ethos.

Bulaq's most famous shrine is the tomb of Sultan Abu 'Ala, in a side room of the Abu 'Ala mosque located near the bridge between Bulaq and Zamalek. The holy man Abu 'Ala lived in the fifteenth century and was known for his bravery and his ability to cross the Nile River without a boat. It is said that the saint was a common laborer whose holiness was demonstrated by many miracles; for instance, at his funeral his coffin flew through the streets, eluding all who tried to catch it. My friends and I often stopped in the mosque between errands to join the women resting near the tomb. I sat as my friends went to pray and to touch the tomb's grillework. We also attended many processions there during Abu 'Ala saint's day and in nearby lanes during the month of Shaaban (just before Ramadan) when many of the minor shrines in Bulaq celebrated their saint's day.

One such humbler shrine is located next to a Bulaq secondary school, whose renovation periodically blocks the shrine. This shrine contains only one room, and the tomb in the center, like most, is covered by a green cloth with gold-embroidered Quranic verses. These vestments and the cone-shaped turban topping them are paraded and changed during the shrine's yearly saint's day. A Muslim woman, a Coptic woman, and I visited this small shrine one day. We located the caretaker to unlock the shrine. After circumambulating the tomb several times in the same way that pilgrims to Mecca walk around the Ka'aba, we stopped for the guardian to lay his hands on the Coptic woman's sick child and to murmur a blessing; she tipped him and we left.

Baladi women visit similar neighborhood shrines throughout Bulaq during daily errands, whereas the shrines near the cemeteries on Cairo's periphery are a popular spot for a full day's outing. Women may join friends for trips to shrines deemed especially effective for curing infertility or children's sickness; they return to the same shrines to fulfill vows that might include the lighting of candles, gifts of money, meals for the poor, or animal sacrifice. Each shrine on Cairo's outskirts is reputed to alleviate a specific problem.

One of the most popular cemetery shrines is that of Imam el-Shafa'i, a ninth-century judge famous for his just rulings, who died after founding one of the four major schools of Islamic law. Even in death, he is thought to retain his powers of arbitration, which people seek in visits as well as in letters sent by post to the tomb. In a content analysis of these letters, Egyptian sociologist Sayyid Oweiss found that the most frequent requests to Imam el-Shafa'i seek revenge, redress of grievances, and relief from such disasters as bad health (including blindness and paralysis) or a collapsed house. Some letters describe circumstances threatening friends, family, possessions, or employment. Oweiss concluded that correspondents consider Imam el-Shafa'i a living person with power to mediate their problems, as a ministry official might, and to enlist the help of other saints (Oweiss 1965). Oweiss notes in his study the position of Islam on mediation by saints: "The religion of Islam does not approve of dependence on saints if that impedes the believer's relation to God. . . . The religion of Islam considers the making of vows [to saints] to be an ignorant and backward practice" (Oweiss 1965:126–127).

Women visit other shrines near the cemetery to treat psychic dysphoria, to reverse sterility, to secure a spouse, or to reconcile quarrels. Local shrine pilgrimages imitate Mecca pilgrimages in such customs as seven circumambulations, but local pilgrimages add popular Islamic features such as vows to return with turkeys, candles, henna, special foods, and tips for shrine guardians if their vows, aided by the saint's grace, are answered.

Baladi Islam may be modified by afrangi religious leaders. For example, during my research, the mosque imam removed a concrete pillar from outside the shrine of Siddi Qubba (known to cure infertility); women who had customarily circumambulated this pillar remarked that since it was un-Islamic it was best it had stopped. With no fuss and no muss, they simply searched for new pilgrimage spots. There was no sense of confrontation, but rather the baladis assimilated the afrangi view saying "it was good the imam was there to tell us."

Companions for visits to religious and other outings are often chosen from a woman's apartment building—simply because they are easily recruited at the last minute. A similar afrangi event might be to gather at a home to read the Quran, or to listen to a Quranic reader or even catch a popular religious program on TV. Since the 1970s many pious afrangi Muslims have listened to Shaykh Shaarawi every Friday on television, and I often heard discussions of his latest pronouncements on "religious duty" or "optional fasting" when I drank tea with my Doqqi and Maadi friends. Afrangi women pray much more rarely in mosques than baladi women. At major shrines such as Hussein next to El-Azhar, the crowd at the door is a mix of baladi women and men from both baladi and afrangi backgrounds.

One day in 1974 friends of mine from the Shaykh Ali house— Mahrusa, her daughter Mona, Fatima, her daughter Nabila—and I planned a typical baladi women's excursion to visit the shrines near the cemeteries at the edge of town. It was to be Nabila's third visit to Siddi Qubba, completing a ritual triad. Siddi Qubba is renowned for answering the prayers of aspiring brides and women who hope to become pregnant. Um Sharaf, who lives across the street, decided to join us at the last minute. Later that year, after Fatima moved from the Shaykh Ali house, she rarely joined Mahrusa for outings even though when they were co-residents they had regularly prayed and played together.

Our goal was to visit the shrine of Siddi Qubba to present the requests of the barren Nabila, but any trip so close to the great arbitrator Imam el-Shafa'i merits at least a cursory visit there. As we approached the tomb, Fatima lifted her hands in prayer and intoned: "Oh great solver of disputes and man of justice." She then switched to a conversational tone to describe how this saint adjudicates complaints: "At the end of the day one finds his tomb full of letters and money. You either write a letter or make your request orally. I once had a request fulfilled." Here and at every other shrine, we "visited"—the popular Islamic expression for walking around the shrine seven times, counterclockwise. Some of our group got carried away during our visits and started to circle a pedestal at the head of the tomb of Siddi Qubba. Mona sternly admonished the women that such innovation was forbidden in Islam and would nullify their visit. The women immediately switched to circumambulate the entire grave. When Nefissa, a Helwan woman my friends had met on earlier visitations, stopped to discuss her search for a husband with a man at the gate, Fatima rebuked her for dabbling in *amal* (black magic); the man gave Nefissa bread and salt for good luck and advised her not to talk to men until she returned to see him. Both of these examples indicate the wide parameters of popular ritual and the role of participants in defining a "relative orthodoxy."

After we had visited Imam el-Shafa'i's tomb, and some of the women had prayed, we visited several other shrines: Shaykh Lizza, Shaykha Dandarawi, Siddi Qubba, Shaykha Raba'iyya, Shaykha Khadra, Shaykha Sukkariyya, and back to Shaykh Lizza and Imam al-Shafa'i. The fourth, fifth, and sixth shrines are those of women saints. Our visits were sometimes cursory and sometimes prevented by closed gates. We were joined by other women in our search for one shrine. They asked if we were planning to make the Mecca pilgrimage. Mahrusa replied that her husband and brother had traveled and that we would "sing and rejoice for them" when they returned. "May your turn be next," the questioner replied politely. Along the way we commissioned some little boys to guide us, and Mahrusa remarked: "God willed that those boys who knew the way be there to help us."

We arrived at our destination, Siddi Qubba, as the Quranic reading preceding the noon prayer rang out over the outside courtyard, packed with women in black dresses sitting on straw mats laid out by an old woman who would be tipped for her services. The woman repeated "Every Friday may you be well" to each potential customer and invited women to move onto "her" mats, for a price, of course. One woman replied that it was fine to sit on the ground for, after all, Gamal Abdul Nasser was buried in the ground, and we all return to it! A nearby worshipper responded with a vigorous "Pray to the Prophet"—as if to erase such blasphemy. A man threaded his way among the crowd to solicit customers for his business of tying money in scarves until after the prayer, when he unties each scarf, metaphorically untying the woman's problem, and tells her future. Nabila thought this practice nonsense.

As the time for call to prayer neared, women gathered around the four-foot concrete post rising at an angle from the center of the courtyard. Someone said the post had been there "forever," but the concrete seemed new. By the next year the shaykh had removed the post because it was un-Islamic, but women told me that the man continued to untie scarfs. I found this incongruous, but women explained: "That's how he makes his living; how could he stop?" That Friday some women muttered that people were too eager to gather at the pillar. When the Quranic recitation stopped, during the expectant pause that precedes every Friday noon's call to prayer, almost all of the young women (those who wanted to marry or to become pregnant) rose and put their left hands on the pillar. Each held seven stones in her right hand. As the call to prayer commenced, they began to walk counterclockwise, each throwing a stone with her right hand at each turn. Some threw the stone over the right shoulder; others threw it anywhere. As they circumambulated, the women repeated this verse: "Siddi Qubba will solve one's problems [literally, untie one's knots] and help one; I will bring him a turkey when it happens." One woman had brought a turkey that day, which she gave to the mosque attendant.

The popular Islamic practice of pillar circumambulation and vow making did not keep the baladi women from also participating in the "orthodox Islam" Friday noon prayer from their position on mats outside the mosque. They also listened intently to the Friday sermon, although one women did ask how long she needed to stay after the popular ritual for it to be efficacious. Two girls arrived late and asked others if there was still time to circumambulate. Everyone concluded that since the noon prayer had not commenced, there was time. At the end of the prayer, Fatima walked up to me, playfully untied my scarf, and asked, "Did you get untied?" She meant by this: "Did you relax, solve your problems?"

When the men had dispersed, we women entered the mosque to "visit" the tomb and read the Quran. A circle of young boys surrounded Shaykh Ibrahim. A blind girl with sunken eyes, who had been in the courtyard with us, sat in the front row with the boys, but when Nefissa tried to join the front row, the shaykh motioned her to the back with the rest of the women. After we read the printed passage, we chanted well-known verses, such as *Surat al-Yassin* and the Fatiha. Fatima leaned over and told me to say my "Amens" louder. After the reading, women crowded around the shaikh to ask advice. He doubtlessly disapproved of the popular pillar ritual in the courtyard, but he was willing to counsel. For a woman who wanted to marry, he prescribed nightly readings of the Quran, prayer, and a follow-up visit to see him. To a woman suffering from infertility, he said that her operation had been performed at a disreputable hospital, that her husband should be examined, and that she should return if her problem persisted. Our friend Nabila managed a question as the shaykh hurried out the door after a quick circumambulation of the tomb; he told her to pray, to be patient, and to have her husband examined. Fatima, who had scorned black magic, and who preferred prayer to popular ritual, said of the shaykh: "He is a man who works miracles; he places paper in people's hands and they can read it."

We left Siddi Qubba and went next door to Shaykha Raba'iyya, where we sat inside the mosque and lunched on fried potatoes, cheese, and bread. Mahrusa explained that this saint died unmarried and is thus particularly sensitive to women's requests for husbands. The mosque guardian allowed several of us to wear, like a necklace, the brown wooden prayer beads that hung on the wall in a glass case while we circumambulated the tomb seven times.

Next we went to Shaykha Khadra, but found the shrine closed and padlocked. Next we went to Shaykha Sukkariyya. Nefissa had brought sugar, candles, and henna; she had forgotten the candy prescribed by popular lore, but no one seemed concerned about her unintentional omission. In baladi culture, as well as in learned theological debates, intention is critical and unintentional acts are much less significant. Many times I have seen a woman complete an amulet only to discover that she forgot a critical element, for example, salt. At that juncture she typically says that since her omission was unintentional, *bil-baraka* (by grace) the amulet will still be efficacious.

The Shaykha Sukkariyya shrine was outside, and the women processed on a ledge around a pit. Some tossed their seven stones over their right shoulder, and some tossed them into the pit. Seven times, Nefissa stuck her head through an opening in a rock wall at the side of the pit, repeating each time: "Oh, Shaykha Sukkariyya, queen of the people who plea; I will bring you sugar, henna, candy, and candles." Nefissa told us that the girl attending the shrine threw Nefissa's sugar down into the pit, placed her candles around the opening and lighted them, and mixed her henna and patted it on the stone around the rock window. She also put some henna on Nefissa's left hand; when I asked Nefissa why, she said, "Because the girl said so."

The afternoon waned as we trudged back to the bus stop at Imam el-Shafa'i. Nefissa, who worked as a clerk in the Helwan electric company, had befriended Sakkina and Fatima on their first visit to

Siddi Qubba. Nefissa, high-school educated, explained the attraction the shrines held for her in a personal narrative of piety volunteered as we walked along debating the sincerity of the man taking money at the gate:

> I had never even visited Imam el-Shafa'i until three weeks ago, when I went to make a vow to be kept if my wish were granted. There I met the man in the green gellabeyya with whom you saw me the day of our trip. He wanted to do black magic on my behalf. The same day I met two girls who said that they were going to Siddi Qubba, and they took me along. No one but my sister knows that I have visited these shrines; other people would criticize me, although they themselves might do the same thing secretly. Some of my co-workers saw me at Imam el-Shafa'i, but when they mentioned this, I denied that it was I. My parents are dead. My sister and I keep to ourselves. One cannot do anything or see anyone or people will talk. Visiting places like Siddi Qubba relaxes me and clears my mind.

Interestingly, although Nefissa was the most educated woman of our group, when we visited the mosque of Shaykh Lizza, she refused to go in, saying that he had not granted her a vow she had made there.

Nefissa is a young woman who (like Nadia, whose wedding we discussed in Chapter 1) lives in the grey zone between afrangi and baladi. She is educated, works as an office employee, and dresses in modern, European fashion and not in the Islamic dress of many women her age. She feels comfortable in the company of baladi women, but she tries to hide her popular Islamic expeditions from fellow workers. An orphan with little economic security, she feels desperate to marry. Even as I write this, Nefissa may have abandoned shrine visitation for the egalitarianism of dress and the nonromantic ties of "brother" and "sister" of the Islamic revival community chosen by Azza. If not, it is certain that the Nefissas of the next generation will not define their problem as the search for a husband at Siddi Qubba, but as the quest for a better life in which they can find money for an apartment so they can marry. For them, religion may be orthodox and revolutionary as it already has become for many young Muslim believers. But for other baladi women like Mahrusa, saints and shrines will remain an essential part of life. After all, the popular Islam practiced at shrines makes women more comfortable and their lives more meaningful. They see no conflict between these practices and their orthodox observance of prayers, fasting, and benevolent deeds. All these practices are part of the ritual complex that embroiders the everyday life of baladi women and that helps them solve problems, spread resources, and explain their situation. Some of the religious ritual we have considered in this chapter reveals social relations of a baladi quarter at the same time it expresses individual piety. It is to the social aspect of baladi ritual and performance that we now turn, to explore rituals of recognition, conflict, and restitution.

5

Baladi Performance:
"Let Me Tell You What Happened"

Baladi women's cultural performances, whether staged quarrels over access to favors or private expression of social relations during a life passage, are situated in everyday baladi discourse. They exemplify the baladi "modality of communication," baladi culture's "categories, discourses, cultural linguistics, and hermeneutical means of understanding" (Fisher and Abedi 1990:iv). A culture's interpretive positions structure understanding not only of grand schemes such as political ideology but also of such specific cultural rituals as children haggling for pocket money and adults "not paying attention." Bulaqi women's rituals often bridge the public and private and often reflect the have-nots:haves dichotomy so central to baladi discourse. Such mundane rituals as food distribution may express both personal emotions and social relations.

I discussed in Chapter 1 the relationship of narrative and text to specific context. For example, Ellen Basso presents Kalapalo mythological narrative and musical ritual as allowing "a special freedom of situational usage in contrast with other forms of discourse" (Basso 1985:5). Glassie describes the Ballymenone *ceili* tale as connecting the immediate situation (tonight's *ceili* or storytelling session) to the cultural (the values enacted by a neighbor) (Glassie 1982:42). While baladi spontaneous performances lack the codified "cultural text" of folkloric and poetic performances, they do follow recognized formats, including social philosophizing and elaborate distributing, which in turn express cultural expectations about social relations.

Back Lane Society: Cheek to Jowl

One should not be misled by the social facade of a baladi quarter where women, balancing a child on one shoulder and clutching

131

plastic sacks of vegetables, exchange news at the corner fruit stand. Street scenes present only the public face of sociability. A woman who appears engaged in easy repartee may be solidifying or cooling relations. Greetings and visits are the ritual format for negotiating social boundaries, and there are finely calibrated degrees of sociability along a continuum of "being on speaking terms" in baladi society.

Baladi sociability fields the demands of crowded, urban life to filter the social demands on a woman. Baladi sociability relies on the spoken word of honor when one borrows or promises, and shuns the written contracts of afrangis who do not trust each other or their own memories. Human relations are paramount, and an authentic baladi person shares in the joys and sorrows of others and is always prepared to assist. But, to retain her sangfroid in crowded conditions, a baladi woman needs to gain social distance by establishing social boundaries marked off by such cultural conventions as "paying attention to someone" and "breaking off speaking."

Aside from unavoidable "neighborliness" there exists a baladi female society of the hearth and the street that is independent of men and intersects with both public and domestic spheres. Baladi women, virtually self-sufficient in female friendships, congratulate each other, counsel correct action, test ideas about household projects and personal business. They take refuge with women friends when their spirits are low. They pool tasks to lighten drudgery. A baladi woman is not intimidated by the intricate urban bureaucracy of the immediate world outside her quarter, or by the farther world of northern Africa and the Levant. Her belief that she needs only the right address, name, or instructions written on a piece of paper to find any place or to complete any business is summed up by the saying "One can travel around the world using the written instructions in her hand."

Baladi women form few if any close relations with men; their brothers tend to be their closest male friends, and their natal family is their refuge in times of trouble. They quip that men are "made of paper" and count for naught. It is the women who understand life, who bring men and women together in marriage matches, and who outwit officials and merchants.

One day we sat cleaning rice and peeling vegetables. Amina, annoyed with her sister-in-law Suad, reminded us how she had brokered many marriages, including that of Suad. Amina heightened her voice's pitch to recount marriages arranged.

See how I have done more than my brothers or my husband to

make our family strong and happy. Suad should be grateful to me for encouraging her husband to marry her. [Here Amina embarked on a long list of unions she had fostered, ending with the dramatic statement . . .] It is I who suggested all the matches, who made them work, who listened to everyone's tales about them. Why, I was the penis which "knit" the family together!

Amina elaborates on her matchmaking to equate it with the male role of procreation. She satirizes virility and implies female sexual dominance. Baladi women spice up discussions and quarrels with suggestive language and gestures. Despite such vivid sexual language, a woman's relation with her husband is traditional, and she tempers her language in front of her children.

Bulaq is a busy quarter that attracts outside shoppers and contractors in addition to the normal flow of visitors. A woman sees and interacts with countless people every day, but she arrays them on a continuum of categories of interaction that runs from close kin to stranger:

1. Close ("kinlike") friend (*habiba*)
2. Relative (*qariba*)
3. Neighbor (*gara*)
4. Fellow villager (*baladiyya*)
5. Acquaintance (*m'arifa*)
6. Partner in commerce, customer-merchant (*zibuna-tagira*)
7. Stranger (*ghariba*)

With time, an urban migrant's relations with those not kin or baladiyya may become more generalized and enduring, and begin to resemble the ideal primary "kinlike" relation, described by baladi women as habiba or "dear friend." Fatima reported on the death of her baladiyya Aida to a group of women neighbors:

Aida went home last night and climbed a wooden ladder to the roof to feed her birds. As she descended, her foot slipped and she fell with the ladder tossing her into the air shaft. She fell on her face so that her teeth were knocked out and her face was destroyed. But we were quiet and went to a doctor to get a certificate that she died a natural death. Otherwise they will take the body for an autopsy and mess around with it.

I went to visit at Aida's house last night, and again this morning when I had finished my housework, and sat with the women from eight till noon. . . . Um Arabi was there this morning.

Why did she go since she and Aida had quarrelled?

Because Aida was Um Arabi's baladiyya. Also when Um Arabi's husband died Aida came to condole her, and it is a matter of reciprocation.

Did you condole your baladiyat back in the village when the bride died?

I don't go to my village any more. There is no one there who is dear to me. I consider the people in Cairo baladiyat, my *habayeb* [dear friends], because I have been here so long.

In general, baladiyat are expected to ask after one another and to attend each other's life crises, and indeed they provide a quasi-kin support in a new and strange city. But Fatima, in her twenty-plus years in Bulaq, has found that fellow residents there take the place of baladiyat.

While resembling kin, the relation of "dear friend" is not specifically marked by a kinship term because such expressions as "sister" or "maternal aunt" are general nouns of address for any woman. A habiba is described as "someone like my sister" or "someone like woman X" where the speaker and "X" have a privileged relationship. A habiba is someone who has no expectations, who visits to ask after one, who gives extra gifts outside the formal reciprocity system. A habiba is the prototype of baladi sociability—a friend who is compatible, expressed as sharing *wid*. To share wid is to "hit it off." While reinforced by shared experiences, wid either exists between two people, or it doesn't—an interpersonal "chemistry." One day Um Amal regaled us with the tale of a woman she had met by accident in the market:

I was just laughing with this woman yesterday who is half crazy and who told me that everyone in her family is sick. Who knows if they are really sick or if she was just saying that so people would not envy her? This woman and I meet at social occasions because she is a distant relative.

About four years ago, this woman came to me and told me that my husband was going out with a girl in the woman's apartment building. I confronted my husband the next day and he called the woman a liar. I am not sure to this day who was right but since then there has been no wid between this woman and me. I never need anybody for anything.

Baladi women are both socially and economically

interdependent, but they joke about the popular proverb: "We have eaten bread and salt together, and must thus ask after one another" and say they avoid eating with others lest they later be obligated to"ask after them"! Baladi social relations wax and wane, played out in baladi codes of information management, hospitality, and social recognition.

Back Lane Codes of Social Relations

Information Control

In densely inhabited baladi quarters it is nearly impossible to conceal activities, or to avoid seeing someone with whom one has had a tiff. Continual neighborhood coming and going requires a surface sociability. Baladi women chat with neighbors while they peel garlic, mend clothes, or wash. They share news of births, broken engagements, or deaths—which can not be hidden from neighbors. Special guests may visit behind closed doors, but other visitors who sense their presence may drop by on other pretexts.

However, baladi women control information via an intricate "dispatching" system and via spontaneous cultural performances of news. In baladi society one earns the right to know. Children have low social status and deserve partial explanations. A mother may not mention her destination when leaving so children will not beg to go along. The less an outsider knows about household triumphs and sorrows, the less able she or he is to interfere or to envy good fortune. A visitor seeking someone may be told the precise location if she is a close friend, or may be given such vague replies as "She is with her friends" or "She went to shop." One favorite dissimulation used with low-status visitors, including those seeking favors, is "She'll be back any minute," which translates into anything from a minute to a week!

The response "We will send for her" is reserved for important visitors such as messengers from a husband working abroad. The visitors are plied with tea while a child is dispatched to locate a baladi woman on the move. This "dispatch" system uses children to retrieve women moving among friends, market, and bureaucracy. A child often gleans extra information along her or his path that is fed back to the family. A child appears and says simply: "My mother/father wants you." Close friends and relatives continually "send for" each other to inspect sale items, mediate a squabble, or hear news out of earshot of an assembled group. Gaining a friend's "private ear" removes the need to wait for everyone to go home.

Intentionality, the fashioning of events, pulses through every moment of baladi life. We noted the importance of *niyya*, intention, in our discussion of popular Islam, where unintentionally forgetting an ingredient of an amulet does not dilute its power. In the baladi social realm, "to send for" someone is a cultural category that, much like hospitality, expresses the wish to invite, the wish to see. To calm someone left out of a social event, one intones "We sent for you but you were not there." Similarly, in the West one says: "I phoned you to invite you to a party, but you were not home!" While phone answering machines now keep Westerners more honest about their communication attempts, so watchful neighbors corroborate baladi dispatch attempts.

Hospitality and Reciprocity: The Social Lubricant

Daily greetings—ritual performances of social relations that include elaborate invitations to visit and remonstrations for past absences—are another feature of baladi sociability. Hospitality is the lubricant of social interaction. As Westerners say, "See you soon," or "Drop by sometime" without specifying a time, so Egyptians say: "Come and drink tea!" The invitation can be elaborate "We have been waiting for you; where have you been for so long; please come to our house"; or abbreviated "Please enter" (*itfaddilli*). To decode flowery expressions of hospitality for social messages is to parse baladi sociability.

When two women meet who have not talked for a long time, a typical exchange might be:

Zainab: How are you?

Salma: Thanks to God.

Zainab: I have been asking after you.

Salma: I too have been asking after you, with vigor.

Zainab: Why haven't you come to see me?

Salma: I am busy with my children and house.

Zainab: How are your children?

Zainab then asks about other family members' affairs and receives a news report whose length depends on the women's relation and on the time which has elapsed since their last meeting. The meeting ends with:

Zainab: Be sure to come see me.

Salma: May you return with strength.

Zainab: May God give you strength.

In baladi women's meetings, polite exchanges are calibrated to circumstances. A neighbor who passes frequently may simply call out "May you have strength" and not await a response. Since baladi women are in the streets on business, not pleasure, they expand and contract polite exchanges according to their circumstances. In a clinic or office, they may join strangers similarly immobilized by the bureaucracy, to swap tales about the new television, the last trip to the village, or the man who just beat his wife. On the other hand, a baladi woman rushing on an errand, balancing child on hip and water pail on head, will abbreviate narratives of divorce or death.

Invitations are the script for performances of social relations. As with "sending for," so with hospitality it is the *intent* that counts more than the actual event. While invitations to "Come, drink tea" make little sense when proffered in some contexts—such as by a woman on an errand miles from home—the potential hostess confuses no one because listeners understand her words as words of intention. Two Bulaqi women that I met by accident at a mechanic's shop far from their homes, automatically invited me to accompany them home for a visit!

Baladi culture stresses generosity, and greetings are chock full of invitations to share resources—home, food, time. In baladi culture, to flaunt good luck or abundance is to invite envy. Thus to offer to share abundance is to make it less vulnerable to envy. Who is actually offered what marks social relations and social distance. When I visited in an Egyptian village, before each meal we ate in front of the house, the head of the household invited anyone sitting along the irrigation canal to join us. No one ever did, but no one could accuse the family of stinginess, for they had established neighbors' rights, in principle, to eat with them.

In reality, my host's invitation served more as a ritual exclusion than inclusion. Inclusion was less ritualized. As a guest in this village household, I felt shy about plunging into the food, and held back awaiting an invitation. But I received no flowery welcomes such as those proffered up and down the lane. Rather, I was motioned to my place with a perfunctory "itfaddilli" placing all food at my disposal, and my fair share of meat, or other delicacies such as eggs sizzling in heavy fat, was unceremoniously plunked down in front of me. If I politely refused, I unintentionally triggered elaborate phrases saved for true guests, wherein my host insisted that no one but me was to eat the food meant for me.

Commentators remark that Egyptians are more hospitable than some Middle Easterners who never invite outsiders to their homes. I suggest, however, that the Egyptian physical threshold of private is merely differently constructed. One can drink tea in their homes, but one cannot cross Egyptian social, personal boundaries any more easily than those of other Middle Easterners. Strangers may be temporarily incorporated into private physical space, while there they are retained at a "public distance." Fatima recounted the following tale of such social orchestration as she sat with neighbors discussing her day of collecting cheese payments, introducing it with "What I do to collect!"

The other day I met Rida by chance in the street. What good luck, I thought to myself. I have been trying to catch her for her ghee payment she missed last month. When she asked me to come for tea, I immediately accepted, so we went to her house to drink tea and I met her mother. I decided not to ask right away for her payment but to let my visit be social. I would return later to collect.

This was luck, for every time I go to Rida's friend Nabila, who introduced us, Nabila never knows where Rida is, and always finds some excuse not to show me Rida's house.

But, imagine! Today I decided to go back to Rida's house, surprise her, and get my money. I arrived to find the woman I met there that day saying that she knew nothing about Rida, for Rida did not live there. Can you believe, Rida had contrived another woman's home as hers so that I would never be able to find her to collect my payments!

Fatima had met her match! When she exploited normal hospitality, her debtor fabricated a house and mother!

As discussed in Chapter 4, food is an index of social relations. Anyone can drink tea together, as Fatima discovered with her customer, but heavier foods indicate social mutuality. Food changes hands during trips to and from the village. Urbanites take urban products such as soap and lentils to their rural relatives, and return with rural products such as cheese and rich pastry made from the rural ghee. When I went to the village I asked my friends what to take; they helped me to carry parcels of candies, lentils, and sugar on the train. The day before I returned to Cairo, my hostess said: "Tomorrow morning we will make bread and *futir* (a rich, layered pastry) for you to take." I responded, "I want nothing." At this point I was told to be quiet. The next day, I passively accepted my share of breads, including biscuits rushed over by the daughter-in-law several kilometers away, and carried it all home to give to friends.

Food sharing indexes social relations as much in the breach as in the observance, as demonstrated one day when Badriyya, who had just returned from the village, passed out bread, biscuits, and futir. First, she dispatched the best two futir to her mother-in-law's house, and then she started to divide the rest of the basket with her other relatives and neighbors. When she offered her sister-in-law Suad half a futir and a handful of biscuits, Suad refused them and scowled at her daughter Abir when she started to pick them up from the table. The futir distribution was a ritual litmus test of social ties: in a spontaneous performance, Suad refused her measly share of "village breads" because she judged them less than her rightful share as the sister-in-law of Badriyya.

> *Badriyya:* Here, Suad, is some bread from my village.
>
> *Suad:* No, thanks, I need nothing.
>
> *Badriyya:* Come on, you must taste the bread I made! Here, Abir, take it for your mother.
>
> *Suad:* [scowling] Abir, don't you touch that bread!
>
> *Abir:* But, mother. . . .
>
> *Suad:* Come, Abir, there is no place here for us with these people.

Calibration of social ties via this ritual of food distribution is similar to Christmas gift giving in our society, in which one does not give a parent a mere handkerchief, or one's school teacher a sports car. The specific reciprocity of an exchange like Suad's and Badriyya's is similar to the give and take of speaking relations.

"To Recognize or Not To Recognize"

Baladis calibrate social ties by who receives what and by who speaks to whom. With forced physical proximity, the only distance achievable is the social one of "no speaking." Two people who have totally broken off relations will refuse to enter the same room. Such a social state can be very inconvenient in a baladi quarter, so most socially estranged people are "not on speaking terms," are *metkhasmin*. Two such people do not acknowledge each other in passing, nor visit in each other's homes. If they meet in a third person's home, in a hospital room on a visit, or in a shop, they adjust their positions to avoid each other's line of vision. Less serious than to be metkhasmin is to restrict interaction to a formal exchange of greetings. This restriction is common among neighbors with petty quarrels, who describe the state as "I merely greet him/her."

The continuum of "speaking terms" runs from "breaking off" at the negative end to "paying attention" to someone, which means "to value someone," at the positive end. A daughter-in-law's natal family, who harbored her and refused to return her when she was estranged from her husband, was accused of "not paying attention to" or not respecting the husband's family. Baladis speculate whether someone failing to greet them did not "pay attention" or simply did not hear. To "not pay attention" is the first step toward social estrangement.

People break off speaking because they have disagreed, been insulted, or been ignored during a family crisis. Conversely, they may also break to avoid others' problems or to protest exclusion from another's good luck. Since metkhasmin is a recognized status, reconciliation requires a formal ritual act such as congratulation at a life passage or help with a crisis. For example, one woman congratulated a neighbor, with whom she had been metkhasma for months, on the birth of her son by offering the customary *nuqta* (money gift). Another woman returned from a trip to find her estranged sister in her house caring for their ill mother. The woman said: "What could I do? I had to speak to my sister when I found her there in my house." People who are metkhasmin are often reconciled when a third woman invites them to join her. Friends may encourage their friends to reconcile. Conversely, close friends display solidarity and do not speak to those that their friends do not.

For baladi Egyptians life passages are a time for restoration of social ties. One day, as the women of Shaykh Ali discussed nuqta given to Badriyya for her excision, they calibrated "speaking terms." Aniyat volunteered details on the estrangement among women in the Shaykh Ali house in a performance, during which she grew more and more upset about Um Mona and stood to gesture in the direction of Um Mona's room. She set the scene with the following: "Not everyone gave my daughter money. Let me tell you!"

> Badriyya's grandmother and two of her neighbors here in the house have given Badriyya nuqta. Fatima walked over from the room where she recently moved to give my daughter nuqta, and she mentioned in front of Mahrusa downstairs that Badriyya had just been excised. Then she came up to visit. Mahrusa didn't. She and I are metkhasmin. When my son Muhammad's twin was still alive, Aziza [who lived next door] cursed me and I was going to complain. Then Mahrusa's husband, Abu Mona, told us

that we should not fight. I told him that Aziza and I were from the same village and that it was our business.

One day Mahrusa's daughter Mona was carrying my twin son and I went into the room to get him; just then Abu Mona came in and he asked me what I was doing and told me that I had no place there. So I left, but continued to say good morning from the doorway. I told Abu Mona that he had nothing to do with his wife and me, and that we would still ask after each other. Then Muhammad's twin got sick, and Miriam told Mahrusa. She came up and I invited her to come in, but she said that she would sit on the landing. So she sat down in the hallway. Then several days later Muhammad's twin died, and Miriam told Mahrusa, but she didn't come up; she said that when she came before, I didn't invite her in. I said, "How could I have invited you in? It was you who preferred to sit in the hallway!" Since that time she hasn't asked after me, nor I after her; she celebrated engagement of a daughter and a son, but I did not visit. From the time that my twin died, I haven't asked after her. But her children speak to me.

Baladi women tie every step in the rise and fall of social relations to a ritual event, and Aniyat's detailed account of past rituals resurrected on the occasion of her daughter's excision is no exception. It also highlights Abu Mona's meddling not only in the affairs of women, but in those of fellow villagers. Baladi society always leaves doors open. Had Mahrusa congratulated Badriyya on her excision, she could have re-established normal social relations, but there would always be another chance at the next birth or marriage.

Aniyat and Mahrusa remained *metkhasmin* for months, and I never understood the root of the problem, although its consequences were clear. It meant I had to be sure to visit each of my two friends separately when I came to Shakyh Ali house. Once, during 'Aid el Futr, I visited the Shaykh Ali house to find the entire building avoiding Aniyat. Six months later, as I sat in Miriam's room, I discovered the depths of the problem. When I visited my women friends at Shaykh Ali I usually went upstairs first to greet my longest-known friend Aniyat, but this time both Miriam and Mahrusa dragged me off the stairs and told me not to bother. When Mahrusa left, Miriam asked me, "Have you heard the latest about Aniyat?" The words tumbled out of Miriam's mouth—framed with a grand sweep of her hands and a conspiratorial tone of her voice.

You know how Aniyat was always entertaining Badriyya's fiancé? Well, the things that went on! [Miriam rubbed her

hands together suggestively and said no more, but I expressed
incredulity—wasn't it dangerous? Her children were there.]

Well, she just closed the door, and had no shame in front of
the children. Her brother and his entire family came from the
Said to deal with her. You have never heard such a commotion.
They beat her and threw her on the ground. Then they finally
left, but the engagement was broken.

When I saw Aniyat that day I found her more withdrawn than
usual. We talked of the family, of her husband working in Saudi
Arabia, of Badriyya's broken engagement ("her fiancé found another
woman"). Suddenly, I thought back to the previous fall when I had
found her already out of bed washing clothes and cooking four days
after giving birth. At that point she had told me that she and her
sister-in-law were metkhasmin. Now I understood why, although I
would never know whether Miriam's tale was true. Years before,
Aniyat and Mahrusa had been estranged when Badriyya was
excised. Now Badriyya was ready to marry, but the same social
patterns continued.

Baladi Conflict: The Construction of Reputation

Words have power. In ritual, pronouncements assume magical
efficacy (Tambiah 1968). Wikan's study of Cairo poor notes how
women massage their images in informal discourse. To attempt to
look good is human nature; what is baladi is the idiom of image
enhancement. Egyptian baladi women concentrate on "obtaining
social confirmation that they are what their culture says they
should be" (Wikan 1980:144, 125). Many of the narratives in this
study justify the steps a woman took to cure a child, to find a bride
for her son, to find an apartment, or to meet other everyday
exigencies. Disputes are a special case of image negotiation; like
other mundane performances, such as hospitality, disputes index
social relations.

A special case of dispute involves children, either that between
adults over their children, or that between parents and children.
Ultimately no one blames an immature child for being indiscreet,
and so children who may be the reputed source of a secret story can
figure as potent pawns in public discussions. Children balk and
bargain when assigned humiliating missions to borrow food or to
inform a creditor that a parent will delay payment. Children also
haggle for more pocket money.

At the Shaykh Ali house, Mahrusa complained that Badriyya

acted impertinent when Mahrusa asked her to run an errand: "I was standing by the water faucet downstairs when Badriyya passed by. I told her, 'Here Badriyya, take my water pail for me like a good girl.' Badriyya ignored me and kept right on walking. What a way for a proper girl to act!" Badriyya's mother Aniyat responded that Badriyya had done nothing while Mahrusa had committed the grievous error of publicizing Badriyya's impending engagement. Mahrusa retorted heatedly that Badriyya had talked about her engagement openly in the hallway, so it was obviously not a secret.

Mahrusa also complained about Aniyat's middle daughter Maha's surliness and refusal to run errands for neighbors. "Badriyya is pleasant like her mother whereas Maha is self-centered like her father. Ahmad went to Saudi Arabia because he was greedy to earn more money although he drew a large enough salary here with his two jobs."

Such talk indicates Mahrusa's relation to Aniyat at that point in time. At other times when the two women were getting on well, Mahrusa praised all of Aniyat's children! Even when the mothers were not speaking, children of Aniyat had free access to Mahrusa's home. While children can be the idiom of discord, they are not held

Two baladi women in deep discussion at the market

personally culpable. Children are "children of the house" who visit freely and are fed and coddled by neighbors even if the neighbors are metkhasmin with the child's parents. On one 'Aid el-Futr, I found Um Mustafa's son spruced out in white and orange striped cotton shorts and shirt and orange patent leather sandals. During the day almost everyone in the house carried him, even though they did not necessarily greet his mother. Likewise, when Aniyat had a new baby, even house residents who were not on speaking terms said they helped name the baby because, after all, the baby is not at fault.

To be baladi is to be generous. Baladi women assist one another, and when the second can not reciprocate, attribute it to her desperate plight. One ironclad rule in baladi society is that friendships change but neighbors remain civil and rally in crises. When Aniyat delivered in the fall of 1980 and received little extra help from the household with whom she was metkhasmin, the women of the house did not fail to help out at the birth; Mahrusa and Miriam joined the two clinic midwives who came to assist. At the same time, Aniyat's own sister-in-law upstairs did not even visit her because, as Aniyat put it, they had stopped speaking the month before.

When I visited after the birth, the day I found her out of bed working, Aniyat had wrapped her new daughter Maha in clean clothes and outlined her eyes with kohl. Aniyat and I sat down to soup and bread, then the fenugreek traditionally drunk to celebrate birth. She nursed as we ate. Aniyat told me that when she delivered the room was "full of people." Baladi neighbors often rely on each other more than kin, incorporating neighbors in "kinlike" relations where possible. In Aniyat's case, her kin were caught up in rumors about her morality. One woman explained such assistance at birth with: "We're all sisters together and sisters are better than mothers; we help each other." In addition, children, including newborns, should not suffer because of adult quarrels.

As children are innocent, so they also are free to do what they can to wheedle such favors as extra spending money from their parents. Mothers actually encourage their children to ask their fathers for lunch or school tutoring money, particularly in front of the father's friends so he will be shamed into paying. This allows the mother to save more from household funds for a nest egg. I witnessed many similar parent-child bargaining performances, such as the following:

Ihlam: Give me my four piasters.

Mother: I gave you ten to go shopping and you only spent six, so you should still have four.

Ihlam: Never mind, just give me four now.

Mother: No, I am not giving you any.

Ihlam: But the teacher takes four piasters from me every day when he tutors me.

Mother: I have nothing to do with your professor. You are supposed to take that money from your father.

Ihlam: But I went to him and he said to get it from you.

Mother: All right, here is two piasters, and take the other two from him.

Children also bargain over assignment of tasks and over attendance at school. A typical exchange occurred when eight-year-old Wafaa brought in a petticoat that needed mending as she dressed for the afternoon shift of school. As Suad stitched, she sent Wafaa off to wash her hair and return for Suad to "check for lice."

Mother: It's time to put gas on your hair to get rid of this lice.

Wafaa: No, I don't want to. When I do, my friends at school complain that I smell of gas.

Mother: All right, now, sweep the floor before you leave for school.

Wafaa: Why do I always have to do all the work?

Mother: Your sister Saha doesn't know how to sweep.

Wafaa: I wish I could become smaller than all of my sisters.

Mother: Never mind. Soon they will grow up and be big like you.

Wafaa: Where are my two piasters? I asked you to keep them for me this morning because you told me that I would lose them.

Mother: No, I don't have them.

Wafaa: [whining] Yes, you do!

Mother: [placating] If I have any small change with me, then it's yours! [Looking in her pockets and finding two coins.] Here you are.

Wafaa: [taking two pieces of candy, a bracelet , but no books] Good bye.

Mother: Bring those back. You can't have them.

Wafaa: [holding out the candy in her hand] But I only took two candies and the bracelet is mine.

Mother: No! Bring them back.

[Wafaa throws them at the bed, and they fall behind it.]

Mother: Put them in the box.

Wafaa: They went into the box when I threw them.

[Mother starts to sprinkle powdered sugar on feast biscuits while talking to Wafaa.]

Wafaa: Give me a biscuit.

[Mother hands her one, which Wafaa grabs with no comment, and walks out the door taking a bracelet and two piasters.]

Mother: Bring those back!

[Wafaa returns and throws one piaster down and leaves.]

Wafaa [on exit]: May God take the rest away from you!

The above is a typical bartering performance between a child who knows just about how far to push, and an indulgent mother who has her limits. Parents are played off against each other for more than lunch money. Suad and another daughter, Huda, discussed Huda's sore ear until Huda became exasperated and elevated her voice to the high decibels typical of a bargaining performance.

Huda: You know my ear hurts and I want to go to the school clinic tomorrow.

Mother: You just want to go so that you don't have to go to school tomorrow!

Huda: No, I'll go and then I will go to school. Will you take me?

Mother: No. Ask your father to take time off and take you.

Huda: No, I want you to do it.

Mother: It's none of my business.

Huda: But I want you to go with me and then I'll go to school.

Mother: All right, all right, enough, I will do it. [A guest arrived and interrupted the discussion, but Huda was not satisfied and a few minutes later Huda interjected.]

Huda: You'll take me to the clinic tomorrow?

Mother: I told you I would.

Huda: But I was afraid you were just fooling me.

Mother: All right, so I won't take you, if that's what you want!

Such haggling is not that different from the American child in the grocery-store line begging a chocolate bar on a candy rack by the cash register, except it proceeds in a format familiar to baladi children.

The most famous baladi performance is the street dispute

between two women. Most include the standard rhymed insults (*radih*) such as "Oh, you rusty sewing needle" and "You are nothing but a worn out bridge." Beyond these and other stereotypic baladi framing verbal formulae such as "Oh, my despair!" lies the construction of reputation via verbal rendition of daily life details.

Films and literature of baladi life always include a few shouting matches from balcony to balcony or balcony to street; they are well-known baladi cultural performances. A typical example is the following excerpt from an Egyptian novel, *The Events of Zaafarani Alley* by Gamal al-Ghitani, from a forthcoming translation by Farouk Abdel Wahab. While this is not a Bulaqi text, it nevertheless conveys the standard afrangi view of baladi disputes and, since baladis may adopt the afrangi stereotype as their own, provides helpful cultural data.

The Second Quarrel

It happened on the same day at one in the afternoon after Oweis had finished telling the Alley part two of the Tekerli story. . . . The quarrel proceeded as follows:

She [Busayna] called out loudly to Umm Suhair who lived across the street from Umm Yusif. Umm Suhair loudly answered in the name of God and hoping that everything will be all right. Busayna declared that no good will come to this forsaken Zaafarani so long as the hearts were ungrateful and as women who were more like scorpions than people nested there. Umm Suhair realized that this was the prelude for a quarrel. A number of women looked out of their windows. Khadija, the Sa'idi woman, ran to her window joyously repeating "A quarrel! A quarrel!" Busayna noticed that the two windows of Umm Yusif were still closed—a fact that made her cut short the usual prelude leading into every quarrel she fought. She declared that that harlot of a woman, whose tongue was fit to be a strap of leather on which razors could be sharpened, that wife of the train stoker. . . .

At that point Umm Suhair made a gesture, Sitt Umm Nabila shook her head, Zannuba, the divorcee, clapped her hands and shouted "Wow! . . . Wow!" And still Umm Yusif did not open her window. . . . Busayna shouted that some women who were never satisfied by their husbands . . . were losing their minds now, and she pointed her arm in the direction of Umm Yusif's house. She clapped repeating: Wife of the stoker! Wife of the stoker! Oh women of the Alley! Oh Alley of women! She wanted them to be her witnesses against the wife of the stoker who exposed her bare breast when she looked out of the window,

who didn't wear any underwear and who badmouthed her even
though last year she had lent her five pounds Egyptian when
she turned to her in tears begging her to save Tahun . . . Tahun
the stoker! Tahun, the stoker, because part of his inventory was
lost and he was given the choice: pay or go to jail. Then she
regretted later on because good people told her that Tahun al-
Mathun al Matahni al-Matahin had stolen part of that
inventory and sold it in the junk yards of Wikalit-il Balah. . . .
Still, Umm Yusif did not respond. Khadija, the Sa'idi woman,
was certain that if she did, a really big quarrel that would help
her cope with her loneliness would ensue; Umm Yusif, after all,
had a talent for heaping abuse that was not to be sneezed at. So
it seemed there was some mysterious reason making her take
this. Umm Suhair was certain that there was something that
Busayna was holding back. Busayna was now stretching her
body on the balcony, waving with her shoe, declaring that she
was going to beat Umm Yusif on her most sensitive parts (Al-
Ghitani 1992).

Busayna nicely framed her dispute both by situating herself above
the two houses she hoped to address and by proclaiming her intent
to fight to Umm Suhair—thereby alerting the entire alley that a
quarrel was about to ensue. Busayna, clearly frustrated at her
inability to rouse Umm Yussif, attacked her by demeaning her
husband as a mere train stoker, and accusing her of provocative
dress. Busayna reminded the unseen Umm Yusif of Busayna's
generous loan—to save the good-for-nothing husband—which had
not been repaid. The alley braced for a performance whose form was
familiar—a performance that Umm Yusif boycotted.

Street or "public" disputes, because they occur not only in the
street but from balcony to balcony, window to window, balcony to
street, or any other permutation of these venues, provide a rich text
for future narrative recounts. Whether one witnesses the actual
event is of little importance as long as someone saw it and
corroborates the star actors' versions. On my way to visit Samira's
family one day, I passed Samira as she shook her fist at a woman
standing inside a doorway, and from time to time also addressed a
man on the balcony the floor above Samira's family flat. At one
point Samira lifted her black gellabeyya to show him the house
gellabeyya underneath—exclaiming: "See I dress well with no torn
clothes!" At another point she displayed a bruise on her leg,
exclaiming "See what she did to me!"

I had missed most of the dispute between Samira and her sister-
in-law Sakkina and daughter-in-law Rida, but I need not have

worried. Later when Samira joined her family and friends upstairs, she retold the entire incident in great detail. The dispute concerned events in the clinic, where Samira had good relations and where Sakkina sought an orphan to raise for a fee. The argument started when Sakkina accused Samira of blocking Sakkina's request for an orphan.

Samira recounted her dispute as soon as she arrived, and twice more for visitors, each time following the same format. She provided a dramatic frame for her narrative when she swept into the adjoining room and returned with a Quran in a small floral cotton bag. Grasping the Quran, she proclaimed: "I swear by the Quran that this is how it happened," and then laid the Quran in front of her. Samira further enhanced her account with theatrics; she threw off her scarf and grabbed her own hair to demonstrate how Sakkina pulled Samira's hair, and she lifted her skirt to show her fine taffeta slip and her bruised leg. In the midst of her narrative, Samira started to cry: "How can they do this to my fine reputation? I've raised my children very well." The women listening reassured her and told her: "Stop crying, don't be ridiculous, no one believes those women."

Here is Samira's account of the dispute:

I was in the clinic this morning and I obtained Rida's [her daughter-in-law] papers for her, saying "this is for my son because he is sick." I also requested my sister-in-law Sakkina's papers; she was standing outside the door and would not talk to me. The clinic doctor told me: "I will do it for your sake, Samira," and Sakkina laughed. There was a stack of papers with Sakkina's on the top. I took Sakkina's papers and put them in the middle of the desk so they wouldn't fall off. Sakkina started to scream at me, "What are you doing that for?" I told her, "So your papers won't fall off." Sakkina screamed and cursed. I did not respond because I was standing in the clinic.

But when I reached the street in front of the clinic, Sakkina called out again to me and cursed me and called me "Daughter of a Dog." Then she went into Rida's house, where she knows I do not go now. [Samira had previously broken off speaking with her daughter-in-law Rida, but she was still willing to process Rida's papers, which would provide money for Samira's son's household.] I called to her, "Come out, you. If you're going to curse me, come out of there and do it to my face." I went as far as the entryway and Sakkina came out and grabbed me by the hair. She grabbed me and then my foot slipped on the stones and I fell into the drain, bruising my leg. Sakkina was on top of me, hitting me. I tried to bring her down with me. Um Magdi [Samira's upstairs neighbor] came and pulled at me to try to get me to stop. She thought I would not notice. Sakkina was pulling my hair! I have never in my life pulled her hair. Sakkina is older than I am; she is my sister-in-law; how can she do such things to me?

Rida just stood there and said nothing. She could have at least said, "Watch out; this is my mother-in-law, don't do this to her." But Rida said nothing and did nothing.

Then Um Magdi called me a tramp! I said to her, "Oh, Um Magdi, so I am a tramp?" And I lifted up my black gellabeyya to show her my untorn, fine black taffeta slip underneath. I said to her, "From the day when my son died, I have gone like this in black." I think she has forgotten the incident of the red gellabeyya, but I have not.

Then Um Magdi told Sakkina to come into the house and told me to leave. Then I went out into the street and saw Um Magdi's husband standing on the balcony of his apartment a floor above mine, and screaming at me. I told him to come down and fight if he wanted to since, after all, "men act." But he didn't move and I yelled: "My children are all well educated and have diplomas; they have specialized skills. I do not have to marry my daughters off to foreigners." But he didn't budge. My neighbors Um Magdi and Abu Magdi are fine ones to talk. My son brings them medicine as a favor from the factory where he works. Look at them: one daughter married off to a Saudi, although that won't last long. Another about to be married to a Libyan, although she is older than he. Um Magdi's family marries their daughters to people from faraway lands to gain valuable gifts. My oldest daughter is not married yet and people are asking why, but she waited to get an education and a good job. She is not like Rida, who is exactly my daughter's age but has no education and no morals. Whatever you say, I am still the mother of Muhammad and of Abdul Wahab, two sons with education and jobs.

As I was screaming at Abu Magdi about his daughters, my downstairs neighbor Amina came out and said: "Come on home and stop fighting." I decided I had had enough!

Samira's and Sakkina's performance is a clear statement of dissatisfaction with kin and friend relations. Rumor had it that Samira was receiving more than her share of rations of flour and oil distributed at the clinic, while Samira protested that she received nothing extra and that her friends and relatives should be grateful because she obtained favors for them from the clinic doctor and social worker. Sakkina resented the fact that her desperate situation had forced her to take in washing from the clinic, which she did in the middle of the night to hide her poverty. Because of past grievances, Rida and Samira were not on speaking terms. Um Magdi initially joined the fray in an effort to stop it, but Samira clearly resented her neighbor's interference.

As do the women of Giza (Wikan 1980), Samira presents herself as a respectable woman who dresses well, educates her children, and does not "sell" them to foreigners. Samira had dressed modestly, but neatly, in black ever since her son's death several years before, while Sakkina, his aunt, had been known to wear red.

Throughout the dispute, onlookers controlled much of the flow of events. The clinic staff kept order inside the clinic. Um Magdi intervened at Rida's house. Amina finally encouraged Samira to get out of the street. One often hears the expression: "For my sake, stop quarrelling." This allows a protagonist to cease and desist without loosing face, because she ostensibly abandons the fight for the sake of the mediator. Feuds are most often between relatives and most often about shares of resources, which can be anything in a marginal baladi economy from money to personal contacts.

Baladi Morality: Action, Not Appearance

Bulaqis have a strong sense of right and wrong, which guides them in disputes and mundane encounters, as well as in their religious lives. We discussed popular Islam in the last chapter, but here I will note how baladi narratives continually invoke the ideal—the rewarding of good behavior and damning of bad—to remind baladis of the need for uprightness. These tales are not necessarily about religion but they are certainly about morality. The two following were actually told by a man, the father of Karima and Sayyida, as I sat with Karima while she made Ramadan biscuits the night before the feast. The father joined our conversation about Ramadan and seized the opportunity of a pause to say: "Listen to the following story which I heard at the mosque the other day."

> There was a man who had been a thief for sixty years. He lived in a two-story building. On the first floor was a widow who had no money. Her children cried for Ramadan biscuits when they saw everyone else making them. But she had no money, so in the middle of the night, the thief, who said to himself that this woman's children should not be deprived, let himself down on a rope in the middle of her house and left flour and other

ingredients for biscuits, and some clothes. When she woke up she
was very surprised because she found these things and her door
had been shut tight. . . . A saint (*wali*) appeared and told the
thief that all his sins had been forgiven and that he had been
made a wali because of this deed.

Another story I also heard at the mosque was about a widow
who lived in a lane just like that one behind us. Many men came
to her door, and finally the neighbors complained and brought
the shaykh to see what was going on. God made many men visit
her that day, so the shaykh went to her door and told her she
must leave. She said, "but where can I go, so late in the day?"
He agreed that she could stay till the morning. The shaykh
went home that night and had a dream in which he died and
went to heaven. As he was walking along the street, he found
big buildings, but they were all closed. Finally he came to one
with its door open. He entered and found grapes on the table. He
reached out his hand to eat some, but the guard told him, "Don't
touch them! They belong to that woman over there." He looked
and saw that it was the woman he had told to leave her house.
The next morning when he woke up, he went to the woman and
found her gathering her furniture to leave. He fell down at her
feet saying that he would be her watchman. She said, "And did
the grapes belong to you?" Then she invited him in to stay and
see what happened when the men came. The first man came and
said, "My daughter is going to marry and I don't have any money
to prepare the furnishings." She reached under the mattress and
pulled out a five-pound note. The next man came and pleaded
that his wife was ill and needed an operation, and the woman
reached under her mattress and pulled out a ten pound note. The
woman told the shaykh that she did this because money
expended for charity would multiply and come back to her. She
said, "What I give away like this will come back tenfold in
heaven."

So you see, this woman understood a good deed, or *sawab*.
There are three things which follow one to the grave: one's
children; one's money; one's work. The first two things go home
again. It is only one's work and good deeds which remain.
Rather than spending time going to the cemetery and spending
the night there to pray at feast time, one should perform a good
deed like providing a water source.

Karima and Sayyida's father is typical of the Bulaqis who
emphasize moral actions over any folk Islam practices such as
visiting the cemeteries. His story is apocryphal, but its point is

clear: never judge a person's action by appearance; good deeds follow one to heaven.

Baladi women can only aspire to have money under their mattress to distribute, and although Karima's father said the story was about a woman who lived in a lane such as theirs, only a successful merchant woman would have so much money. Baladi women talked mundane, household-centered good deeds. When Aysha's son burned his hand, the neighbor who helped Aysha bandage it told Aysha to be sure to lend someone a colander. I asked the neighbor what she meant, and she replied: "When Aysha buys a colander and lends it to anyone who comes to ask for it, she will gain a sawab that she lost when her son's hand was burned." At that point another visitor pulled a small bronze dish out of her bag and said that it was a "fright cup" which she had borrowed from a recently returned pilgrim who brought the cup from Mecca. She explained:

> You put seven dates in the cup and leave them out at night. In the morning the mist comes down on the cup from the heavens and you drink it. One should do this three days in a row. The cup should be passed around. People bring it back from the pilgrimage as a sawab.

Lending "fright cups" and more mundane food and utensils is an example of the many small gestures that can be made to fulfill one's Islamic duties. A good, authentic, hospitable baladi shares household items as part of baladi mutuality.

Baladi Restitution: Procession and Response

In rural areas, at life passages of circumcision and marriage, women feel a social duty to walk in colorful parades that display vast amounts of food and clothes, and display the state of social ties. In urban areas, women exchange money gifts of nuqta, but some urban migrants continue to exchange food and clothes and process with baskets on their heads through clogged streets rather than along scenic, shady irrigation ditches. These processions are symbolic presentations of the nourishment of food from women, the managers of life, fertility, and household, to other women. Grapes and oranges cascade among macaroni and *sharbat* (fruit drink) for all bystanders to see. One woman balances a basket on her head and a drum under her arm to beat a rhythm for chants throughout the walk. When the procession arrives, women of the hostess's house respond, and sing

back and forth for ten or fifteen minutes, allowing ample time for
visual consumption of the display. Finally, the women are clapped
into the house where they deposit their gifts. There is nothing
haphazard about these presentations; a woman from the family sits
near the deposit point to mark down in a notebook each gift by
quantity and giver. This record will be consulted when it is time to
reciprocate the gift. When Fatima invited me to her village for her
son's engagement, I had the opportunity to witness two such
processions.

The groom's procession is first. Muhammad's relatives had all
arrived in the village and the women busied themselves arranging
the thirteen dresses that Muhammad had purchased for his fiancée,
Sabah. By noon they were placed on thirteen separate trays with
oranges, grapes, cones of sugar, toffee, rice, macaroni, and sharbat
tumbling among the dress folds. The women of the family heaved
the trays to their heads and set off, with Fatima leading the way,
clapping and singing. Sabah's house was only a few minutes away;
the women arrived and were met by the women of Sabah's house
who "clapped them in" to a room where they deposited the trays.
They then returned to the courtyard where they sat drumming and
singing for an hour and a half while the men left to write the
engagement. The women sang traditional wedding songs with
standard exchanges such as: "Look at the mother of the bride"—
"We're looking" or "Think about the life to come"—"We're
thinking." For circumcision processions, one merely substitutes
"circumcised one" for "bride" or "groom" in a leader-follower series
of rhymed responses. Many extol the mother-child relation or the
family reputation. The leader improvises stanzas and the listeners
chime in with set responses.

As the women sang, the bride sat in the courtyard in a blue floral
taffeta dress with her long hair combed out and held back with
bobby pins. A woman remarked on Muhammad's childless cousin
Nagat who was vigorously drumming: "May God compensate her,"
that is, may she become pregnant as a result of her vigorous
celebration here. When they heard the men returning, the women
left the courtyard to stand by the irrigation ditch and peer up the
road. The men proceeded straight into the courtyard the women had
vacated, and sat down for lunch! The women relocated outside the
wall. Some slipped away, while others remained to eat.

That night I accompanied Fatima and some of the family to pick
up the trays. During a round of tea drinking, Sabah's mother joked:
"Shall I bring you rice or futir tomorrow?" Fatima laughed and said
"Bring nothing." That short exchange was to be the kernel for a
disintegrating relation between the in-laws. The next day, on the

way to market, the women from Muhammad's family speculated on how the family of the bride, Sabah, would respond to the gifts of the previous day. The bride's mother's comment about rice or futir did not go unnoticed. One of Fatima's daughters, Nabila, reported that the bride's mother had taken her aside and said: "You can take the rice and futir to Cairo; we have also bought two male ducks for five pounds for Muhammad's grandmother." It was immediately agreed that it looked like trouble, that the bride would not respond with the expected bolt of cloth for a suit for the groom. The women also criticized the meal presented by the bride's family and noted the lack of tomatoes in the sauce.

The response procession by Sabah's family was the next day. At breakfast, Fatima's sister-in-law announced that Sabah's family was not bringing a suit for Muhammad and that they were in the midst of making futir. Fatima said angrily: "Who asked for futir anyway? Doesn't my son deserve a suit? I will not accept the futir if they don't bring a suit too." A daughter-in-law, Saadiyya, who was related to Sabah, decided to go see her family and find out what was happening. Throughout the day the tension grew as we tried to guess the contents of the anticipated procession. A merchant arrived to look at the family grape arbor, but was soon embroiled in the discussion. He gave his opinion: Sabah's family had an obligation to answer the gifts by the same standard; Muhammad's family should refuse gifts that did not include material for a groom's suit. He left advising Fatima not to be shy to refuse inappropriate gifts.

The daughter-in-law returned, saying her parents told her they "had no word" and could not influence the bride's family to send a suit. Fatima retorted that the bride's family should have been instructed by relatives to buy cloth for the groom. The scene was charged for a dispute. The first was between Saadiyya and her sister-in-law Nagat:

Nagat: If Sabah's family does not bring a suit, may they all fall ill.

Saadiyya: It is shameful to talk this way. You should not curse my family.

Mother of Nagat: I have raised my children well and given them everything. Why do I have to arrive at the day when I hear them curse one another? Why do I have to listen to my daughter-in-law Saadiyya tell my daughter Nagat how to behave? Why do I have to suffer this ill behavior in my own family. Who is at fault?

[At this point a man who happened along on a donkey selling turnips said, familiarly, to the mother-in-law, "Please let me tell you one word! None of this is important."]

Mother of Nagat: I refuse to accept this. How can I raise my children with correct manners and then find these accusations ringing out on my very doorstep?

Saudiyya: All I did was tell Nagat that it was shameful to curse. Would not you, mother-in-law, have done the same thing?

Finally the argument fizzled, but the lines were clear. Mother would defend daughter against daughter-in-law. Mother would protest poor treatment by outsiders of her family. Of course the initial engagement was accomplished via the very same lines, the family of a daughter-in-law of the house, but now the stakes had changed.

Soon another daughter-in-law, Zakiyya, returned. She was not related to either side of the argument and remarked brightly: "I just saw a woman from Sabah's family carrying a big tray for the sweets, and she said that the bride's family was making futir. I made no comment but I thought 'Why all this futir anyway?'" The group coalesced around Zakiyya. She had guessed their mood without being there. They all wanted the chance to agree that there was no need for futir and certainly none for sweets, that all they wanted was the suit. The anticipated procession would apparently include the most unwanted pile of futir in village history! Um Rushdi, a neighbor, happened by. With her arrival, Fatima and her in-laws joined forces to recount a narrative of all their intelligence work on the content of the procession to be.

At 11:00 A.M. we heard drumming in the distance. The procession party was on its way! But what was their reception? Saudiyya, who had been washing dishes in the irrigation ditch in front of the house, scooped them up and retreated inside. Zakiyya and Fatima peeped out and scooted back in when they did not see any sign of a suit. They would not extend the customary "clap in welcome" to such a paltry showing.

This placed the household in an awkward situation. To leave the procession totally unwelcomed was unthinkable no matter how unwelcome they actually were. Codes of hospitality require a modicum of welcome. As a compromise, two daughters-in-law from Cairo stood in front of the house clapping lackadaisically. There was no pause for ten or fifteen minutes of exchanged songs as there had been at the bride's house. Rather, Sabah's mother dashed for the half-open door to the sitting room and pushed her women

relatives through the door to deposit their gifts—perhaps nervous
that the door might slam shut before she could deliver the goods.
Fatima stood by the wall and refused to look at the women entering,
but rather wailed "Do you not appreciate the worth of my son? No,
my kind brother-in-law, you will not make me quiet. I will not cease
to complain." Fatima's sister-in-law, the hostess, asked Sabah's
family if they would like to stay for tea. "No, we must rush back to
our house. We have much work." One was hard pressed to imagine
what the work could be, since Sabah's family had just stayed up all
night baking futir and were doubtlessly very tired, but the point of
social ritual is not fact but intent. Sabah's family knew better than
to stay and chance verbal abuse, if not the physical return of an
unacceptable gift.

After they left, Fatima declared: "I did not show my face to
the mother of the bride. I did not greet them." Then she sat
down and started to sob. Sabah's mother, still unloading trays,
pretended not to notice Fatima's wails, but she did send the
trays back immediately—obviating the need for a ceremonial
return visit at night to fetch them. This was the leanest social
occasion I saw in my three years in the field. It was, in effect, a
nonevent.

While the procession had been vacuous, its evaluation was not.
The cacophony of comments crescendoed as soon as Sabah's mother
was out of the door.

—These women were too eager to leave. She who brings enough
is not afraid to honor her hostess with her presence.

—Did you notice how the mother of the bride did not even look
at Fatima?

—See the poor quality of futir? Why, it is full of air bubbles.
Our children could make better. They were obviously in a hurry.
The whole lot required less than two pounds of ghee. What a
cheap family they are.

—Did you notice [mimicking the women with their swinging
hips] how the bride's party came singing "Bahri, bahri, we are
going to the North." Where else would they go?

—See how Sabah's mother gave orders "Empty those baskets"
as if they had something of worth to empty. We should just
throw the futir in the street.

—It is clear that they knew they had not brought enough. They
did not want to meet our eyes.

Fatima disposed of the futir quickly. She gave futir to her relatives and saved some to distribute in Cairo. She gave the two ducks to Saudiyya to sell in the market for her. The women shelled the corn, and divided it and the potatoes. Fatima remarked that her husband could have taken everything to Cairo, that there was no reason for her to travel. Nevertheless, she did—perhaps because she was already committed to accompanying me on the train back to Cairo.

The procession was form without substance. The event met the standards of style—complete with drumming, clapping, and singing, but it began to disintegrate when the substance, the requisite suit for the groom, did not appear. There was lukewarm response from the hostess's house, although lethargic invitations were actually proffered at appropriate points. The women visitors rushed to dispense of their goods and did not stay for tea. However, the groom's house did not return the goods, so the ritual, empty though it was, had occurred: "The bride has answered with gifts for the groom."

I wondered what would have happened without the moderating influence of Fatima's brother-in-law. He restrained her in the sitting room. Would she have thrown out the women and their gifts had he not been there? Later Fatima told me that her husband was standing down the road, saw the procession, and sent his brother to calm his wife. He had heard Fatima saying all morning: "If my husband will not talk, I am not ashamed to. I will not beg. It is my money, after all, that is paying for the bride's gifts." In the end Fatima held her peace, perhaps because her husband and his brother (her host) restrained her, perhaps because she knew it was of no use to complain. When I visited her a few weeks later, I was surprised to find her mellowed. She said, after all, Sabah's father is scheduled for surgery. What could they do? Fatima had known all along that there would be no suit. The ritual processions and responses had allowed Fatima to work out her disappointment. It had been a true performance of catharsis and creation of meaning (Early 1985).

The give-and-take of engagement presents can be quickly forgotten if families are truly in need. One hopes for ample presents but one needs most of all a loyal, hard-working spouse. Baladi society values the human element (loyalty, for example) as much as the material. Fatima was disappointed at her son's engagement but she forgave all in the face of the plight of Sabah's father and the reality that nothing more was forthcoming from Sabah's family. The next year, Sabah and Muhammad married and moved into Fatima's room. She and her husband moved across the lane and a new chapter of family life began.

The baladi cultural performances examined here are flamboyant interludes in the quiet flow of everyday life. They index social relations and social reputation. They allow personal expression of frustration: at seeing one's son receive paltry gifts from in-laws, of watching one's sister get the lion's share of goodies, of being humiliated by neighbors' inattention to one's life crisis, of not attaining the benefits of afrangi or foreign economies in which only husbands work and they have much money to spare. These cultural performances embody the baladi ambivalence toward the afrangi, as they also embody the tension between personal, specific situations and their general, cultural explanations.

Not all social negotiations occur with the flair witnessed here. Are the performances drama? Humdrum life? Exclusively baladi? Exclusively Egyptian? Baladi performances are part and parcel of baladi everyday culture—they enunciate baladi culture with a vigor and a clarity that cannot be equaled in a reconstruction of their text. It is in the glimpses one receives from the original narrative that one encounters the essence of baladi savvy: one ever moralizes and one ever enhances one's reputation. That, in a nutshell, is at the heart of baladi sociability.

6

Daily Life and Well-Being

Women's role as life-giver is ritually emphasized at circumcision and marriage processions in which women carry food cascading from trays on their heads. Fertility and social ties *are* the most important resources for a baladi woman's household management and business. A baladi woman's skill at playing with a stone and an egg shines in her forging of extrafamilial alliances in a kin-oriented society. She does this to marry off her children, to find jobs for relatives, to cultivate customers in the informal economic sector, and to better her downtrodden status.

Escape from Poverty with Honor: Marriage and Virginity

Marriage: Match and Maximization?

The search for the appropriate groom is fraught with frustration. Ihlam, who had been a nurse in Ras el Barra before she married, was now a widow with two daughters, who ran their deceased father's lathe shop. Ihlam talked while cleaning vegetables for lunch with some neighbor women and me about her daughter Ibtisam. She introduced her account with the standard baladi verbal formula: "It has been hard to find a match for Ibtisam. Let me tell you what has happened."

> First there was Fuad, who met Ibtisam when he visited his sister living next door to us. They were engaged three years ago. We thought he had a steady job working as a mechanic, but we found out after they were engaged that he had resigned to go to work in Beirut. Every year he put us off for another year, saying

soon he would get an apartment and they would marry. He borrowed thirty pounds from me before he went to Beirut, and then went behind my back to borrow sixty more pounds from Ibtisam's father. In all he took ninety pounds, which was more than the price of the bracelets that he gave Ibtisam when they were engaged. Now we are thinking to ask him the difference between the bracelets and the ninety pounds and tell him goodbye. . . . Three years ago Ibtisam was happy with Iman, but now she says he is old.

The reason is because she has met Nabil. Nabil is a friend of Naguib, the fiancée of Samiyya next door, and Samiyya introduced them. One evening, Naguib and Samiyya, Naguib's mother, and Nabil all came to visit without any notice. They came while we were fasting, and we had not even eaten our sunset meal. They started talking about marriage and told me that I should be happy that as a Christian, Nabil had converted to Islam, even though his family disowned him. I said that there are many Muslims in the world, so why should I be happy that one more converted. . . . I told Ibtisam that Nabil will never reconcile with his family and she agrees, but she still wants to marry him. I will spend about one thousand pounds to prepare Ibtisam for marriage. Why spend this and then one year later have Nabil's family come and say he must come back to them? I want Ibtisam to be happy and relaxed, and she will be neither in this marriage. When these kinds of things happen, the families get angry. If you [addressing me] were to convert to Islam, could you tell your family you did it for me? I don't think so. I have nothing against Christians but families must stay together.

Ihlam was not keen on this romantic match. Unsure whether Nabil had converted to Islam to marry Ibtisam, Ihlam wanted to avoid a man estranged from his family and inheritance—a man who might prey on Ibtisam's share of her father's shop. Arranged marriages are common in baladi society. Even Ibtisam's romance had started via neighbors, not from a chance encounter. Baladi young women may, however, have a say in courtship, if only by rejecting untenable candidates.

Baladi mothers seek favorable matches for their children; there are numerous accounts of the lucky woman who escaped baladi poverty through a propitious match with an outsider—be he afrangi or foreigner. Yet Bulaqis criticize blatant opportunism. Ihsan told me one day:

Guess where I was last night? At the marriage of my sister-in-law Sumayya to a Jordanian she had only just met last Wednesday! My husband and I went to sit with the wedding guests awhile so that the family would not be angry with us, but we took no presents. Haven't we given them enough? . . . Wasn't I sick in Gala' hospital and no one came to ask after me when I lost the twins? In any case, I don't care, because it is as if the family of my in-laws have sold their daughter to the Jordanian. I heard that they accepted a bride price of two hundred pounds, but some people said that it might have been five hundred, and that the groom would bring all the furnishings.

There was no "morning-after" visit by the families to inspect the marital sheets. The bride and groom were in a furnished apartment, so there could be no examination of the blood. Anyway, these days everyone is "sport" [Egyptian for "trendy"] and they do not bring a midwife the night of the marriage to check the blood.

Ihsan, the realist, is not shy to label "selling" of a daughter for what it is and to impugn her in-laws for stinginess. Earlier we heard Samira attack her neighbors for selling off their daughters. In the discussion of baladi and afrangi weddings we heard Mahrusa of Shaykh Ali house criticize her nephew for marrying a rich girl whose family was not even polite to the nephew's mother. Mahrusa herself married her daughter to a man from Saudi Arabia.

Mahrusa, originally from southern Egypt, grew up in the Cairo district of Imbaba, where two of her maternal aunts still live today. Mahrusa's oldest son is married to one of their daughters. Her husband is a policeman who retired during my research in Bulaq. Mahrusa complained that he was always underfoot, and he soon learned to stay in the coffeehouses! Sometimes he visited his old job just to kill time. He also began to sell scarves and sleepwear both to occupy his time and to supplement his pension; when I returned in 1982, he had a new job as a cashier in a shop.

Mahrusa has seven children. When we first met, the oldest, Muhammad, was in the army, and the youngest, Ahmad, was in fourth grade. By the time I returned in 1980, Mahrusa's children had spread to the four winds. Her two oldest sons and her eldest daughter, Mona, were married and living in Saudi Arabia. The next son, Omar, still worked as a butcher a mile from home. The next daughter, Suad, was engaged and the next, Azza, turned religious. The youngest, Ahmad, was the only child still in school. Suad worked in a seamstress shop and Azza stayed at home and helped her mother.

Mahrusa has reached the sublime time of life when a woman can slow down and savor the small pleasures of the day while her daughters pick up the slack in household routine. Her silver-gray hair frizzes almost straight back the few times she lets it escape from her scarf. One hardly notices the crinkled lines in her face because it is so animated, as she sweeps her hands or rolls her eyes to emphasize a point.

One day as we sat talking about Mona's wedding, after she and her husband Hassan, a Saudi school teacher, had left for Saudi Arabia, a former neighbor dropped by for tea. The obvious question was "what's happened?" and with that introduction Mahrusa took her tea glass, arranged her legs comfortably, leaned back against the wall, and introduced her narrative of her daughter Mona's meeting with Hassan with the characteristic frame "Let me tell you how it was." Listeners' questions are in italics:

One Friday my seamstress friend Fatahiyya, who lives near *Akhbar al-Yawm* newspaper, dropped by to ask me to accompany her to pray at the mosque. . . . As we walked to the mosque, Fatahiyya mentioned that a Saudi man she knew was coming to her house that evening to look for a bride. I said "Why not tell Mona?" Fatahiyya said that Mona would not be interested, that Mona resents arranged meetings with prospective grooms, and Mona curses anyone who tries to, saying she does not want to marry. I told Fatahiyya: "As you like."

After prayer, I invited my friend to lunch. After lunch, she proposed to Mona that she come to help her cook that afternoon. . . . Mona said that she wasn't going anywhere that day; she had made up her mind. . . . About sundown I told Mona that she should go see Um Ali, as she had "sent for Mona" to come see her at Fatahiyya's. Mona said no, but finally I persuaded her. I suggested she take a bath and get dressed. She refused, and she went in a melaya liff without dressing or combing her hair.

When Mona arrived at the seamstress's house, Um Ali greeted her delightedly: "Oh, here's Mona!" From this, the Saudi, Hassan, knew that Mona was the woman Fatahiyya had told him about the first night he arrived in Bulaq. However, the nurse Nawwal, who had brought Hassan to Fatahiyya, wanted him to marry one of Nawwal's relatives, so she forbade Fatahiyya to send for Mona. Nawwal met Hassan at Shoubra hospital, where she works as a nurse, when Hassan visited his ailing father there. Fatahiyya would have sent for Mona the first night if Nawwal had allowed her. Um Ali and Mona exchanged long kisses. Hassan said: "That's enough kissing."

Then Um Ali told Mona: "Come in and meet my nephew" [referring to Hassan]. She said this because she knew how Mona would react if she thought she was being introduced to a prospective groom. Mona sat down and talked with Hassan. Hassan later told us that this was the fifteenth day he had come to the seamstress's house and that luck had brought Mona that day, because he had not planned to return. Hassan understood what Fatahiyya was up to when she refused to tell him where Mona lived, saying that he need not bother to go to her house because her parents were always away at work [Mona could not entertain him alone], and that Mona still saw her old fiancé.

Hassan wanted to read the Fatiha to confirm an engagement the very night he met my daughter, but they tried to dissuade him. He came to our house anyway, and asked for Mona's father. I had just finished praying, and told him that Mona's father was still praying. Later Hassan, a devout Muslim, told Mona how impressed he had been to find his future father-in-law at prayer. We went that night to read the Fatiha at Fatahiyya's house. Her mother told us: "I hope you don't come back again; you drank all my tea, even the extra tea I brought when Um Ali came to visit."

The next morning, Mona had planned to spend the day at my sister's house in Imbaba. I told her not to go. What if Hassan should come? And sure enough, by the time Mona had dressed, Hassan had arrived. I was just coming out of the water closet and I saw someone. He came right up the stairs and made himself right at home; I did not recognize him at first. He stayed and we all ate a big lunch.

After Hassan left, I went to tell Fatahiyya about his visit, so she would not think that I was doing something behind her back. Why, I had even asked him when he came, why he came without Fatahiyya and Nawwal. He said that he had no use for them. When I went to Fatahiyya's, I found the door open but I knocked anyway, as I always have ever since her mother complained about visitors who burst right in. I knocked and Fatahiyya called out: "Come in, the door is open." I told her that I knocked to be socially proper. Fatahiyya was standing in the middle of the room, and she slipped her melaya liff around her as I entered. Nawwal was also there. I asked if she were on her way out. She said yes.

I told Fatahiyya and the nurse that Hassan had visited, and they said that they had seen him pass in the lane, carrying a big bag. I said that he had brought nothing. They asked if I fed him lunch. I said I didn't even give him tea. That way, if Fatahiyya says to him: "Mahrusa didn't even feed you," and he answers: "Why, she gave me a big lunch," Fatahiyya will be embarrassed ("caught from here and from there").

The two women were leaving to give a patient an injection. Fatahiyya's mother told them: "Do not pass by Um Mona's house." When we reached my lane, I said to them, "Either you visit me now or I will never set my foot in your house again." They came up. As we sat talking, Nawwal said that they wanted sixty pounds each for their role in Mona's engagement. I would have given them ten pounds each without their asking, but when they demanded so much as if it were their right, I changed my mind and gave them nothing. Later on Fatahiyya asked me to give the nurse a little something to satisfy her, but I have not seen her since. Nawwal, the nurse, advised me to ask Hassan for a big bride price with extra furnishings and dresses. I responded: "Are we going to sell our daughter? Didn't we once spend three years entertaining a potential groom and throw him out in the end when he proved worthless?"

I sent my daughter Azza to buy *kefta*, and just as she returned with it, Hassan arrived with a big box of candy and several kilos of grapes. He asked, why the kefta, and I responded that it was for my two guests. I stood here by the bed, and watched as the two women exchanged glances. They ate very little. At one point, Nawwal took Hassan into the other room and, according to what he told me later, claimed that we were going to give them each sixty pounds and asked what he would give.

I asked Mona to serve the candies and grapes, and as she did Hassan told her to shake his hand. He put a watch on it. Mona jokingly asked if people in Saudi Arabia wore watches on their right hand. When my husband returned, I met him in the street to tell him about Hassan's plan to get engaged now. . . . We made the arrangements for the engagement in a few days. Since Hassan was planning to leave for Saudi Arabia in fifteen days, we allowed Mona to go out with him, with the children [as chaperones]. I wanted him to go and return happy, not upset. He visited every day until he left.

What about your relation with Fatahiyya, given that you paid her nothing?

I have visited her twice, and have not seen her since. I went to condole her when her maternal aunt died. Fatahiyya asked me if I wanted tea. I answered no, that I had just drunk some. She responded: "So, you don't drink tea with us?" I said no, that

I would if I wanted it, but that I had just had tea. My second
visit was to greet Fatahiyya's mother since she had been in the
village when I condoled Fatahiyya. They treated me poorly. I
don't see Fatahiyya anymore. She comes to call on an old woman
who lives right around the corner from me, and they go together
to pray, but she does not even look my way.

Mahrusa's narrative recalls minute social details of visits and
hospitality in order to index social developments. Baladi social
practices of sending for someone, of signaling relations by visiting or
not visiting, and of hospitality (offering/not offering food;
entering/not entering doors; coming upstairs to visit/staying in the
lane) redound throughout the account. Mahrusa represents herself as
socially impeccable, and Fatahiyya as socially improper. Mahrusa
forces hospitality of kefta on Fatahiyya and Nawwal and she
visits Fatahiyya and then her mother to pay condolences so that no
one can say that she was the one to break off relations with them.
She also admits to planting misinformation about her hospitality in
hopes of embarrassing Fatahiyya. Fatahiyya, on the other hand,
does not want to visit or eat and her mother even begrudges Mahrusa
a cup of tea.

Whether or not the visits, gifts, and meals occurred just as
Mahrusa described, the details of her account of hospitality are a
perfect mirror image of social relations. Mahrusa presents her
two women friends as greedy, and uses their avarice to justify
her nonpayment. Poorer baladi people are not shy to ask for
tips, particularly from outsiders such as Hassan. That Mahrusa
spoke openly of these requests indicates how common "pay offs"
are in baladi society. This is one subject about which it was
difficult to collect information because it was so sensitive. I might
walk into a clinic examining room and see the pile of piasters a
nurse was collecting but be told that they accepted no tips. I
sensed that much money passed hands for strategic information
about jobs or for assistance in the bureaucracy, but I could never
confirm this.

Mahrusa's story highlights the power of serendipity,
transforms an ordinary social event into a tale of a heroine and hero,
and conveys mixed emotions of a family both sorry that a daughter
will be taken far away and happy that the daughter will have
opportunities. Mona might never have met Hassan if Fatahiyya
had not started to feel guilty, and if Hassan had not visited one last
day to the seamstress. The timing of Hassan's meeting with Mona is
providential; the seamstress delayed her invitation, and by the
time Hassan met Mona he had tired of the petty, made-up girls of

the quarter. Serendipity is a popular baladi theme; things "happen" because people meet by accident, because someone falls sick, and so on.

Just as Mahrusa's narrative critiques Fatahiyya in the parlance of hospitality, so it praises Mona and Hassan in typical baladi idioms of authenticity and piety. To be baladi is to be authentic, and Mona's true beauty was natural. To be baladi is to be savvy and independent; Mona was feisty and refused to pander to Hassan. In fact, Mona's mother had to struggle to keep Mona from going to Imbaba the day after she and Hassan met. Even when Hassan presented her a watch, Mona poked fun at him and did not ingratiate herself with profuse thanks. Hassan was religious and patient. He was pleased to find Mona's parents praying; he returned several times to the seamstress's house.

Mona is presented as a kind of baladi Cinderella, a heroine who epitomizes natural baladi beauty without cosmetics, sitting next to afrangi-like, made-up young women of the neighborhood. Hassan is a hero in his religious devotion; much as Prince Charming overcame the stepsisters' plotting to rescue Cinderella, so Hassan by sheer dint of the number of visits to the seamstress, finally defeats the nurse in her efforts to keep him from Mona—who has in the meantime stayed home and cooked like a wretched Cinderella.

Mona's own engagement narrative differs little from her mother's, except for her elaboration on her independence. She related it after her marriage the next summer. To hear Mahrusa tell it, men have little or nothing to do with marriage partner selection. Mona's account is short—she squeezed it in while we drank coffee near the Hussain mosque while we waited for her husband to return from Friday noon prayers.

> I was invited to visit this seamstress that we know, but I was having my period and was reluctant to go anywhere. However, there were people there—not my husband's family, but friends—that I wanted to see, so I decided to kill two birds with one stone and go. When I arrived, I found girls all dressed up with fancy makeup; I was in my melaya liff. I wondered why they were all there, and asked the seamstress; she said, "Oh, there's nothing." Then later I met Hassan and sat on the balcony. I wanted to leave, but my friends said to wait. And in the end Hassan said he wanted me. The seamstress wasn't happy because she had wanted him to marry someone else; so she said no, that he couldn't possibly want me. When Hassan wanted to go ask my father for my hand, the seam-

stress said that he would not be home; then Hassan went and found my father praying the evening prayer. He was very impressed.

Hassan said: "Let's read the Fatiha," and we did. The next morning I wanted to visit my aunt in Imbaba, but my mother asked what if Hassan should drop by? By the time I had dressed, he had arrived, and he sat with us and ate lunch. Then I wanted to go to Imbaba. My mother told me no, what if he comes back! Then two sets of guests came, which prevented me from going anywhere. And then Hassan returned with candy for everyone, as well as a watch for me, which the seamstress protested was for her. Hassan said to the seamstress: "Are you my wife? Why should I bring you a watch?" The seamstress tried to make trouble and to tell Hassan that I didn't want him, so we decided to become engaged so that no one could talk. I bought material that cost three pounds a meter for a dress; I found it prettier than the material he chose for five pounds a meter. The material cost eighteen pounds and the flowers cost seven pounds. The seamstress shop where my sister Suad works sewed the dress for me in two days for twelve pounds. People thought that I rented the dress since it was sewn so fast.

By her account, Mona disdained matchmaking and refused to be completely squelched by Hassan. Nevertheless, she does not dwell on the decision process about the marriage, and one can only assume that she might have used a veto if she felt strongly. By her mother's account, Mona had already rejected one suitor.

Mona's parents realized some material advantages from Mona's marriage, although they did not feel they had "sold" their daughter to an outsider. Rather, they saw the financial contributions of their new son-in-law as a kind of salvation that meant such benefits as the installation of electricity and pilgrimage to Mecca for both parents. When I saw Mahrusa after her return from the Mecca pilgrimage, she was full of the tales of life in Saudi Arabia:

We were in a boat for three days. Toward the end, we became ill because there was a storm and the boat tossed and turned. The boat crew joked with us and claimed that Pharonic spirits caused the boat to rock so much. They said that so we wouldn't be afraid. The doctors came around and told us not to drink lemon juice because that would only made us sicker. They gave us some

pills that did the trick, but by the next time the doctors made
their rounds, they had run out of the pills.

I paid the Egyptians who organized the tour or I would not
have gotten permission to go to Saudi Arabia. But after I arrived
I stayed with my son-in-law. It would have been better if I had
stayed with the group because Hassan wouldn't let me go out
unless I was all veiled and in his car. . . . On the ninth day of the
month of the Haj we went to Mt. Arafat. Then we went to
Muzdalah where we stoned each of the three devils seven times
three days in a row. . . . Then we went to Mena, and then to
Medina where we stayed in a tent for seven days. Hassan would
go out and get us food.

Mahrusa discovered her son-in-law's limits. Mona's life in Saudi
Arabia was not all she had fantasized. Mona had told us she would
have a maid and be free to dawdle with her adoring children. She
would have a car to whisk her about. Pictures she sent her parents
confirmed the car and the—presumably lovable, certainly chubby—
children. Mahrusa said her daughter complained that it was hard
to "keep help." Mona had been determined not to live a cloistered
life like Saudi women. In her pictures she was swathed in Saudi
clothes, but her face was never veiled—at least to our camera. There
is no doubt that Mona's life was more comfortable in Saudi Arabia
than in Bulaq. But she was also more restricted. Mahrusa told us:

While I was in Saudi Arabia, my son-in-law Hassan made me
veil almost like a Saudi woman, and would allow me to go out
only in the car. During the pilgrimage everything was covered
except my face; it was naked, so to speak, as was Mona's. But we
could keep our faces uncovered only because Mona told her
husband, "Do you want them to think that I am Saudi? There is
nobody here who knows us; I should be able to go with my face
unveiled." That's my Mona: always speaking up!

This narrative fragment brings the narrative cycle full circle.
Mona remains the baladi heroine. Hassan, always an outsider but
initially resembling the devout, ideal baladi man, here begins to
fall from grace and to appear like the afrangi with their attention
to looks. To retain some freedom of dress, Mona appeals to her
husband's elitism—his foreign wife should not look Saudi. Mahrusa
valorizes Mona as the immigrant escaped from the burden of
everyday Egyptian life. The story of Mona and Hassan is a kind of
ballad of baladi life. To be baladi is to retain one's authenticity
above all, and Mona does just that.

Virginity: First-Night Trauma

Marriage can be traumatic for any bride, but particularly so in a society where the wedding night symbolizes the union of two families and proof of the honor of the bride's family. At the beginning of this chapter, Ihsan criticized her in-laws for "selling" their daughter to a Jordanian, and implied that trendy Egyptians had abandoned the ritual exhibit of virginity on the wedding night when traditionally the midwife, and sometimes the spouse, produced blood with digital penetration. Modern couples may forego the ritual, but Egyptian women who are not virgins at marriage still besmirch the family honor. In the past such a woman might have been killed by her family to expunge the dishonor, but even today the pressure for virginity remains strong. The Egyptian feminist physician Nawwal Saadawi has written of the personal crisis that afflicts a woman who is socially chaste but biologically not a virgin.

> I went with her [a patient who had been accused of not being a virgin at birth] to her father's house and explained the situation . . . that his daughter was a virgin still, and that her hymen was elastic and would not tear until she delivered her first child. The father was astonished when he listened to this technical account. He hit one fist against the other and cried out in anger, "This means that my daughter was wronged" (Saadawi 1976:3, passage translated by D. Bowen).

Although there are few honor killings of nonvirgin daughters these days in Egypt, one that occurred in the home village of my friend Fatima while I was in Egypt was dramatic. I had met Fawzi's new bride when I went to the village with Fatima, and was surprised to hear from Fatima a few weeks after our return that she had died. On a return visit, Fatima settled back for a long chat, saying "Did you know that Fawzi's wife was not really sick?" Who could do anything but listen spellbound after such a verbal frame for a story?

> When Suad married Fawzi, she had "something in her stomach." Everything went fine on their wedding night, because Suad produced blood. But the next night, Fawzi woke up and said: "What's that! I hear something. There is something moving." Then he began to examine the bed and his wife, and he said, "What's this! I feel something moving in your stomach." Suad said she had a stomachache. Then Fawzi asked to look at her stomach and found it very big and he said, "No, it can't be just a stomachache." Then Suad said, "You did this to me." And he said, "How could I have done it? I hardly spoke a few words

to you since we became engaged." Then he took her to her father, and she told her father about the three men who had slept with her.

Her family took her to the doctor's clinic and they opened her stomach. She was eight months pregnant and they took out the baby. If the mother lived, she lived; if she did not, it was just as well. They threw the child in a big garbage can. After all, it was a bastard child.

Poor Fawzi, he is a very good person, and he could have complained and taken all the dowry, but he said nothing.

Even while recounting this sad tale, Fatima's wry sense of humor led her to add sound effects of what Fawzi heard in bed. Fatima appeared sad about Suad's death, and later that day said: "Would that Zakiyya's new baby girl had died rather than Suad, for the baby had not yet begun a life."

However, the cultural expectation that a bride be a virgin was strong in Fatima's tale and although Fatima and the women in the village appeared melancholy, all said that Suad should have known better. A ten-year-old girl told me one day many months later: "If someone suggested that [sexual relations] to me, I would say 'You impolite thing,' and hit him. If I ever acted 'that way' my mother would beat me. Even to be with boys is shameful. If one steals while one is young, one grows up that way."

Traditional Egyptian women joke together about sex. When they cook bread, they sometimes make explicit replicas of female and male parts from raw dough; they never bake the models but they chuckle over them. However, when women are with their husbands, they display modesty and reticence—particularly on their wedding night. A few months after Suad died, Fatima's sisters-in-law in Menoufiyya were sifting flour. As the women became whiter and more ghostlike from flour dust, and as afternoon shadows lengthened across the room, the women fell into a kind of punchy "slumber party" camaraderie. Talk turned to men and to sex. Zakiyya, rolling on the floor with laughter at her sister-in-law's story, offered her own:

After my wedding, we consummated the marriage in the same room in which we now sleep. I was scared and tried to find a window so I could jump out! Ahmad was patient and just laughed. My father-in-law kept pounding on the door to see what had happened. Finally my mother-in-law and my aunt came in and held me and Ahmad used his finger with a piece of gauze which was bloodied. My father displayed it when people brought money, and then my family took it and washed it. My sister-in-law was de-virginized by a midwife.

That night I was embarrassed, and could not sleep, so I played with the embroidery on the sheet. After a while, I calmed down and Ahmad told me to take off my clothes, but I only took off my outer dress; then he took off his clothes, but that big thing scared me so much that he put his clothes back on and just laughed. You should know [directing her words toward me] that when a man starts to play with you he will go for your breasts and see if that gets you excited, and then he will work his way around. Finally, I relaxed, but the next morning I was embarrassed to dress in front of him.

I came out of the room the next day and there were many people going back and forth and coming into my room to congratulate me. I was hungry but I was shy to eat in front of them. Then I told my mother-in-law that I was hungry and she brought me four pieces of meat with sauce and I ate it all.

After a few more tidbits on marital bliss by other women in the room, talk turned to the dead bride Suad. Zakiyya led off:

Come and I will tell you a lesson. When Suad married Fawzi, she was seven months pregnant. The family said there was blood the wedding night, but do you remember how the day of the wedding she was wearing a tight dress with a full skirt, walking along trying to pull her stomach in, with her rear sticking way out? When Fawzi was lying on top of her, the baby started to move around. Fawzi took a long knife and said, "Tell me who did this to you, or I'll cut your stomach and put you on the road and say a truck ran over you." Suad told him, "so and so." Then they took her to the clinic for an abortion. She would have recovered, but her father's brother said that he would kill her himself. Her father agreed and one morning they put poison in her tea.

[Here Zakiyya's sister-in-law chimed in:] It is shameful to do what she did. . . . The man is not to blame. He is like a dog who comes when you call him.

In the flour-sifting session, the women had a good time discussing sex, but clearly any rowdiness outside of an all-female group was unacceptable. Zakiyya's account of her nuptial night demonstrated culturally appropriate reticence and modesty. Likewise, her account of Suad's death offered no critique of the family's right to kill an errant daughter. Her sister-in-law went even farther to characterize men as sex-driven creatures who are not responsible for their actions. Another day during my visit, village women washing wheat in the irrigation ditch mused that even a young girl knows the facts of life, and wondered how Suad's pregnancy could have happened: they then rushed to speculate which in-law might have forced himself on Suad. The implication that she might have had no choice was the only recognition I heard that the matter might have been out of Suad's hands.

Fatima's husband Omar had his version of Suad's story, which he recounted for me one day several months later in Bulaq as we sat waiting for Fatima to return from selling her cheese. We had been talking about an impending marriage in the same village, when suddenly Omar looked hard at me and lowered his voice:

> You know that bride Suad who died awhile ago in the village? She did not die from an operation; they poisoned her. Don't believe anyone else when they tell you what happened. I know the truth. Fawzi took Suad to her father, saying: "I do not want Suad hurt, but I will have nothing to do with her. Take her and give me a *feddan* of land and all will be forgotten."
>
> Suad's father told Fawzi he would think about it, and to go home. After Fawzi left, Suad's uncle convinced the father that they should kill Suad, so they put poison in her lunch, and when she became ill, they took her to the regional clinic to be examined. But it was just for appearance because, for heaven's sake, they could not let the clinic staff examine her there and discover that she was pregnant. The family honor would have been ruined. So they took her and brought her back to die in the house. Fawzi was beside himself with sorrow when he heard.

It is clear that the three versions of Suad's death are different, and I can't be sure of the true version. Each version reflects cultural realities for the teller, and all three convey the message that it is the woman who is responsible for her virginity. Fatima did not mention poisoning either because she did not yet know that part of the story or because she wanted to protect me. The women were sorrowful about the death, and Omar was even angry, but they also pitied the groom left without a wife. Omar's account presents Fawzi in the most sympathetic light. It is possible that Suad died from an attempted abortion, although it is also possible that her family preferred to keep her pregnancy a secret and that the clinic trip was a cover-up for a poisoning.

Sometimes, a tragedy similar to honor killing occurs when a despondent bride trapped in an unbearable match kills herself. One day at Zainab's, a neighbor who stopped to chat remarked: "The girl who poured gas on herself and lit herself on fire is the daughter of Um Hamid, who lives in the lane of your uncle." Zainab responded:

> Oh, her. I have seen her being beaten many times by her family because she would not go back to her husband, someone three times her age. Once she was almost hanging from the window to escape them. It is probably better that she burned herself, although suicide is forbidden in Islam. According to Islam, someone who poisons herself holds the poison in her hand the day of resurrection and anyone who throws herself from a mountain will never enter heaven.

The new bride had lived by the Behig clinic. Zainab immediately knew the place: "Yes, I passed by that house and they told us that a butane container blew up and killed the new bride. But I know that they were only covering up, as the neighbors told us that the young bride had been married off by her greedy family to an old merchant."

Marriage is an important vehicle of social mobility for some women, and Mahrusa's and Mona's narratives point up the role of baladi social capital and baladi conventions in this process. Theirs is also a story of international labor migration, for after Mona's marriage, two of her brothers—sponsored in part by Mona's husband—went to Saudi Arabia to work. Conclusions from the above cases of bride death and suicide should be guarded. There are no figures available to make a case one way or another, but family honor killings are rare, and much rarer than suicides from unhappy marriages. Baladi women can be ribald and disdainful of men, including future and present husbands, when they are with other women. Their talk somewhat resembles that of Western women, but on two things they stand apart. Once men are present, women assume a timid decorum. They do not question social mores that hold a woman's chastity responsible for family honor. I suspect that in their hearts they may know that traditional Egyptian sexual mores represent a double standard. But that was never expressed by any of the baladi or rural women I knew.

The Body Political: Social Healing

As Foucault (1980) has contended that the body is a template for social and political processes, so baladi discourse on health, fertility, or general well-being provides an important perspective on the baladi sociopolitical context. Further, baladi (and other) women's narratives may be situated at the private-public intersection as women strategize to enroll their child in the right school or to find a job for a relative via their informal social networks.

Two favorite historical references that recur in baladi tales are the "good old days" of opulence under the English during World War II and the reforms under Nasser, who sought equality for all. The contradiction between these two references does not bother anyone. Cosmopolitan medicine was introduced to Egypt by Muhammad Ali, who founded the prestigious Qasr el 'Aini medical school in the early nineteenth century. By the time the British arrived in 1886, Western medicine was well established. The British introduced public works clinics in traditional areas of Cairo; several still operate today, more than thirty years after Egyptian independence. Older Egyptians speak in glowing terms of the days of shiny British medical equipment as if the forceps and scalpels were instruments of salvation. Tales of British munificence during World War II abound; a popular one relates what it was like to wash clothes for the British: "By the time you finished washing, you had a mound of pound notes that had been left in their pockets." Another favorite tale describes the British barracks giving away kilos and kilos of meat. One friend reminisced about her operation in Kitchener Hospital where "everyone was dressed in sparkling white and they rolled me into a shiny operating room."

Baladi Well-Being and Afrangi Politics

One day at Shaykh Ali, as neighbor women drank and talked about plans for independence day, Miriam reminisced about taking her children to Nasser's tomb the previous independence day. There "people" had tried to buy her daughter, Nadia. The soldiers had pushed the people away, but not before they gave Nadia a pin with Nasser's name on it in English. Then Miriam, primed by her account about Nadia, continued with a tale of the wonders of Nasser. Her account reveals the mix of private and public (children, education, and clothes versus politics, armies, and occupiers) so typical in women's everyday discourse. It is, after all, women who usually procure health care, education, international remittances, and security benefits from the official bureaucracy to support their families. Her account also divides the world between insiders (baladi) interested in personal welfare and outsiders (afrangis) interested in political manipulation.

Haven't you heard about the guard who saw Nasser come up and pray the morning prayer in his white gellabeyya in which he was buried? They took the guard to the hospital and said he was crazy, but Khalid, the son of Nasser, said the guard was perfectly sane because his [Khalid's] father was a *nabi* [prophet]. Nasser's family gave the guard money for his children. They had him medically examined and found him perfectly sane. Nasser performed other miracles too.

What?

He took destitute people and gave them clothes. Nasser said that everyone should be educated. Before his days, the school took ten pounds for clothes and imported books and only the rich children graduated. But now there is knowledge for everyone so that one doesn't sell onions on the street while the other has a desk job. Nasser nationalized all of the *pashas* and laid down the steps that Sadat [followed].

In the beginning there was a man named Muhammad Naguib who ruled about two years, but he was all politics and they got rid of him, and put him in a prison in Helwan where he still lives today.

Has Nasser performed any other miracle like leaving his tomb to pray?

He has performed many miracles such as providing food for everyone and helping people find houses. . . . The Virgin Mary performed many miracles. An angel told her she would deliver a baby, and her mother told her her father would kill her, so Joseph the carpenter offered to take her away. Three midwives came to touch her, to see if she was pregnant. One touched her legs and aged; one touched her arm and aged; one touched her eyes and aged. Mary and Joseph left Palestine for Bethlehem, and found a place in a sheep stable. She didn't give birth like other women. The child came out of her right side. The man's sheep increased from ten to a thousand. Then as they were fleeing and the "people"—the English army—were coming, she saw a man sowing watermelon; she told him that if people came looking for a baby boy, to tell them he passed that way while the man was sowing. So the English army came that evening, by which time the watermelon had already matured, which usually takes four months, but this was a miracle. So when the farmer told them the baby boy had passed by when the farmer was sowing the seeds, he wasn't lying.

The Virgin Mary performed many miracles, as did Miri Girgis al-Romani [a Coptic saint]. They used to throw one girl a year to the mermaids in the Nile at the time of the yearly

flood. One year the lottery fell on the king's only daughter, and
his wife prayed to the gods, but the king petitioned Miri Girgus.
The girl, dressed in gold and diamonds, was left in a kiosk by
the river for the mermaids to come and eat. But Miri Girgus came
and was not afraid, and he killed a crocodile with his weapon
and it was so heavy none of the men would carry it. But the girl
carried it through the town with ease. This was the Pharonic
time; after that, they threw statues into the river.

Miriam's narrative commingles the private world of the family,
education, and work with the public world of politics, revolutions,
and nationalizations. It juxtaposes the secular realm of guards and
occupations with the sacred world of the Virgin Mary and Jesus.
Miriam creates a political saint in the domestic sphere of clothes,
food, and education. In so doing she transforms historical discourse
into tales of native saints and sinful occupiers.

These saints and sinners replicate the insider (baladi):outsider
(afrangi) opposition. Nasser, an authentic Egyptian and insider who
knew the people's real problems became a kind of prophet in the
eyes of Miriam, herself a Copt. Miriam's worldview mixes Islam
and Christianity; the good people are the genuine Muslims or
Christians, those who serve. Small wonder that when she casts
about for a word to describe the pursuers of Mary, Joseph, and Jesus
that she chooses the English army as a ready-made example of
outsiders and oppressors. For Miriam, both the British army and
Muhammad Naguib confined themselves to "politics," and ignored
the private, the domestic, the *real* problems of everyday life.
Miriam's cultural performance sums up the everyday and the
baladi: one cannot be a saint, or for that matter a successful secular
leader, without paying attention to the private, the mundane.

Miriam's reference of historic figures set the scene for another
personal narrative by another Shaykh Ali neighbor, Mahrusa, who
intercalated her story in the flow of personal narratives. Mahrusa
reminisces about her children's childhood while commenting on the
afrangi, foreign, occupier, British world. Note the domestic concerns
of nutrition and health, and the public institutions of clinics and
aid.

When I had my next-to-youngest, Ahmad, birth control pills
were not available, and when they finally became available I
was already eight months pregnant with him. Before I could
start taking them, when Ahmad was one and one-half years old,
I became pregnant with my youngest, my daughter Azza. When
Azza was six months old, my sister asked me why I had not

started the pills. I told her that I heard that they dried up milk. But my sister convinced me to take them, so I did and, sure enough, my milk dried up, so I bought formula. I was already weak and the pills made it worse, so I went to the clinic to buy the pills that sold there for a shilling because those were less debilitating than the yellow ones I purchased at the pharmacy.

One day I went to the Ministry clinic with my two youngest children, and the staff said that there was no treatment that day but that there was free flour. They gave me a paper. I took it home and threw it under my pillow. [Women store their money and official papers under their pillow or mattress.] But later I looked at it and saw it was for two big bags of flour, ten kilos of milk, and several kilos of ghee. But I needed to go to Sayyidna Zainab to receive it. My husband was against the idea and said it would be too much trouble. But finally a woman upstairs took Mona and went to fetch the goods. They ended up helping to line up all the women waiting and by the time they reached the window they received only a portion of what was written, but then who can complain about free food? (Early 1985b:176)

Later, in a more apocryphal version of this narrative, Mahrusa said the neighbor returned so laden with goods that she had to rent a horse-drawn cart, and Mahrusa gave portions to each of the neighbors. This baladi theme of the opulence of the old days mirrors the ambivalence baladis feel toward the afrangi, toward an historical occupying force that was simultaneously oppressor-occupier and benefactor-supplier of, here, medical technology. Another day, Mahrusa regaled us with a tale of British clinics, where the ambivalence about accepting afrangi largess remains, but here coupled with baladi skill at dissembling.

My relatives told me that the clinic was for the very poor, so I wore a house dress with long sleeves to cover my gold bracelets. My daughter Mona was so clean that the British clinic nurses liked her. The nurses slapped women whose children had pacifiers and told them that this was bad for babies, so I hid Mona's pacifier inside my dress. The nurse said that Mona was very clean and that I should bring her every week. Mona's eyes hurt her, which is why I took her that day. I said, "Fine, I will return, just do not hit me," and I took Mona several more times to get her eyes cleaned. The other women did not understand why I received all that attention. (Early 1985b:176)

Mahrusa shines here as she presents herself as she perceives the British want to see her, just as in stories of the savvy baladi women duping the dimwitted afrangi office worker. The equivalent of the afrangis in the medical sphere are, of course, the Egyptian Ministry of Health professionals who now staff all the slightly tarnished English clinics. Baladi women constantly remark on the neglect of clinics, as in the birth story of the Nubian woman.

The Infertility Syndrome of Mushahara

A baladi Egyptian woman works hard to keep her family healthy, in part because of the social capital at stake; her children will care for her in her old age. For her, infertility is not only a physiological but also a social problem. This is why so much ritual and social energy is expended to control reproductive powers—both as a commodity of honor as in virginity and as a resource as in fertility. The baladi cultural syndrome *mushahara*, infertility or insufficient lactation, is both physiological and social—caused by improper action (outlined in Chapter 4). Mushahara is the body politic writ individual. A woman with fertility problems is a woman with social problems. At the end of this section Feriayla recounts her tale of frustration with fertility—a tale that integrates her critique of public health and government services in her personal saga of infertility.

The life forces symbolized in the circumcision and funeral processions already described are closely linked to the syndrome of mushahara. These two observances are loaded with cultural restrictions that ritually contain the potent forces associated with procreation (fertility) and infertility. Neither someone who has attended a funeral nor a recently excised girl or circumcised boy should enter the room of a recently married or recently delivered woman.

Baladi ethnophysiology draws many connections among dimensions of fertility in mushahara. An unexcised girl is in a liminal stage. She cannot become fertile unless she is excised, but at the time of excision she should be a premenstrual virgin. Not yet fertile, she can nevertheless affect others' fertility by touching or passing in front of them. The woman afflicted by mushahara may in turn cure herself of infertility by placing male circumcision blood or her own virginal blood from her wedding night (which she has saved on cloth) on a vaginal suppository. This blood is potent enough to reverse infertility.

A popular cure for infertility is to vow at the shrine of Siddi Qubba. Fatima's daughter Nabila joined the shrine trip reported in

Chapter 4, but alas, by the time I left Egypt neither shrine vows nor clinic treatment had changed Nabila's luck. Her sister Feriayla was also desperate to conceive. In August 1974, when Fatima still lived in the Shaykh Ali house, I found her daughter Feriayla on a visit to her mother from Mohalla Kubra to recover from an operation for sterility. On that particular day, I wrote in my notes that Feriayla "went into a long, virtually unrequested monologue which detailed her trials in the hospital." Feriayla yearned for sympathy and moral support. She had had this operation before, but her husband, unwilling to wait the requisite forty days for intercourse, had "ruined" it. Subsequently he married a second wife, who bore him children. Pregnancy was on everyone's mind that day. A neighbor was pregnant, and Fatima had just said to her: "Are you fantasizing, experiencing food cravings associated with pregnancy? Gaze at our foreign friend [myself] so that your girl will look like her." Feriayla, not pregnant, seized the opportunity of a lull in conversation to express her feelings of frustration in a poignant narrative.

> I have been married for more than twelve years. In the beginning, I had a miscarriage at three months, and have not been able to become pregnant since. My husband threatened to divorce me if I didn't have this fertility operation. I had one before, but it didn't work. This time I went to the Spinning Company hospital in Mohalla, but they did not seem to know what to do to cure me. So I went to a Ministry of Health hospital. There they took me upstairs, where they said to come back the next day. They took x-rays, and told me that I had a growth in my womb that should be removed if I wanted to have children, but that the operation might be difficult. I agreed to the operation. I stayed in the hospital for sixteen days; then I rested for two weeks at home. Then I came here to Cairo to stay with my mother and recuperate since I was very lonely at home alone.
>
> When I had the operation I lay on a big table with a mirror hanging overhead. There were three men and three women looking down at me. I fell when they were lifting me up on the table; I asked them to bring me water. The anesthesia was very strange. When I was in the hospital the head doctor came to see me every day. He was a very good man and seemed to know what he was doing. But the nurses were awful. When I complained to the doctor about their care, one nurse refused to do anything for me. [The nurse was angry that a patient had dared to complain.] She would not bring me a clean gellabeyya, even

when I gave her a five-piaster tip. Once on the way to the toilet I had an accident and I gave the nurse some money to clean it up.

Every day in the hospital, my husband brought me food when he finished work. He is a better cook than I am; he taught me to cook when we married. Once the doorman allowed me to leave the hospital and get some food. Once I felt very tired and they took my blood pressure and listened to me with the stethoscope. The doctor wanted to give me a shot to make me sleep, but I would not let him. I had heard the stories, after all, about how they sometimes give you a shot and you never wake up.

Feriayla sighed and settled back after she finished her personal narrative. The women in the audience had clucked with sympathy along the way and Feriayla had received the support she craved. Her account packaged a critique of government health services with a personal frustration. But daily life is not only marriage and health. It is also business—be it international labor migration or local credit and vending.

Livelihoods: Migrants, Workshops, and Merchants

The International Link

Many Bulaqi women have a husband, child, or other relative working abroad, and some women travel themselves to work as domestics or to procure goods to sell door-to-door back in Egypt. One day, my Menoufiyya peasant friend Zakiyya mused:

When I married, my husband gave me a gold necklace with seven strands. My father-in-law needed money to buy the corner lot where we now grow corn, and he asked me to sell my necklace or to borrow money from my father. My father had no money so I sold my necklace for thirty-two pounds. We used this, plus the money from selling a mule, to buy the land. When my father-in-law received money, he returned the thirty-two pounds and we went in with a relative on a water buffalo for a hundred pounds. Every year we sold a calf from the buffalo and split the money. Then the water buffalo died, and I bought sheep with my money. Then I put my money into the tea and cigarette shop that we operate out of our house. I bought a gold necklace for twenty pounds but it was stolen last year while we were picking cotton. I told my husband that we should open an actual grocery to try to make ends meet in the household, but a friend of his who was already in Saudi Arabia sent for him to take a construction job, and now he sends back every few months more than we made from selling a calf once a year!

Zakiyya's case is typical: a couple engages in petty vending, such as cigarettes and tea, and realizes that with an enlarged business venture or someone working abroad, they can supplement their income, keep up with rising costs, and afford a few luxuries such as a television. Much of international work is based on personal contacts, such as a seamstress who went on pilgrimage and met some Saudis. According to the story, they later came to visit her in Bulaq and were so pleased with her sewing that they brought her to Saudi Arabia to sew for them. Such women are probably glorified domestics, but they can save money that they can invest in further work in Egypt.

Often women mobilize social networks to help to find a job for male relatives with contractors seeking day laborers for Libya or with hotel owners seeking staff for the Gulf. Most often the work offered is manual and unskilled, but these jobs often pay inflated wages with handsome benefits, and can be secure. The family of the person who works abroad receives money orders and checks. To cash them, a woman must have a personal identity card and negotiate signatures and approvals. Widows, particularly of soldiers killed in combat, must wind through an enormous bureaucracy to receive their benefits. There is no published list of steps; a woman learns by asking. Although the details—drafts, currency conversion, or welfare forms—may be strange to a baladi woman, the process by which she acquires the necessary information is not. Accustomed to continual banter with bystanders—whether about the latest development in the food cooperative or about which check approval to obtain next—the baladi woman forges ahead in the tangle of paperwork by honing her bureaucratic techniques. Wary that afrangi government bureaucrats will obfuscate benefits and "park" papers, women persevere in "pushing" their files.

Baladi families with members working abroad devise various impromptu methods of passing information internationally by word of mouth with other travelers, or by written or recorded message. The traveler carrying the message may be a complete stranger but she or he is greeted like an old friend and grilled by eager family members. Such an event occurred with Mahrusa in the Shaykh Ali house. Her son Ahmad, who worked in Saudi Arabia, sent a letter with a visitor unknown to the family. The traveler, carrying a Samsonite attaché, said that he had just arrived from Jedda yesterday, and had come all this way to say hello. He took a cassette tape and money, which he asked them to count, from his attaché.

Mahrusa: We are so happy to meet you. How is Ahmad?

Visitor: Very well, and he greets you. But he is upset that the last cassette tape you sent contained only the children's voices and not his parents.

Abu Mona [Mahrusa's husband]: Ahmad is not a person for me, is not my son, is nothing. I no longer "recognize" him, nor will I send him any words, nor listen to any words he sends me.

Visitor: Had I known you felt this way, I would not have bothered to come.

Mahrusa: But the children will listen to the tape.

Abu Mona: No one will listen to Ahmad's words. Why, there were the two watches from Port Said for my wife and me. Ahmad took them back. When my wife went to visit, Ahmad took one of the gold chains she had received from her son-in-law and gave it to his [Ahmad's] wife.

[Abu Mona went on detailing incidents where his son had not given what he should to the family. Every time his wife tried to silence him, Abu Mona said "Be careful! Don't silence me!"]

Visitor: Do not be so angry. He is your son after all.

Abu Mona: I have become accustomed to a certain style of life and do not look to my children for support, but it is my right as a father to expect some support from time to time.

Visitor: Maybe Ahmad is spending too much on his wife.

Abu Mona: Ahmad has completely lost himself, and spends everything on his wife, and does not even think of us.

Visitor: Why don't you record something and I can take it to play for Ahmad after the feast? Why don't you listen to the tape I brought from him and see what he has to say before you answer?

Such scenes recur as families seek to settle arguments with distant members via mediation of messengers trapped in the middle; these unlucky messengers often add their own opinions (such as the one above that the son may be overspending on his wife) to try to calm the recipients of their message. Families also seek to embellish the meager information provided through cassettes or letters. (The bulk of Ahmad's cassette, to which the family did finally listen, was Quranic readings with only minimal news.)

Aniyat's husband Ahmad used to return from work at two and nap before going to his second job in a nearby coffeehouse owned by a fellow villager. He worked there until midnight, and was rarely at home except to sleep. To make extra money he had fashioned a cart to rent for ten pounds a month to ice cream vendors by summer and hot chickpea-drink sellers by winter. Eventually, he decided to seek his fortune abroad driving trucks in Saudi Arabia, where he heard people earned good wages, and from where friends returned laden with consumer goods. Aniyat, like many baladi women, learned to process remittances from abroad and to run her house on her own.

Ahmad sent frequent letters to his family from Saudi Arabia after he arrived there and found a job driving trucks. On one of my visits, the children asked eagerly if I wanted to see their father's letters. I agreed—hoping to discover something about the life of a migrant worker. About that I learned little. About the personal discourse of letters—where gender relations predominate, and where affect outweighs content—I learned much. In baladi society, a husband's letters never address his wife by name, although neighbor women may be greeted by name. The letter follows an expected sequence of fond inquiries about children and everyone but the wife. The following is my reconstruction of the letter from Ahmad that his children read to me.

To my honorable son, Muhammad, I send greetings from Saudi Arabia. I also send my greetings to———[here Ahmad wrote all the names of neighbors in the Shaykh Ali house: the man next door, the two bachelors on the landing, the brother of Aniyat who lives upstairs, the Coptic neighbor Miriam's husband, Miriam, Mahrusa's husband, Mahrusa, two women on the ground floor, the landlady Um Ali and her sons, Aniyat's friend Um Sadaq next door and her two sons, and the fiancé of Ahmad's own daughter Badriyya].

I am in good health and I miss all of you and send you my greetings with the birds of the dawn. I look forward to the day when I see you again.

Um Muhammad, be sure you do not join Miriam's money-saving society. Ask Samir to return the electrical tools he borrowed from me. I will bring wonderful things for the children and the house. I will bring Mona a watch. I will bring you a beautiful dress. I send my greetings and I wait anxiously until I will be with you again.

[There was a final paragraph of flowery greetings to the family and to the household.]

Although greetings comprise some two-thirds of Ahmad's letter, he never greets his wife Aniyat by name, and he directs instructions and gift promises to her obliquely as "mother of Muhammad." The letter communicates affect, that Ahmad misses family and friends, but offers little information. One learns nothing about his work. His instructions are the typical ones baladi men repeat even when at home—for example, not to join savings associations that will put the family in debt.

The Workshop Shadow Economy

Baladis may pursue unskilled wage labor abroad, but for skilled workers there are many opportunities in Bulaq. It is a place of hole-in-the-wall workshops, featuring fine carpentry and ironwork; Bulaq also houses large lumber and metal warehouses. Many large creditors like Hamida are bankrolled by husbands with workshops and warehouses. Both the credit system and the workshops are part of the typically baladi "shadow economy" straddling the informal and formal economic sectors. Shops are registered and taxed, but

A Bulaqi seamstress

some transactions (such as provision of raw materials at "black market" rather than government-controlled prices or of specially made spare parts) are informal and personal.

Women enter the workshop economy when their help is needed by the family. Ihlam's two daughters, Ibtisam and Raisa, assumed the supervision of their father's lathe workshop upon his death. They knew enough about soliciting work, keeping books, and supervising workers from the days they spent there with their father to carry on. There was no formal apprenticeship; they had simply hung around enough to absorb operation of the family business. Ihlam spoke of her husband Ibrahim's workshop in the midst of a conversation with neighbor women about children and birth control—a conversation sparked by a recent neighborhood birth:

> Our family is one of few children. I used "pills" [suppositories]. I did not want to have many children, but I was very young and did not know anything when I married. Ibrahim told me about the pills. At that time, he was working for a foreigner in Maaruf Street and the man's wife was using them and so he told me about them. . . . Ibrahim worked as the foreman of the workshop of the foreigner, but he was taking sixty pounds a month [not a bad salary for that time] and this was not enough for us. He smoked and drank a lot and we had a car and used to go out for lunch in Helwan, or in a French restaurant on Fuad Street. So Ibrahim opened his own workshop, a lathing one, here in Shanin Street, with a partner, who now since Ibrahim's death is trying to get the shop for nothing.

Not only the partner, but also a stepbrother and a stepsister had claims on the workshop and, as the competing claims mounted, Ihlam and her daughters began to talk of liquidation and of consulting attorneys. One night, Ihlam and Ibtisam discussed courses of action:

> *Ihlam:* I will not go again to that worthless lawyer Muhammad Fuad, whom I gave a deposit that he now refuses to repay. I had to get a court order to get my money back.
> *Ibtisam:* There are certain procedures for liquidation; a lawyer must be appointed and salaried to watch over the affairs. There must be an escrow. But you must be very careful, because declaring bankruptcy means that the bank deducts all the debts that you owe first, and that means that they put a lien on your house, and then you go looking for a way to live. . . .

Ihlam: Raisa continues to sit supervising the workshop. She
takes no salary because she wants to get rid of the debts of the
workshop. She recently took fifty pounds from her post office
savings to buy a piece for the lathe machine. She is continuing
her father's practice of giving a meal to the workers during
Ramadan. Her half-brother Muhammad sits there doing
nothing every day and takes 1.70 pounds a day as his wage, plus
thirty piasters as his share in the workshop. Raisa's half-sister
takes three pounds a month for her share in the workshop.
    I tell the girls that if they are tired, to go ahead and sell
their share in the workshop, but they do not listen. They want
to settle it all so everyone gets a fair share.

Ihlam and her daughters were thrust into the middle of a
complex court case over the family inheritance, but the daughters
quickly became experts on escrows, liens, and shares. When I
watched Raisa in the workshop, she ordered raw materials, kept
the books, set the tasks for the day, and paced the work of the three
tradesmen and some half dozen apprentices. She was the one who
negotiated prices and delivery schedules—not her half-brother who
had grown up far away from the workshop and had little idea of its
operation.

Creditors and Customers

To have a workshop like Ibtisam's requires substantial capital, but
to become a small scale merchant peddling candy in the street or
cheese from the village requires minimal capital. A big-
time merchant dealing in furniture and clothing for many
customers also needs sizeable capital from work abroad, successful
trade, inheritance, family workshop profits, or a gainfully
employed relative. Although the term *dallala* can mean "door-to-
door" merchant, Bulaqis usually reserve the term for "big-time"
merchant women who are often creditors, and I use it here in that
sense.
    Family problems may originally catapult a woman into business.
A vendor needs only a few pounds to buy some fruit or sweets to sell in
the street. Women who might otherwise never venture into the
informal economic sector will resort to street vending when they are
in dire straits. The wife of a hashish dealer who was imprisoned for
several years, Um Hanafi was forced to support her family. One day
while I was waiting to have a gellabeyya sewn to wear in the
village, I overheard Um Hanafi tell some women how she became a
vendor.

When my husband went to prison, I had no way to support myself, so I began to sell grapes in front of Gala' hospital on 26th of July Street. I continued selling for two years. Let me tell you how rough life was when I worked. I woke at 3 A.M., rode a cart to the wholesale market at Rod el-Farag, bought fruit, and was back by 6 A.M. to pick through and clean the fruit. I sat selling fruit in front of the hospital all day, and returned home in the afternoon so tired that I would sleep at once, laying my head on anything I could find. Then I would wake and look at my watch—a plain one that I had before my husband sent me such a fancy one from Libya—and make tea and dress the children for school before leaving the house again at 3 A.M. In those days my house was very chaotic. I had no time to clean (Early 1993a).

Um Hanafi had no family or friends in Bulaq who could help her when her husband was jailed, so she picked a business that was safe and needed no capital, street vending. She went on to say that her husband had now gone to Libya to work and she would be joining him. It is a sign of her social desperation that she, unlike most women with Egyptian husbands abroad, decided to travel and live with her migrant-laborer husband.

Fatima is a prototypical baladi merchant woman; Chapter 2 covered physical location and movements about the city by such women. Originally from Menoufiyya, Fatima lived in Bulaq with her government-employed husband. She returned to Menoufiyya after a quarrel, at which time she (like Um Hanafi) was pushed into petty food vending. She finally returned to Cairo, where she used her nest egg from vending to market ghee and cheese, on credit, from the weekly market in her hometown. I was never able to learn exactly how much Fatima made from her trade, but she saved enough to marry off her son, at some 250 pounds, and to send him to Saudi Arabia to work there for a few years—nicely rounding out her rural-urban ties with Cairo-Gulf ones. The experience of international labor migration was not all pleasant for Fatima. She fell ill, but her son sent her little support and poured most of it into his own new natal family (Early 1985).

Fatima is a typical example of the women in the informal sector, a category continually underenumerated in national censuses. A Michigan State University survey reports that women comprise the largest number of participants within the food products subsector of the informal economy and that women own and operate 42 percent of the dairies surveyed in two governates (Badr et al. 1982:34–36). Fatima is of course a merchant, not a producer.

Fatima attributes her ability to sell and to provide credit to her schooling.

> I was the only girl in our family who went to school. I used to wear a long blue apron and a scarf around my head, but my brother would take the scarf and roll it up into tight knots because he envied me for being so bright. . . . When we were walking to school my brother would hit me from behind and tell me, "Make yourself dumb like I am in school.". . . When I passed the sixth grade, I needed to take the train to another town but my father didn't allow me to go alone. I was left at home, but after a year or two my husband came and asked to marry me.
>
> If I could not read and write how could I remember the money I collect? I write it down in front of the customer and when they finish paying their bill, I mark it off in front of them.

I examined Fatima's books to try to understand her system. She would write a family name on line one—sometimes repeating the name followed by "for her sister, another customer." The next line would be the number of kilos bought, followed by a total number of

A Bulaqi family, with mother in house gellabeyya and daughter dressed in Islamic muhaggaba style

pounds charged for the lot. Successive lines would mark payments and when the end was close Fatima wrote a number with "remaining" after it. Every week she bought about twenty kilos of ghee and some cheese, and she seemed to make a profit of some twenty to thirty piasters a kilo, netting her four to six pounds a week—not a bad sum at a time when a government employee started at twenty pounds a month. She described the higher price she charged for customers buying on credit not as interest, which is forbidden in Islam, but as follows: "If you gave me your money right away, I could use it to buy more ghee. But this way I must be patient, and you pay me more for my patience."

It was clear in the three years I spent visiting Fatima that her monthly collection of payment from the fifty-plus customers in her notebook was as much a social occasion as a business one. She relished the excuse to visit and told me that her customers "held on to her" and did not let her take her money and leave.

Social relations also formed an important part of the business of another baladi businesswoman, Zainab. Since creditors need help cultivating trustworthy customers (there are no formal "credit checks" in the informal economic sector of baladi credit) and tracking down clients who owe monthly payments, they retain assistants who have the social capital of dense networks of kin and friends. Zainab was such a woman for the creditor Hamida. Zainab spoke of Hamida as her "dear friend"; their relationship, clearly both business and social, was what I have described elsewhere as a "quasi-kin" relation (Early 1977). Such a mixture is typical of patron-client relations in Cairo. When Hamida's son was drafted, Zainab carried a homemade casserole and accompanied Hamida on her search from army camp to army camp. Zainab recruited customers for Hamida, and followed up to extract monthly payments from them. Zainab helped Hamida cook for special occasions. Hamida, in turn, gave Zainab informal commissions on customers and sent Zainab's children special treats on birthdays and feast days.

As Fatima sent her son to work in Saudi Arabia, so the tides of international labor migration and of kinship played roles in Zainab's work as a creditor's assistant. When her husband traveled to Iraq to work as a truck driver, Zainab began to look for a way to supplement her income in between irregular payments from her husband. To save rent, Zainab moved back to live with her parents in Bulaq, where her repertoire of childhood friendships, coupled with her spirited personality and perseverance, made Zainab a successful, sought-after expeditor and assistant. She was respected as a woman of her word and as a good mother. My memory of Zainab is of her talking to neighbors—either hanging out her window or leaning against the door, or setting off to help someone. Zainab's dependence on social capital dictated a highly social life. While part of it was Zainab's personality—she loved the bustle of visiting and finding out the latest news—part of it was also business.

Zainab's work for Hamida was casually arranged, and I was never able to determine how much she earned, but the combination of commissions, gifts, favors, and social contacts clearly made it worth Zainab's while. For instance, Zainab would troop off with a friend to the clothing and furniture markets in Wikalat al-Balah to meet Hamida. The friend might decide on a purchase at the shop of Hamida's business associate and, with Hamida's guarantee to the shop owner, settle the matter. Zainab would collect monthly installments and, as with Fatima, never discuss interest. Rather, Hamida simply stipulated, say, twelve monthly installments of ten pounds each to cover a purchase of one hundred pounds.

One day I went with Zainab, Hamida, and Zainab's neighbor Sherifa to procure a bed for Sherifa. We crossed Bulaq el-Jadid street and went down a lane to a small shop with some chairs for sale. When we first asked for beds, the sales clerk said to come back Friday, but the owner soon appeared, recognized Hamida, and took us to a nearby building to see two small storerooms of furniture. Sherifa found the bed she wanted and we returned to the shop to discuss payment. The conversation between the owner and the women was full of exclamations about the quality of the furniture; as Sherifa zeroed in to look at a bed the owner enhanced the auspiciousness of the moment by saying, "Look, but first pray to the Prophet." The merchant-creditor discourse was packed with mutual assurances of the best assistance and purchase terms possible.

Hamida: How much is the bed if we pay in full?

Owner: Twenty-one pounds, but if you buy in installments, it is twenty-five pounds.

Hamida: Come now, we are old associates and I have brought you many customers.

Owner: But this is a solid bed, not like the ones you will find down the lane.

[Here there are several bargaining rounds.]

Owner: The final price: four pounds down and two pounds a month, for ten months.

[The owner produces an agreement and fills in the blanks. Sherifa signs and Hamida countersigns.]

Sherifa: I will write my address but you will never need to know it because my payments will always be early.

Hamida: See the good clients I bring you.

Store clerk: But Rida, one of your other customers, still owes us her pound from this month.

Hamida: Why didn't you come to me? I would have made sure you received it.

After we left the shop, a lively comparison of stores ensued.

Zainab: This shop is far better than "Ideal" at which we had planned to buy. I have more confidence in them.

[She had earlier commented how dusty the bed was because it was "parked" in this shop unlike the fast moving merchandise of Ideal. Once we had left Hamida, Sherifa compared her with another dallala, Karima.]

Sherifa: Before we could start out this morning, I had to clean two chickens for Hamida. That is why we did not have time to go to Ideal. Karima is better than Hamida and does not ask for so much.

Zainab: Hamida borrowed fifty pounds from Karima the other day, even though Hamida has money. Karima has lots of money in her wardrobe, even though she says that she is not well off. She knows more people than Hamida.

It was clear to me that the women were dissatisfied with Hamida's performance—either because the purchase took so long, or because of the final price, or both.

I often saw the baladi system of "sending for someone" in operation at Zainab's. It was the only way for Zainab to query a woman in private about installments or purchases; Zainab sent a child to whisper in the ear of a woman blocks away or in the next room, to join Zainab alone. Zainab visited high status women herself. But installment collections were not always such a private event if a customer were especially recalcitrant. Then an informal performance to announce Zainab's ultimatum might well occur in the midst of the social discourse of the street corner or the home threshold:

Zainab: You know that Hamida has been patient and, because I requested the favor on your behalf, waited for your payment.

Customer: God knows that I have just had a disaster.

[Details follow here of sick child, collapsed house, and so on.]

Zainab: All right. For your sake, I will personally intervene, and promise Hamida that you will pay next Saturday.

One can well imagine the scene if the unlucky customer failed to pay on Saturday! Zainab would attack the delinquent woman for breaking her word of honor and damaging Zainab's reputation.

Hamida's husband owned a car repair shop, while Zainab's husband drove lorries for others. Hamida dangled over a dozen gold bracelets on her arm; Zainab had dramatic gold earrings and a gold tooth. While patron-client relations such as Hamida's and Zainab's are stacked on the side of the patron, Zainab calibrated her obligations from time to time by "getting lost" in the back streets of Cairo when Hamida asked for more household help than Zainab deemed reasonable. After all, Hamida was famous for detaining a women for hours on a simple errand; when Hamida asked her help with washing dishes and cooking, the woman knew she had better help if she wanted to accomplish her business. Zainab's life was a whirl of raising her own family and doing favors for dallalas. The day we went to buy the bed, I noted Zainab's following activities between 10 in the morning and 2 in the afternoon: making tea for Sherifa; accompanying Sherifa to buy the bed; dressing the children for school; cleaning vegetables for her family's lunch; going to buy macaroni; talking with Zahra about what happened at the clinic; visiting the gold merchant and putting a gold cap on; visiting her seamstress friend to check on Karima's dress; and visiting one of Hamida's clients to claim an installment payment.

The status of patron-client relations is ultimately expressed in the baladi parlance of "speaking" and "not speaking." One dramatic occasion was when Zainab's only son was rushed to the hospital after a fall from a ladder. At the time, Zainab and Hamida were estranged. Hearing of the emergency, Hamida seized the opportunity for reconciliation, collected some of her friends, and swept through the streets bearing an expensive box of sweets. When the two women greeted each other at the hospital, their social performance signaled the discourse of reconciliation:

Hamida: When I heard the news of your son's fall, I was beside myself and could not rest until I came to see him.

Zainab: I am grateful for this visit. How is your family and children? I cannot get along without you.

The last is a common social pleasantry, which rings very true here. For Zainab, a profitable work relation, as well as a social relation, was re-established. Zainab and Hamida became even more closely connected when Zainab's niece and Hamida's son Muhammad were engaged to be married. When Zainab's husband returned from Iraq, he disapproved of Muhammad, saying that he took too many hallucinogens, and insisted that the engagement be canceled. Unavoidably, Zainab and Hamida broke off speaking and this condition would not be easily reconciled with a social performance such as the one at the hospital. This social development drastically curtailed Zainab's income; one of her neighbors commented: "She lost her leg by doing that." But there would be other opportunities for Zainab, for her capital—social contacts—was not lost.

This chapter's examination of daily life has centered around themes of fertility and productivity, themes that flow through every hour of baladi life. Baladi savvy forges favorable marriage alliances, and converts social ties to business capital. Bulaqi women operate in a social and economic arena that bridges the domestic and public, and that stretches from the village to Cairo, and from Cairo to the outside world of the Gulf and North Africa.

Daily well-being is a "package deal." Informal business ties are influenced by plans for marriage and by states of health. The government is personalized in visions or in bureaucratic experiences. Through it all, the baladi woman is no simpering, secluded lady. She picks from baladi and afrangi, from kin and non-kin, from folk medicine and cosmopolitan medicine, from informal and formal economies, and from the hearth and the market to nurture her family and to energetically stretch her resources.

7

Conclusion

This study has presented baladi women's cultural accounts of life passages, gender roles, religious rituals, social boundaries, health, and business (1) to demonstrate the dynamism and ambivalence of the baladi:afrangi cultural opposition, and (2) to document expression of sentiment and emergence of context-specific meaning in personal narratives and other baladi cultural performances. The traditional:modern cultural opposition mirrors the disparity baladi Egyptians face daily between their life situation and an ideal life. This opposition is a kind of symbolic signpost for baladis who experience the irony of drifting from one side of the divide to the other. Baladis yearn for afrangi consumer goods, medicine, and technology at the same time that they mock afrangi morals, stupidity, and hypocrisy. To be baladi is to be honorable, but baladi culture is not a weak panacea for poverty in the sense of "We may be poor but we are moral." Baladi culture is a rich tapestry into which a baladi woman weaves elements of reciprocity, recognition, and other social codes needed to navigate in society.

We have listened to what the women of Bulaq have to say and heard the mundane interwoven with the exotic. Baladi women are not epic poets, but their accounts of wedding nights or of quarrels with relatives offer rich cultural texts (Weigle 1982). Much of the text in this study is more self-conscious than gossip, but detailed accounts (such as the wanderings of Mahrusa and her daughter from a Bulaqi seamstress to the wedding, to pilgrimage in Saudi Arabia, and back to Bulaq) provide the makings of epic tales of hospitality and alliances. They also express poignant sentiments of modesty, of serendipity, of heroic action.

While I have not presented this account totally free of the researcher's perspective, I have sought to capture as much as possible of the baladi women's everyday life, unmediated by my reflective gaze, as they give birth, name their children, raise families, establish a business, marry off children, and grow old. I have selected the discourse quoted, but it is the vibrant narratives that appear here—the ones I remembered best when I recorded my notes because they were most dramatically set off by verbal formulas that resembled others I heard on other days. I conducted much of my fieldwork simply by staying in the background and listening. I did so because in the fast pace of Bulaqi life, I got nowhere whipping out a notebook and asking, "What do you think about fate?" or "How do you make extra money?"

Baladi women's narratives convey the cultural richness of mundane rituals of a low-income group; they convey not bald mechanisms of maximization but subtle orchestrations of the material and the cultural. By dint of baladi wit, Bulaqi women benefit from afrangi bureaucracy, business, politics, medicine, and morality. They stretch their household budget, convert social assets into business ones, and fashion marriage alliances with afrangis, while guarding their reputation. They dabble in the afrangi formal economic sector, although mostly to bring baladi business, with its personal sales and credit, back to baladi folk. They pick piecemeal from afrangi medicine, clinics, schools, and social services.

I hope that any images of cloistered, timid, and traditional Egyptian urban women crumbled away as the reader witnessed street disputes and encountered women working as vendors and creditors. These women are firmly ensconced at the intersection of informal/private and formal/public economic realms—usually with a feeder line to at least one family member overseas. International labor migration has altered consumption habits, and this promises to revise the simple ethos of the baladi life-style. As baladis begin to outwardly resemble the afrangi (as both groups procure modern gadgets and wear modern and Neo-Islamic clothes), the baladi identity centers in internalized self-images such as authenticity, and in externalized social rituals such as food exchanges.

We have explored baladi cultural concepts of identity, social decorum, piety, personhood, work, and health. Cultural concepts impart meaning to experience but the fit is not always exact. Probably the tightest and most dramatic fit in this book was the interpretations of the bride's death. While all interlocutors were melancholy, none questioned the cultural premise that a woman must come to marriage a virgin. Social tradition dies hard. The conformity between culture and experience was less exact in fields of religion and health, where baladi women were steeped in tradition yet open to modern innovation.

The perspicuity of the women themselves as they judge their own folk beliefs—calling on others to abandon practices such as shrine circumambulations—suggests that women are self-conscious consumers of folk options when they need something cheap. Baladi women are aware that afrangis live differently, that they do not excise their daughters, and that they do not embellish every life passage with intense rituals and reciprocity. In a similar way, rural women recognize their isolation and simple life with such statements as: "The women of the city live with their eyes open and see another world. Here I talk of water buffalo and clover, but there they talk of politics and markets."

The richness of baladi culture shines through in ritual life cycles and the accompanying social discourse of alliances in support of business and family. Bulaqi women's accounts reveal an eclecticism which reverberates through all of everyday baladi life. One activity is a template for others. Baladi women combine traditional kinship criteria for a son-in-law, for example, with modern criteria for upward mobility. They blend baladi personal contacts with afrangi market relations to generate business in the informal sector. Devout Muslims, Bulaqi women fashion a workable personal piety from orthodox ritual (prayer, fasting, Quranic reading) and popular Islam (shrine visitation, vows, amulets). They memorize bits of the Quran, pray the required prayers from time to time, fast fastidiously during Ramadan, and aspire to go on pilgrimage even though they may also paint garishly unorthodox pilgrimage murals. A baladi woman can find a panoply of religious personages to assist the destitute in the cemeteries surrounding Cairo. She can write a letter to the jurist Imam el Shaf'i and then visit him to query the best course for a personal dispute. She may visit one of the women saints known to specialize in pregnancy and health. She may circumambulate the saint's tomb in a blatantly unorthodox imitation of the Meccan pilgrimage on an outing that is both ritual and social—complete with picnic lunch. She may leave her home and problems behind in Bulaq to seek solace in the quietude of the Qarafa.

This study reveals the dynamic aspects of baladi eclecticism in religion and health. On the one hand, we met women who followed the popular Islamic practices of shrine visitation and vows to cure their children, but when these failed, they resorted to clinics. On the other hand, we met women like Laila who render cosmopolitan medicine lab tests into a kind of magic, and end up relying on time-honored folk practices such as pigeon sacrifice. While baladi women were not bound by traditional explanations, they effectively used "cultural rationalizations" for explanations of infant death. The account of the infant Maha's death reveals that a dying infant should not suffer unduly, cannot die under its mother's gaze, and that such an infant is not yet a person. The baladi concept of fate summarizes these explanations, but it is used only as an a posteriori explanation for death. When Maha's neighbors talked, they combined the cultural explanation of fate with their own suggestions that the baby had been neglected.

Some of the baladi women I knew were more orthodox in their observance of Islam than some of my afrangi women friends. These Bulaqi women prayed five times a day, assiduously followed the itinerant mosque classes sponsored for women in local mosques by the Ministry of Religious Endowments, and made the pilgrimage to Mecca at great personal sacrifice. Some of their daughters practiced an Islam that stipulates that they cover their heads and dress conservatively.

Fertility and productivity are two complementary motifs weaving this study's stories together. There are exotic tales of the syndrome mushahara (infertility) in such rituals as circumcisions and funerals, which culturally contain the potentially disruptive forces of fertility and infertility. There are more mundane personal tales of attempts to become pregnant, such as Feriayla's use of the twin recourses of shrine vows and hospital operations.

In business accounts, women describe the launching of their productive career—often in the shadowy realm between home and market so typical of baladi foraging strategies. Fatima tells how she quarreled with her husband and ended up started a thriving cheese and ghee business; her account includes frustration with family and appreciation of her friendship with her urban neighbors and customers, whom she describes as "like fellow villagers."

An important resource for the baladi woman is her savvy, her ability to avoid "breaking the egg." There is Zainab, with a barren stone of no business capital, but who has a fertile egg of neighborhood friendships that can be parlayed into contacts for a creditor. There is Ihlam, who single-handedly pursues, and obtains, an apartment after years of living off a smoke-filled courtyard. We have peeked at the lives of the women of Shaykh Ali in particular and of Bulaq in general to unpack some of the cultural understandings and practices that enunciate the baladi:afrangi symbolic opposition. It is not a simple we:they or poor:rich opposition but an undulating wave of stories one likes and stories one believes. Everyday problems are not always easily solved and so one spins a tale, a cultural explanation, to mitigate the disjunction between what is happening and what one wishes would happen. This occurred when Um Amal read the coffee grounds of the distraught father. This is what happens when Bulaqis celebrate children's circumcision or marriage with a grand party while worrying about the possible ill effects of envy on the circumcised child or the newlyweds.

It is the spontaneous set off by traditional markers that tells us the most about baladi culture. The self-image of destitute but savvy is played over and over again in social encounters. We have explored the everyday life of baladi women as they raise families, run households, and start businesses. We have witnessed social performances that afford social distance in harsh physical proximity.

We have seen abundant social disjunctions; there is time to wish things were different, to generate alternative stories both in normal discourse and on the periphery of rituals of life passage and of faith. Women evaluate family ties while they prepare for a subu'a ceremony; they exchange market and marriage lore as they pile food on trays to process and congratulate the family of a bride. Fatima's reaction to her son's engagement procession illustrates the emergent meaning of performance; Mona's description of her wedding night, the expression of sentiment.

Mundane performances, positioned as they are in everyday discourse or on the edge of formal ritual, exhibit such intricate innuendoes as "breaking off speaking" in the social interaction of a crowded, baladi quarter. A woman tilts her body away from an estranged woman who enters to visit a common friend in a hospital room; a neighbor studiously ignores a birth celebration next door to demonstrate that she and the mother have not yet reconciled after their children's quarrel. Baladi women pick an appropriate rite of passage as a forum for re-establishing ties with each other. Social estrangement and reconciliation is the score for a symphony of biographic diversity, and of economic ventures succeeded and failed.

Individual sentiment is colorfully channeled through social ritual. A child haggling with her mother for spending money expresses individual will in a culturally familiar format. Two sisters disputing the reception of a family friend meld cultural themes of hospitality and sibling responsibility at the same time that they express individual frustration at limited resources.

Bulaqi women's everyday discourse is resplendent with information on problem solving and social relations. Does this make them similar to women the world over, given women's proclivity to be "relation oriented" (Gilligan 1982:22)? Perhaps. Does it mean poorer women turn to social resources in lieu of material ones? Sometimes.

What do we learn about everyday life? That it is immersed in the matters of well-being and business; that it offers colorful treatment of mundane rituals. What do we learn about baladi culture? That it is defined by the baladi:afrangi opposition at the same time that it defies that opposition. The baladi strategy is not a weak plea by the underprivileged, but a dynamic option wrought by an energetic culture.

Through it all shines the motto of "Mix the appropriate cure at the appropriate time and place." This is, indeed, the central message of this book. Baladi women celebrate life by drawing on both baladi and afrangi realms to raise their children and to better their lives. They partake of their cultural potluck supper in a way that makes them distinctively baladi. And at the same time, people the world over are eating other potluck suppers.

Glossary

Note that words are transliterated and defined as heard and used in Bulaq, with no long vowels and no differentiation between hamza and 'ayn. Please see the Preface for explanation.

Abu: father of
'afarit: afrangi spirits
afrangi: modern, inauthentic
'Aid el-Adha: Muslim feast of sacrifice on the tenth day of the month of pilgrimage
'Aid el-Futr: Muslim feast at the end of Ramadan, the month of fasting
'Ashura: Muslim feast celebrated in Bulaq with special pudding
asyad: baladi spirits
'awliyya': holy women and men; saints (singular, *wali*)
'ayb: shameful, disgraceful
balad: community, town, country
baladi: traditional, authentic
baladiyya: fellow villagers (plural, *baladiyat*)
baraka: grace
bedu: bedouin; tribal nomad
bint al-balad: woman from a traditional urban quarter
dallala: woman merchant or creditor (plural, *dallalat*)
dayya: midwife
effendi: gentleman; bureaucrat; white-collar worker
Fatiha: opening verse of the Quran
fellah(a): peasant; implies regional identity of northern (Delta) Egypt (plural, *fellahin; fellahat*)
futir: rich, layered pastry; also flat, round bread for cemetery donations

gallaba: the downtrodden, the oppressed

gara: neighbor

gellabeyya: a woman's housedress or a (usually black) light gown worn over a housedress; a baladi man's robe

ghariba: stranger

habiba: close, loved friend (plural, *habayeb*)

haj: pilgrimage; *hajj(a)* Mecca pilgrim

hara: small lane

haram: forbidden; *harama:* forbid, protect

haramlik: women's (*harim*) section in 19th century houses

hasid: envy

hijab: amulet, curtain

hijriyya: Muslim lunar calendar, figured from time of Muhammad's migration (*hijra*) to Medina

hilal: permitted

ibn (ibna') al-balad: man from a traditional urban quarter; literally "son of the town or country"

iftar: evening meal in Ramadan (*fatara:* verb—to break fast)

ihmal: irresponsibility

imam: prayer leader

infitah: policy of economic liberalization initiated by the late President Anwar Sadat

itfaddil(li): please; an invitation to eat, visit, and so on

Ka'aba: the sacred shrine of Mecca, which was revered even in pre-Islamic times

kaff: palm of the hand; amulet in shape of palm used to ward off evil eye

kak: rich cookies made at *'Aid el-Futr*

ketb el-kitab: engagement

khamaysa: amulet made of five (*khamsa*) parts

khawaga: foreigner or Europeanized Egyptian

khayr: goodness

kos kossi: small balls of steamed dough

kucheri: lentil and macaroni dish

kuttab: Quranic school for memorization of Quran and reading

mahr: payment by groom used to furnish married couple's house

m'arifa: acquaintance

mawlid: saint's day

mawsim: feast day (plural, *mawasim*)

melaya liff: baladi women's black outer garment, worn draped over house dress

metkhasma: not on speaking terms (plural, *metkhasmin*)

moda: modern, fashionable dress

mu'allima: "master," a woman who is a coffeehouse or store proprietor; known to be tough and masculine in her ways

muhaggaba: woman wearing Islamic garb, including head, arm, and leg cover

mushahara: infertility or insufficient lactation

muwazaffa: office, white-collar employee (plural, *muwazaffin*)

nasib: fate

nazra: vow

niyya: intention

nuqta: money gifts exchanged at birth, circumcision, and marriage

qarafa: cemetery

qariba: relative

Quran: the holy book of Islam revealed to the Prophet Muhammad

radih: rhymed insults used in baladi women's street disputes

rahma: food distributed to the poor, especially at cemeteries on feast days

ruqaq: a thin bread made for *'Aid el-Adha*

Saidi(yya): a person from southern Egypt, the Said

sawab: good deed

sebil: fountain or jug that provides water to the public as a good deed

sharaf: honor

sharbat: fruit drink

shaykh: learned man

shaykha: learned woman; woman who holds *zars* and fashions amulets

subu'a: naming ceremony seven days after birth where *sab'a habub* (seven grains) are distributed in amulets

suhur: predawn meal in the month of fasting, Ramadan

sunna: religious custom

tabikh: a heavy stew

tahara: excision (female circumcision); male circumcision

Um: "mother of," commonly used with first son

'ulema': religious scholars

wali: saint, religious man

wasfat baladiyya: home remedies

wasta: influence or intercession

wid: special friendship; "hitting it off"

yi'abir hadd: acknowledge a person socially

zagrutta: ululation

zakat: alms

zar: ceremony of spiritual purging

References

Abu Lughod, Janet. 1971. *Cairo: 1000 Years of the City Victorious*. Princeton: Princeton Univ. Press.

Abu Lughod, Lila. 1985. "A Community of Secrets: The Separate World of Bedouin Women." *Signs: Journal of Women in Culture and Society*. 10:637–657.

———. 1986. *Veiled Sentiments: Honor and Poetry in a Bedouin Society*. Berkeley: Univ. of California Press.

Allen, Barbara. 1978. "Personal Experience Narratives: Use and Meaning in Interaction." *Folklore and Mythology Studies*. 2: 5–8.

Attiya, Nayra. 1982. *Khul-Khaal: Five Egyptian Women Tell Their Stories*. Syracuse: Syracuse Univ. Press.

Barker-Benfield, G.J. 1973. "The Spermatic Economy: A Nineteenth-Century Sexuality." In Michael Gordon, ed., *The American Family in Social-Historical Perspective*. New York: St. Martin's, pp. 336–372.

Badr, M., et al. 1982. "Small-Scale Enterprises in Egypt: Fayoum and Kalyubia Governorates." Working Paper No. 23. Department of Agricultural Economics, Michigan State University and Zagazig University, Moshtohor, Egypt.

Basso, Ellen. 1985. *A Musical View of the Universe: Kalapalo Myth and Ritual Performance*. Philadelphia: Univ. of Pennsylvania Press.

Basso, Keith H. 1984. "Stalking with Stories: Names, Places, and Moral Narratives among the Western Apache," in Bruner 1984.

Bauman, Richard. 1977. *Verbal Art as Performance*. Rowley, MA: Newbury House.

———. 1986. *Story, Performance, and Event: Contextual Studies of Oral Narrative*. Cambridge: Cambridge Univ. Press.

Beck, Lois, and Nikki Keddie. 1978. *Women in the Muslim World*. Cambridge, MA: Harvard Univ. Press.

Beeman, William O. 1982. *Culture, Performance and Communication in Iran*. Tokyo: Institute for the Study of Languages and Cultures of Asia and Africa.

Betteridge, Anne. 1980. "The Controversial Vows of Iranian Women," in N.A. Falk and R.M. Gross, eds., *Unspoken World: Women's Religious Lives In Non-Western Countries*. New York: Harper and Row, pp. 41–58.

Boullata, Issa J. 1989. "Arabic Oral Tradition." Guest editor of special volume of *Oral Tradition*. 4:1–2.

Bourdieu, Pierre. 1977. *Outline of a Theory of Practice*. Cambridge: Cambridge Univ. Press.

Bowen, Donna Lee, and Evelyn A. Early. 1993. *Everyday Life in the Muslim Middle East*. Bloomington: Indiana Univ. Press.

Briggs, Chuck. 1988. *Competence in Performance: The Creativity of Tradition in Mexicano Verbal Art*. Philadelphia: Univ. of Pennsylvania.

Bruner, Edward M. 1984. *Text, Play, and Story: The Construction and Reconstruction of Self and Society*. AES proceedings. Prospect Heights, IL: Waveland Press.

Campo, Juan. 1983. *Muslim Homes: The Religious Significance of Domestic Space*. PhD dissertation, Univ. of Chicago.

Caton, Steven C. 1990. *Peaks of Yemen I Summon: Poetry as Cultural Practice in a North Yemeni Tribe*. Berkeley: Univ. of California Press.

Chock, Phyllis Pease, and June R. Wyman, eds. 1986. *Discourse and the Social Life of Meaning*. Washington, D.C.: Smithsonian Institution Press.

Clifford, James, and George E. Marcus. 1986. *Writing Culture: The Poetics and Politics of Ethnography*. Berkeley: Univ. of California Press.

Cloudsley, Anne. 1984. *Women of Omdurman: Life, Love and the Cult of Virginity*. New York: St. Martin's Press.

Crapanzano, Vincent. 1973. *The Hamadsha: A Study in Morrocan Ethnopsychiatry*. Berkeley: Univ. of California Press.

———. 1980. "Rite of Return. Circumcision in Morocco," in Warner Muensterberger and L. Bryce Boyer, eds., *The Psychoanalytic Study of Society*. New York: Library of Psychological Anthropology.

Davis, Susan S. 1983. *Patience and Power: Women's Lives in a Moroccan Village*. Cambridge, MA: Schenkman.

DelVecchio-Good, Mary Jo, Byron Good, Michael M. J. Fischer. 1988. "Discourse and the Study of Emotion, Illness and Healing." *Culture, Medicine, and Psychiatry*. 12:1–7.

Denny, Frederick M. 1983. *Islamic Ritual Practices*. American Council of Learned Societies.

El-Doktor. 1951. *Khitan al-Binat* (Female excision). Special supplement to the May 1951 edition of the magazine *The Doctor*. Cairo.

Early, Evelyn A. 1977. "Social Networks of Cairo *Baladi* Women." Paper presented at Middle Eastern Kinship conference, Kuwait City, Kuwait.

———. 1978. "Entrepreneurship among Lower Class Egyptian Women." Uppsala, Sweden: World Congress of Sociology.

———. 1982. "The Logic of Well Being: Therapeutic Narratives in Cairo, Egypt." *Social Science and Medicine*. 16:1491–1497.

———. 1984. "Women's Narratives and Theories of Social Action." San Francisco: Middle East Studies Association.

———. 1985a. "Fatima: A Life History of an Egyptian Woman from Bulaq," in Elizabeth W. Fernea, ed., *Women and the Family in the Middle East: New Voices of Change*. Austin: Univ. of Texas. pp. 76–83.

———. 1985b. "Catharsis and Creation: The Everyday Narratives of *Baladi* Women of Cairo." *Anthropological Quarterly*. 172–180.

———. 1988. "The *Baladi* Curative System of Cairo, Egypt." *Culture, Medicine, and Psychiatry*. 12:1, 65–85.

———. 1989. "Women's Presentation of Everyday Experience in Narrative:

Its Relevance for Curriculum Development." Khartoum, Sudan: Workshop on Women's Studies in Sudan.

———. 1993a. "Getting It Together: Baladi Business Women." Forthcoming in *Arab Women and Development,* Tucker, 1993.

———. 1993b. "Fate and Fertility." Forthcoming in *Everyday Life in the Muslim Middle East,* Bowen and Early 1993.

Falassi, Alessandro. 1980. *Folklore by the Fireside: Text and Context of the Tuscan Veglia.* Austin: Univ. of Texas Press.

Fernea, Elizabeth Warnock, and Basima Bezirgan. 1977. *Middle Eastern Muslim Women Speak.* Austin: Univ. of Texas Press.

Fernea, Elizabeth Warnock. 1985. *Women and the Family in the Middle East: New Voices of Change.* Austin: Univ. of Texas Press.

———. 1993. "The Veiled Revolution." Notes on Fernea film "The Veiled Revolution." Forthcoming in *Everyday Life in the Muslim Middle East,* Bowen and Early 1993.

Fischer, Michael M.J., and Mahdi Abedi. 1990. *Debating Muslims: Cultural Dialogues in Postmodernity and Tradition.* Madison: Univ. of Wisconsin Press.

Foucault, Michel. 1980. *Power/Knowledge.* New York: Pantheon Books.

Friedl, Erika. 1989. *Women of Deh Koh: Lives in an Iranian Village.* Washington: Smithsonian Institution Press.

Gaffney, Jane. 1987. "The Egyptian Cinema: Industry and Art in a Changing Society," *Arab Studies Quarterly* 9:1.

Geertz, Clifford. 1983. *Local Knowledge: Further Essays in Interpretive Anthropology.* New York: Basic Books.

al-Ghitani, Gamal. 1992. *The Events of Zaafarani Alley,* translated by Farouk Abdel Wahab. Manuscript.

Gilligan, Carol. 1982. *In a Different Voice: Psychological Theory and Women's Development.* Cambridge: Harvard Univ. Press.

Gilsenon, Michael. 1973. *Saint and Sufi in Modern Egypt: An Essay in the Sociology of Religion.* Oxford: Clarendon Press.

———. 1976. "Lying and Contradiction," in Bruce Kapferer, ed., *Transaction and Meaning.* Philadelphia: ISHI. pp. 191–219.

Glassie, Henry. 1982. *Passing the Time in Ballymenone: Culture and History of an Ulster Community.* Philadelphia: Univ. of Pennsylvania Press.

Goffman, Erving. 1974. *Frame Analysis: An Essay on the Organization of Experience.* New York: Harper and Row.

———. 1981. *Forms of Talk.* Philadelphia: Univ. of Pennsylvania Press.

Gornick, Vivian. 1973. *In Search of Ali Mahmoud: An American Woman in Egypt.* New York: Saturday Review Press.

Gran, Judith. 1977. "The Impact of the World Market on Egyptian Women." *Middle East Report.* 58:3–7.

El-Guindi, Fadwa. 1981. "Veiling *Infitah* with Muslim Ethic: Egypt's Contemporary Islamic Movement." *Social Problems.* 28:4, 465–487.

———. 1990. "On Making an Ethnographic Film on Egypt—*El Sebou':* Egyptian Birth Ritual." *MERA Forum.* 13:1.

El-Hamamsy, Laila. 1973. "The *Daya* of Egypt: Survival in a Modernizing Society." Caltech Population Program Monograph. Pasadena, California.

Hammam, Mona. 1979. "Egypt's Working Women: Textile Workers of Chubra el-Khaima." *Middle East Report.* 82:3–11.

Hanna, Nelli. 1983. *An Urban History of Bulaq in the Mameluke and*

Ottoman Periods. Supplement of *Annals Islamologiques*. Cairo: French Oriental Institute.

Al-Jibarti, Abd Al-Rahman. 1958. *'Aja'ib al-Athar fi'l-Taragim wa'l-Akhbar* (The marvels of biographies and history). Reprint of original volumes published 1870–1871, 1882, and 1904–1905. Cairo: Dar as-Sha'ab.

Kapferer, Bruce. 1979. "Mind, Self, and Other in Demonic Illness: The Negation and Reconstruction of Self." *American Ethnologist*. 6:1, 110–134.

Kennedy, John G. 1970. "Circumcision and Excision in Egyptian Nubia." *Man*. 5:2, 175–191.

Labov, William, and Joshua Waletzky. 1966. "Narrative Analysis: Oral Versions of Personal Experience." *Essays on the Verbal and Visual Arts*. AES 1966 proceedings. Seattle: Univ. of Washington Press. pp. 12–44.

Leprette, Fernand. 1939. *Egypt: Land of the Nile*. Translated by Lillian Goar. Cairo: E.T.R. Schindler.

Lewandowski, H. 1958. *Ferne Lander, Fremde Sitten*. Stuttgart: H.E. Gunther.

McPherson, Joseph W. 1946. *The Moulids of Egypt: Egyptian Saints Days*. New York: AMS Press.

Maher, Vanessa. 1974. *Women and Property in Morroco*. New York: Cambridge University Press.

Makhlouf, Carla. 1979. *Changing Veils: Women and Modernisation in North Yemen*. London: Croom Helm.

Manning, Frank. 1983. *The Celebration of Society: Perspective on Contemporary Cultural Performance*. Bowling Green, Ohio: Bowling Green Univ. Press.

Marcus, George E., and Michael M.J. Fischer. 1986. *Anthropology as Cultural Critique*. Chicago: Univ. of Chicago Press.

Marsot, Afaf. 1978. "The Revolutionary Gentlewoman," in Beck and Keddie, eds., *Women in the Muslim World*. Cambridge: Harvard Univ. Press.

Meinardus, Otto. 1967. "Mythological, Historical and Sociological Aspects of the Practice of Female Circumcision among the Egyptians." *Acts Ethnographica Academiae Scientiarum Hungaricae*. 16:387–392.

Mernissi, Fatima. 1975. *Beyond the Veil: Male-Female Dynamics in a Modern Muslim Society*. Cambridge, MA: Schenkman.

El-Messiri, Nawwal Nadim. 1975. *Relations between the Sexes in a Harah of Cairo*. PhD dissertation, Indiana Univ. at Bloomington.

El-Messiri, Sawsan. 1976. *The Concept of Ibn al-Balad*. Master's dissertation, American Univ. of Cairo.

———. 1978a. "Self Images of Traditional Urban Women in Cairo," in Beck and Keddie, eds., *Women in Muslim Society*. Cambridge, MA: Harvard Univ. Press.

———. 1978b. *Ibn al-Balad: A Concept of Egyptian Identity*. Leiden: E.J. Brill.

Mills, Margaret. 1991. *Rhetorics and Politics in Afghan Traditional Storytelling*. Philadelphia: Univ. of Pennsylvania Press.

Mitchell, Tim. 1989. "Culture Across Borders." *Middle East Report*. 159:4–6.

Nejm, Ahmad Fuad. 1976. "Nass el-'Ulata." Lyrics of a popular Egyptian song.

Nelson, Cynthia. 1974. "Public and Private Politics: Women in the Middle Eastern World." *American Ethnologist* 1:3, 551- 563.

Nelson, Kristina. 1985. *The Art of Reciting the Qur'an*. Austin: Univ. of Texas Press.

———. 1993. "The Qur'an: The Sound of the Divine in Daily Life." Forthcoming in *Everyday Life in the Muslim Middle East*, Bowen and Early 1993.

Oweiss, Sayyid. 1955. *A Comparative Study between Roxbury and Bulaq*. PhD dissertation, Boston Univ.

———. 1965. *Malamih al-Mujtama' al-Misri al-Mu'asir* (Features of modern Egyptian society). Cairo: Dar as-Sha'ab.

———. 1970. *Hadith 'an al-Thaqafa* (Discourse on culture). Cairo: Anglo-Egyptian Press.

Paige, Karen Eriksen, and Jeffery M. Paige. 1981. *The Politics of Reproductive Ritual*. Berkeley: Univ. of California Press.

Robinson, John A. 1981. "Personal Narratives Reconsidered." *Journal of American Folklore*. 94:371, 58–85.

Rosaldo, Michell Z., and Louise Lamphere. 1974. *Woman, Culture, and Society*. Stanford, CA: Stanford Univeristy Press.

Rugh, Andrea. 1982. "Foreword" in Nayra Attiya, *Khul-Khall: Five Egyptian Women Tell Their Stories*. Syracuse: Syracuse Univ. Press, pp. vii–xxii.

———. 1984. *Family in Contemporary Egypt*. Syracuse: Syracuse Univ. Press.

———. 1986. *Reveal and Conceal: Dress in Contemporary Egypt*. Syracuse: Syracuse Univ. Press.

Saadawi, Nawwal. 1976. *Al-Mara' wal-Jins* (Women and sex). Cairo: Dar as-Sha'ab.

Salvador, Mari Lyn. 1986. "Symbolism and Ephemeral Art: An Analysis of the Aesthetic Aspects of the Festos do Divino Espirito Santo." In *Il Colóquio Internacional de Simbologia: Os Impérios do Espirito Santo na Simbólica do Império*. Instituto Histórico da Ilha Terceira, Angra do Heroisma, Açores.

Shaaban, Bouthaina. 1988. *Both Right and Left Handed: Arab Women Talk about Their Lives*. London: The Women's Press.

Sonnini, C.S. 1799. *Travels in Upper and Lower Egypt: Undertaken by Order of the Old Government of France*. Henry Hunter, trans. London: John Stockdale.

Stahl, Sandra. 1977. "The Personal Narrative as Folklore." *Journal of the Folklore Institute*. 14:9–30.

Tambiah, S. 1968. "The Magical Power of Words." *Man*. 3:175–209.

Tedlock, Dennis. 1983. *The Spoken Word and the Work of Interpretation*. Philadelphia: Univ. of Pennsylvania Press.

Thesiger, Wilfred. 1959. *Arabian Sands*. New York: Penguin Books.

Toussin, al Amir. 1928. *Kilimat fi Sabil Misr* (Words about Egypt). Cairo: Sulafiyya Press.

Tucker, Judith. 1985. *Women in Nineteenth Century Egypt*. Cambridge: Cambridge Univ. Press.

———, ed. 1993. *Arab Women and Development*. Bloomington: Indiana Univ. Press.

Turner, Edith. 1987. *The Spirit and the Drum: A Memory of Africa*. Tucson: Univ. of Arizona Press.

Turner, Victor. 1982. *Celebration: Studies in Festivity and Ritual*. Washington, D.C.: Smithsonian Institution Press.

———. 1985. *On the Edge of the Bush: Anthropology as Experience*. Tucson: Univ. of Arizona Press.

Turner, Victor, and Edward M. Bruner. 1988. *The Anthropology of Performance*. New York: Paj Publications.

Waterbury, John. 1978. *Egypt: Burdens of the Past, Options for the Future*. Bloomington: Univ. of Indiana Press.

Waugh, Earle H. 1989. *The Munshidin of Egypt: Their World and Their Song*. Columbia: Univ. of South Carolina Press.

Webber, Sabra J. 1991. *Romancing the Real: Folklore and Ethnographic Representation in North Africa*. Philadelphia: Univ. of Pennsylvania Press.

Weedon, Chris. 1989. *Feminist Practice and Poststructuralist Theory*. Oxford: Basil Blackwell.

Weigle, Marta. 1982. *Spiders and Spinsters: Women and Mythology*. Albuquerque: Univ. of New Mexico Press.

Wikan, Unni. 1980. *Life among the Poor in Cairo*. London: Tavistock.

———. 1982. *Behind the Veil in Arabia: Women in Oman*. Baltimore: Johns Hopkins Univ. Press.

Zenie-Ziegler, Wedad. 1988. *In Search of Shadows: Conversations with Egyptian Women*. London: Zed Books.

Index

Abu 'Ala, Sultan, 29–30, 123
Abu Lughod, Janet, 7, 62; study of bedouin women by, 23
Afrangi culture, 2; opposed to baladi culture, 53–63
Agency for International Development (United States) (USAID), 2
'Aid el-Adha (The Great Feast), 94–95
'Aid el-Futr (The Small Feast), 94
Amal, 17–20, 134
American University (Cairo), 1, 3
Amina, 132–133
Aniyat, 8, 58, 140-142, 144; life of, in Bulaq, 41-43; husband of, 55; tells of death of infant daughter, 100–101; excision of daughter of, 104–105; receives letter from husband in Saudi Arabia, 185–186
As-Sukhariyya (Mahfouz), 62
Atimad, 98–99
Attiya, Nayra, 24–25
Aysha, 153
Azza (daughter of Mahrusa), 120–122

Badriyya (daughter of Aniyat), 42, 49, 104–105, 139, 141–144
Baladi culture, 2; and Bulaqi women, 4–6, 26–27; and narrative, 10–12; as concept, 51–53; opposed to afrangi culture, 53–63; gender roles in, 67–75; household and daily life in, 75–80; maximizing behavior and, 80–84; social relations in, 135–136, 139–142; eclecticism in 199–202. *See also* Morality; Popular Islam

Basso, Ellen, 131
Bibar, Sultan, 30
Birth, 95–99
Bulaq Abu 'Ala: location and research advantages of, 2; baladi women in, 4–6, 26–27; history of, 29–34; daily life in, and Cairo, 34–40

Campo, Juan, 114–116
Caton, Steven C., 23
Childhood rituals and daily activities, 106–107
Circumcision rituals, 87–89, 102–106
Conflict, 142–151
Coptic feasts and fasts, 117–118
Copts and Muslims: relations between, 48–49; women's dress among, 73; ritual mutuality between, 118. *See also* Ritual
Credit, saving, and money management, 68–69, 79. *See also* Dallalat
Cultural performances, 131–135, 169, 197. *See also* Conflict; Restitution

Dallalat (merchant-creditors), 188–195
Death, 109–111; marriage and, 171–175
Decorative motifs: on murals, 114–116; in feast-day ornaments, 116–117

213

About the Book and the Author

Traditional, urban Egyptian women—baladi women—extol themselves with the proverb, "A baladi woman can play with an egg and a stone without breaking the egg." Evelyn Early illustrates this and other expressions of baladi women's self-identity by observing and recording their everyday discourse and how these women—who consider themselves destitute yet savvy—handle such matters as housing, work, marriage, religion, health, and life in general.

Based on more than three years of research in Bulaq Abu 'Ala—a jammed popular quarter north of the fashionable Nile-side hotel district of Cairo—Early's work reveals important cultural themes by minimizing the reflective gaze of the researcher and allowing spontaneous discourse and narrative recountings to "catch" culture in action.

Evelyn A. Early has conducted anthropological research on the Shi'a of south Lebanon and on everyday life, popular Islam, and medicine in Cairo. She has also studied popular culture in Syria and kiosk pamphlets as a reflection of social history in Egypt. She is coeditor of *Everyday Life in the Muslim Middle East*, and her articles include "Catharsis and Creation: The Everyday Narratives of Baladi Women of Cairo" and "Tradition and Nationalism in Syrian Performance."